Behave as a Fisher of Men

Dr. Christopher Powers

WESTBOW
PRESS®
A DIVISION OF THOMAS NELSON
& ZONDERVAN

This book is a work of non-fiction. Unless otherwise noted, the author and the publisher make no explicit guarantees as to the accuracy of the information contained in this book and in some cases, names of people and places have been altered to protect their privacy.

WestBow Press books may be ordered through booksellers or by contacting:

WestBow Press
A Division of Thomas Nelson & Zondervan
1663 Liberty Drive
Bloomington, IN 47403
www.westbowpress.com
844-714-3454

Because of the dynamic nature of the Internet, any web addresses or links contained in this book may have changed since publication and may no longer be valid. The views expressed in this work are solely those of the author and do not necessarily reflect the views of the publisher, and the publisher hereby disclaims any responsibility for them.

Any people depicted in stock imagery provided by Getty Images are models, and such images are being used for illustrative purposes only.
Certain stock imagery © Getty Images.

Unless otherwise noted, scripture taken from the New King James Version®. Copyright © 1982 by Thomas Nelson. Used by permission. All rights reserved.

Scripture marked (KJV) taken from the King James Version of the Bible.

ISBN: 978-1-6642-3669-1 (sc)
ISBN: 978-1-6642-3671-4 (hc)
ISBN: 978-1-6642-3670-7 (e)

Library of Congress Control Number: 2021911423

Print information available on the last page.

WestBow Press rev. date: 06/21/2021

CONTENTS

Introduction If You're not Fishing, you're not Behaving vii

Chapter 1 Our Marching Orders....................................1

Chapter 2 Seeing the Harvest Through His Eyes 11

Chapter 3 Mission Impossible: Reaching Out to the Dead 22

Chapter 4 Courage to Go..35

Chapter 5 Courage to Go After One................................ 46

Chapter 6 Can God Really use Your Life? 57

Chapter 7 God's Response to Man's Sin 69

Chapter 8 Evangelism in the Hands of Sinners.....................83

Chapter 9 Salvation Plain and Simple.............................94

Chapter 10 The Rejection of the King.............................106

Chapter 11 The Crucifixion of the King 119

Chapter 12 What a Difference a Day Makes 134

Chapter 13 Our Great Salvation................................... 145

Chapter 14 If a Fisher of Men Could Spend Five Minutes in Hell.... 157

Chapter 15 Fishermen and Hunters................................. 170

Chapter 16 When Jesus Comes Again................................ 185

Chapter 17 The Kingdom of God....................................201

Chapter 18 Come and Dine 214

Chapter 19 The Invitation to Generation Now......................226

Chapter 20 A Tender Moment 235

If You're not Fishing, you're not Behaving

Simon Peter said them, "I am going fishing." They said to him, "We are going with you also." They went out and immediately got into a boat, and that night they caught nothing. (John 21:3 NKJV)

THE DAY WAS LIKE NO OTHER, THE DISCIPLES HAD JUST MADE IT BACK to Galilee after seeing the resurrected Savior, and they stood on the shore of the Sea of Galilee contemplating what they should do next as they waited for Jesus to meet them there. They were struggling with what they had seen over a week ago. Jesus was crucified upon a cross, He was buried, then suddenly on the Sabbath day someone came and told the disciples that the body was gone. Peter, as he stood on the shore, must have remembered that, he and John ran to see if it was true. After confirming the story, they go back to the upper room to tell the others. And there behind closed doors Jesus shows himself to His disciples. That must have been a lot to get as grasp of what just happen. Seven days later Jesus shows up again and after meeting with them in the upper room Jesus tells His disciples to go to Galilee and He would meet them there, (Matt. 26:32; 28:7-10; Mark 16:7 NKJV)

Galilee was a familiar place for the disciples, it was a place of rest as many of the disciples were from there, especially Peter. Peter's wife and home was here, and this was his comfort zone. The event recorded in John 21 should have been an opportunity for Peter to lead and put his two-year training to work. So, Peter being in his comfort zone is drawn to the shore of the sea of Galilee and as he heads there six other disciples follow him there. As they stood there, they began to converse among themselves as to what they should do while they waited upon Jesus to meet them there (John 21:1-2 NKJV).

Their actions bring up a good question: Why do we want others to go to hell? When is the last time you brought someone to the Lord? When was the last time you tried? Please understand as a child of God, Jesus did not save us just to sit back and do nothing. The moment you accepted Jesus Christ and surrendered your life to Him is the moment you were given a great privilege which is to behave like Jesus Christ. As children of God, we are to continue to grow our Christ-like behavior as we walk with Jesus Christ. We grow our Christ-like behavior by growing the Christ-like characteristics that Peter discusses in 2 Peter 1:5-7 (NKJV). These characteristics help us to grow as individuals as we follow Jesus Christ. These characteristics also aid us to go about doing the work that Christ has given us to do once we got saved. Jesus has commissioned His children to continue His work of being fishers of men and making others become fishers of men. As we grow those Christ-like characteristics through the teaching and help of the Holy Spirit, He guides us and shows us how to behave as fishers of men.

Jesus said, "Follow Me, and I will make you become fishers of men" (Mark 1:17 NKJV). That is what Jesus intended to do for these men that He was calling to follow Him. Plus, He spent a good part of His ministry discipling them to be fishers of men. That phrase "Follow Me" implies: that to know Him is to love Him, and to love Him is to want to share Him, and to share Him means that you have a desire to see other to come to know Him like you know Him. That means you need to behave as a follower of Jesus Christ and go out and do something: sharing the Gospel. Now for most of the people they like to begin by making excuses instead of making disciples: "Well, pastor, that is just not my thing. I am not that out going, and I just don't know that much about the Bible". Think about what Jesus is saying as a promise "follow

Me and I will make you fishers of men" (Mark 1:17 NKJV). We need to let what Jesus said penetrate our hearts like an arrow, lodging deep down in our hearts, so that we never forget that Jesus the Son, God the Father, and the Holy Spirit is the One Who is going to make fishers of men.

But the problem with some so-called church members or so-called children of God is the fact that they may not know how to bring a lost person to Christ, or it could be the other problem which is they don't truly know Jesus Christ as their personal Lord and Savior. If you are reading this book, you need to have a personal salvation experience with Jesus, if you want to be able to bring some to Christ and see them get saved by grace. Because if you are not genuinely saved it would be like the blind leading the blind out in a lost and dying world. Therefore, you need to admit to God that you are a sinner (Rom. 3:23; 6:23 NKJV), you need to ask Him into your heart (Rom. 10:13 NKJV), and then you need to confess Him as your Savior and Lord (Rom. 10:9-10 NKJV). Ask Jesus to come into your heart and save you this very instant. If you are saved and you do not have that desire to see sinners saved, then you need to ask God for forgiveness for not behaving like Christ. Ask Him to make you like His Son and build up the Passion of the Christ in your heart.

Jesus said, "Follow Me, and I will make you become fishers of men" (Mark 1:17 NKJV). Let's break down this statement and let it penetrate your heart and build up that desire to see sinners come to know Jesus. Notice that this statement is a pointed command, it is not a suggestion. It is not some advice, or an opinion it is a command "follow Me" (Mark 1:17 NKJV). The word "follow" literally means that you look with high regard and high esteem to the one you follow, and you obey and behave like that one (Dictionary 1828). Think about this question: what right do you have to call yourself a follower of Jesus Christ if you are not behaving as a fisher of men? So, let's get this straight, soul-winning, sharing the gospel, being a fisher of men is not up for debate, it is a pointed command. And we need to be honest enough to admit to ourselves, that we are not fishing with Jesus. We need to stop making excuses as to why we do not go out and bring in lost souls to Jesus Christ and admit that the reason we don't go out is because we are not behaving like Christ as we should.

Let me ask you, "How do you fish"? You fish by going fishing, you don't drag your boat down to the lake or river never to put your boat in the water and hope that the fish jump in! Fishing for men is the very heartbeat of God. This can be seen in the book of Genesis, all the way back to the Garden of Eden, when Adam sinned, and God realized that Adam could not get to Him. God didn't run and hide from Adam. No, it was Adam who hid from God. But God tracked him down. And God has pursued man from the beginning, and man has been running from the beginning. I may not be a brilliant fisherman, but I know this about fish; you must go to where they are if you want to catch fish. The only fish that comes to you is the kind of fish you find in the frozen food section of your local grocery store! Jesus said, "I will make you fishers of men" (Mark 1:17 NKJV). That is a personal promise to you, however, with this promise he meant for you to be actively seeking out lost souls to share the Gospel of Jesus Christ with. He doesn't want us to sit back and wait for people to come to us; He wants us to go to them and just behave as a follower of Jesus Christ and let Him do the rest! You know why most of us never witness? You know why most of us never talk about Jesus to our colleagues, friends, neighbors, and families? It is because we are not excited about Jesus anymore. He has become a routine. He has become an "old hat". He just becomes a part of you comfort zone that you have molded to fit your needs.

So, on the seashore there was an opportunity for Peter be the leader, that Jesus asked Him to be, of the disciples. Peter knew what he was supposed to do, fish for men. However, Peter was not thinking spiritually. So, "Simon Peter said to them, "I am going fishing" (John 21:3 NKJV). Now, had Peter put all this training to work right here he could have led these six men by telling them lets go practice what Jesus has taught us to do, let's go fish for men and share the Gospel with our hometown and see them get saved and become followers of Jesus Christ. But no! Peter decides to go fishing (John 21:3 NKJV), without Jesus, and the other six said to Peter, "We are going with you also" (John 21:3 NKJV). Now it is unclear as to why he decided to go fishing.

Maybe he and his wife had bills to pay, which would be perfectly okay, however, that was not what Jesus called him to do. Jesus had called him to "Follow Me" (Luke 5:11 NKJV), not to hear the teaching of Jesus, follow him throughout His ministry, see Him die and be resurrected, only to go back to old way of life. And yet, that is how many Christians behave every Sunday. They hear the message that has been prepared for them by God through the pastors or preachers at their church and then go out unaffected by the message. What is sad is the fact that the disciples saw Peter as the leader of the group, and he led a group astray from doing the kingdom work by his behavior.

But have you ever wondered why Jesus called so many fishermen to be in His enter most circle? That's right seven of the twelve disciples are professional fishermen, not vacation fishermen, but professional fishermen. Something to understand about professional fishermen they are courageous, and if you are going to behave as a follower of Jesus Christ then you are going to have to be brave. Professional fishermen are also dedicated or focused upon one thing, which means that they are not easily distracted. When you get distracted as a follower of Jesus that usually means that you have taken your eyes off Jesus, which can lead to you behaving like that of the distraction. Another thing about fishermen they don't quit! They persevere, which is one of the seven Christ-like characteristics that Peter talks about, (2 Pet. 1:5-7 NKJV). Professional fishermen also know how to work together and take orders, which should be a lesson for us as individuals or as a church to practice unity and harmony if we want to behave as fishers of men.

Now whether you want to argue whether Peter and the other six were right or wrong for literally going fishing, the point remains the same: their efforts were in vain. John 21:3 (NKJV) says, "They went out and immediately got into the boat, and that night they caught nothing". In their training they should have remembered what Jesus had taught them, "For without Me, you can do nothing" (John 15:5 NKJV). And here they are doing something that Jesus called them to give up and follow Him, and to do the work that He had taught them to do. And they go fishing without Jesus's blessing and catch nothing. This is the same kind of situation that happened two years ago which should have jarred Peter's memory, when they spent all night fishing and caught nothing. Listen, when God the Creator is left out of the picture, then men and women cease to see themselves as stewards and behave only as selfish consumers. When morning came, Jesus showed up and taught a multitude and when He was finished, He told Peter to "launch out into the deep and let down your nets for a catch" (Luke 5:4 NKJV).

Again, it is possible, with all that happened in the past week, that Peter was not thinking spiritually about the task that Jesus called Him to, that is why he went fishing. But think, Peter was sincere in following the Lord, and he worked hard, but there were no results. That sounds a lot like pastors, deacons, or even believers today as they serve Jesus Christ. They sincerely believe the teachings of the Word of God, but they labor and toil in vain, because they are not behaving as a fisher of men. They are behaving as fishermen who are fishing without Jesus or they are not fishing as all. And if you are not fishing then you are not behaving.

It is sad that there are church members who have never led a soul to Jesus Christ. It is sad that there are Christians who do not consistently witness for Christ, and there is just a hand full of Christians that are involved in the ministry of evangelism. These statistics are sad because they reveal the true state of the behavior of the individual and the behavior of the church. I believe that the greatest thing that you can do for the world is not be a good citizen, it is not to be a good church member, it is not to be a nice neighbor; but the greatest thing you can possibly do is behave as a fisher of men and bring men, women, boys, and girls to Jesus Christ. However, there are many church members who behave as though the end of their responsibility is to come to church a couple times a week, pray when they can, read the Bible every now and then, and live a life that is slightly different and cleaner than the world around them. They assume that the job of evangelism is the sole responsibility of the pastor, staff, and evangelist.

It is my prayer that this book be an encouragement, a motivator to us to go out and share the Gospel of Jesus Christ and let us all behave has fishers of men. Is a person a fisherman if, year after year, he never catches a fish? Is one behaving as a follower of Jesus Christ if they aren't fishing?

CHAPTER ONE

Our Marching Orders

---

*All authority has been given to Me in heaven and earth. Go therefore
and make disciples of all the nations, baptizing them in the name of
the Father and of the Son and of the Holy Spirit, teaching them to
observe all things that I have commanded you; and lo I am with you
always, even to the end of the age. (Matthew 28:18-20 NKJV)*

BEFORE ASCENDING INTO HEAVEN, JESUS ISSUED WHAT HAS COME TO
be called The Great Commission. A "commission" is "an authoritative
command; a directive" (Dictionary 1828), therefore when Jesus spoke
these words directly to His disciples, and indirectly to us, He was
giving the church her marching orders. He was telling us exactly what
He expected us to do in His physical absence. The disciples took the
Lord's command seriously. They went into the world and shared the
Gospel of Jesus Christ and thousands upon thousands were saved by
the grace of God. Their message was so powerful and their witness so
effective that their critics accused them of "turning the world upside
down" (Acts 17:6 NKJV).

That was then, and this is now! What was given as The Great
Commission has turned into what some have labeled "The Great
Omission". When something is "omitted", it is "left out, undone,
neglected" (Dictionary 1828). Instead of taking the Gospel to the ends
of the earth as the Lord has commanded us, the modern church won't

even take the Gospel to the end of the street! Now that this Coronavirus Pandemic has hit America and the world; churches, pastors, deacons, and other leaders in the church are scrambling to find some way to overcome the "social distancing" to fulfill The Great Commission. Perhaps one of the reasons why God allowed the pandemic to come was to rock the boat a little so that we would behave as fishers of men again. Think about it, we were rocking along and do evangelism the same old way with a few new methods here and there, and "bam!" the pandemic hits. But think who was really doing the work, was it everyone in the church or just the pastors, deacons, and/or church leaders. There is an old saying that 90% of the work in the church is done by 10% of the people. If it was God's intentions to bring about this pandemic, then perhaps one of the reasons was to refocus His children upon Him, the home, and to create a desire to behave as fishers of men. Because one thing this "social distancing" has done it has brought the family and the church family a little closer by building a desire to see people. And we need to get back to the task at hand, sharing the Gospel of Jesus Christ and the best way to do that is by making yourself available to the Holy Spirit.

You see, we as the children of God have forgotten the truth that Christianity is a militant, active faith. Our calling is not to endure to the end; but to storm the very gates of Hell. Jesus said, "I also say to you that you are Peter, and on this rock, I will build My church, and the gates of Hades shall not prevail against it" (Matt. 16:18 NKJV). Our orders are not to sit by while the world drops off into Hell; our orders are to go into the world and tell them the glorious news of a crucified and risen savior who specializes in saving souls, and changing lives and eternal destinies.

While the church has pulled the covers of complacency and apathy over her eyes and has fallen into the deep slumber of self-satisfaction and comfort the world continues to plunge headlong into Hell. Even during the pandemic, it seems as though the church is okay with what the world tells her she can and cannot do. And even though pastors, evangelist, and church leaders are struggling to behave as fishers of men and make disciples to be fishers of men; I fear that the door of evangelism is closing in America. Despite the conditions around us; despite the difficulties, danger, and persecutions; despite every excuse we offer, The Great Commission of our Lord and Savior Jesus Christ still stands! Christ still expects His followers to behave as fishers of men and take His message to a lost and dying world so they might hear the wonderful words of life.

Has the Great Commission become the Great Omission in your life? Are you doing everything you can to find the creative methods of sharing the Gospel of Jesus Christ during a pandemic? In this chapter I want to take a fresh look at The Great Commission. I want to take a closer look at our marching orders that He has given to every one of His children.

God's Unlimited Power

Jesus said, "All authority has been given to Me in heaven and on earth" (Matt. 28:18 NKJV). The KJV uses the word "power" in the place of "authority" (Matt. 28:18 KJV). Power does not mean energy, but authority; the One in control of all things. Just think that Jesus has all the authority in the universe, which means that His word is the final word. He controls everything with just a word. He has authority because God has declared Him Lord. The angels have announced that He is Lord. Everything was created "through Him, and without Him nothing was made that was made" (John 1:3 NKJV). Therefore, we must obey Him and crown Him as Lord. There is an old saying "God said it, I believe it, and that settles it"; listen God settles it whether you believe it or not. Jesus is Lord, the One true God.

Jesus is Lord in heaven and on earth. Since Jesus has power on earth that means that He is in control with sovereign authority over the nations, weather, politics, viruses, nature, animals, etc. With this sovereign authority He can set up and control Christianity. Remember that He told Peter, "on this Rock I will build My church, and the gates of Hades shall not prevail against it" (Matt. 16:18 NKJV). Okay, who is the Rock? The Greek word for rock is "*petra*" which means "rock ledge" which is a solid foundation (Strong's Concordance 1984). So, Jesus is not going to build upon a stone ("*petros*": which means loose rocks)

(Strong's Concordance 1984), but upon "The Rock". Now Peter is not "The Rock" although his name means rock or actually *"petros"*. "The Rock" that Jesus is going to build His church upon, with His Sovereign authority, is the confession that Jesus is Lord, the Messiah, the Son of the living God. This truth is Jesus, with His power, is going to build His church and make Himself the Chief Cornerstone, (Eph. 2:20 NKJV). Jesus is spoken of as the "The Rock" in 1 Corinthians 10:4 (NKJV), which says, "and all drank the same spiritual drink. For they drank of that spiritual Rock that followed them, and that Rock was Christ".

Since the church is built upon faith in the Lord Jesus Christ as the Sovereign Lord in control of all things, who gave His life upon Calvary to save us from our sins, and gives us eternal life; therefore, that means that the church has the power of Jesus Christ with in the hearts of the children of God, and His power is moving in the church so with all that is going on in the world today the gates of Hell cannot and will not prevail against it. If we are going to behave as fishers of men then we need to behave as a follower of Jesus in the power and authority of Jesus who through the Holy Spirit resides in us and goes before us preparing the hearts of lost sinners. Because the Gospel of Jesus Christ transcends every language, every culture, every nationality, every color, ever race, and every rank of people in all the world. All lives matter to Jesus!

Now when Jesus says "in heaven" (Matt. 28:18 NKJV) that literally means, "in the heavenlies"; that is, the realm of spiritual things, and that includes where the angels are, that includes the realm of the demons; it includes all spiritual creatures, it also includes the throne room in heaven itself (Strong's Concordance 1984). He is Lord over them. Angels serve Him and demons bow down before Him and cringe at His authority and power. "If God be for us, who can be against us" (Rom. 8:31 NKJV)? When you put the phrase "in heaven and on earth" together it means that He has authority everywhere. There is no place He does not belong, there is no power that can stand against Him. There are no powers in the heavenlies, no demon power, no Satan power, political power, government power, or world power that can withstand Him.

His Gospel is universal and since He does have ALL authority "in heaven and on earth"; Jesus says, "Go therefore" (Matt. 28:19

NKJV) which it is implied "Go [you] therefore". That does not mean: "Go some of you" because the "ye" in the Matthew 28:19 (KJV), that translates into "you" and both uses in the NKJV and the KJV are plural; it is a universal command to go and share a universal gospel (Strong's Concordance 1984). I believe that it is possible that Jesus gave The Great Commission to at least five hundred people according to 1 Corinthians 15:6 (NKJV). That means that this command was not to a select few, but for every person who puts their faith and trust in the Lord Jesus Christ to save them from their sins. This command is for every generation and is to be applied and obeyed to the life of the child of God, so that they can be made into and will behave as a fisher of men. Let me be a little blunt: If you fail to obey the Lord Jesus Christ in the Great Commission that is high treason against your King!

We Have a Divine Mandate

According to Matthew 28:19 (NKJV) the mandate of the Great Commission is to "Go". This is a word of action! We cannot "go" if we are sitting still. We cannot "go" if we stay in our comfort zones. We cannot "go" if we do not make a move. This verb "go" literally means "as you go", as you pass through this world, we are to carry the Gospel message with us, sharing it with everyone we meet along the way (Strong's Concordance 1984). There are two ways we can do this.

First, it involves our lifestyle. In Matthew 5:13-16 (NKJV), Jesus tells believers to be salt and light. Like salt, our life should create a thirst in lost souls for the Lord Jesus Christ. Our joy, unspeakable and full of glory should cause them to want to know more about why we behave the way we do. The peace in our lives should create a desire in the hearts of the unrest that lost souls have as they see the difficult storms of life pass in ours. As light we should be like a great tall lighthouse which directs its beam toward Jesus. If He is the focus of our lives and we behave as a follower of Jesus Christ, then men, women, boys, and girls will see Him lived out through our life day by day!

Second, it involves our lips. The KJV says, "Go ye therefore, and teach" (Matt. 28:19 KJV). The word "teach" has the idea of "making disciples" as used in the NKJV, or it can also mean "to instruct" (Strong's Concordance 1984). That means you must do evangelism and discipleship. I believe that the two go hand in hand and they do not need to be done without the other. So, how do you make a disciple? Well, you must first bring a person to the saving grace of the Lord Jesus Christ through faith in the completed work upon the cross. Evangelism is telling someone that Jesus is mighty to save. The very heart of God is to save lost sinners. Jesus says, "The Son of man is come to seek and to save that which was lost" (Luke 19:10 NKJV). And if you are not concerned about bringing people to Jesus Christ, you had better examine your heart and see if you are saved. If Jesus is real to you, if Jesus Christ is a blessing to you, wouldn't you want to share Jesus? Salvation is in Jesus Christ and Jesus Christ alone. Jesus said, "I am the way, the truth, and the life; no man comes to the Father, but by Me" (John 14:6 NKJV). Acts 4:12 (NKJV) says, "Neither is there salvation in any other: for there is no other name under heaven given among men, whereby we must be saved". There is no other way; and it is our duty, our privilege, our mandate to live and behave as a follower of Jesus Christ, and to share our faith. Mark 16:15 says this, "Go into all the world and preach the gospel to every creature". The word "preach" comes from the word that means "to herald" (Strong's Concordance 1984). Like a king's herald, we are to pass through the highways and the byways of life and lift our voices to declare the Gospel of grace! The "preach" is a present tense, active voice, imperative mood verb (Dictionary 1828). The imperative means that it is a command. The active voice means that you are to be involved in carrying out this command. The present tense means that it is something we are supposed to be doing all the time.

But not only are we to evangelize them we are to make disciples. The word "disciple" literally means, "to disciple" all nations (Dictionary 1828). It means "to make disciples" of all the nations. In other words, teach them how to behave as a follower of Jesus Christ; by sharing how Jesus has taught you to behave as a follower. Some has asked, "What if they never hear? Are they lost if they never even hear?" Let me purpose a harder question: "Are we saved if we don't tell?" If we believe what we believe, we are to make disciples of all nations, and that begins with your next-door neighbor; that begins with the members of your family; it begins in "Jerusalem, Judea, Samaria, and the uttermost parts of the earth" (Acts 1:8 NKJV). It is the marching order of the church and the children of God to do evangelism and to make disciples.

As you continue to make disciples you also need to mark disciples. Jesus next said, "baptizing them in the name of the Father and of the Son and of the Holy Spirit" (Matt. 28:19 NKJV). What is baptism? Baptism is the outward declaration of what Jesus has done inside a person who now belongs to Jesus Christ. Somewhere down through the years the church or we as individuals have minimized baptism. Jesus never minimized baptism, and He only had a ministry of three years. Here is a trivia question: How did Jesus begin His ministry? The answer: by being baptized. He was fully immersed in the Jordan River. So, how did Jesus conclude His ministry? By commanding to go out and make disciples and baptize them. Baptism symbolizes the death, burial, and resurrection of Jesus Christ. How? When the person is standing in the water, that represents Jesus' death on the cross. As the disciple of Christ places the newly saved person in the water that represents the burial of Jesus Christ. As the person comes up out of the water that represents the resurrection of Jesus Christ. And from there we are to help the newly saved child of God walk and behave in the newness of life. "Therefore, we were buried with through baptism into death, that just as Christ was raised from the dead by the glory of the Father, even so we also should walk in newness of life. For if we have been united together in the likeness of His death, certainly we also shall be in the likeness of His resurrection" (Rom. 6:4-5 NKJV).

We Have a Divine Message

Jesus tells His followers to share a specific message: "to observe all things that I have commanded you" (Matt. 28:20a NKJV). We are to go tell the world about Jesus by sharing a truly clear Gospel message. If there is one message that the devil would like to take out of the church, it would be the Gospel. If there is one message that God wants to permanent in the church is the Gospel. And every time anybody gets saved, we are to make a disciple out of them, and then baptize them, give a graphic illustration of what it was that saved them: the death, burial, and resurrection of Jesus Christ. However, it is not enough to just get them saved. It is not enough to get them baptized. We are to pour the Word of God into these disciples because as we make them and mark them, we are then to mature them. After we have evangelized and enlisted these new saints of God, we must edify them. And they are to begin "to grow in the grace and knowledge of our Lord and Savior Jesus Christ" (2 Pet. 3:18 NKJV). We need to teach them what He commanded us. We are to teach them the message of the Gospel. That it is not about our church or our denomination. That it is not about our preacher or about our standards of dress and music. That it is not about our style of worship. All of those are important, but none of those can save a lost, hell bound soul. We need to teach them the simple message that there is hope for the hurting, there is life for the dead; there is peace for the tormented, that the Gospel "is the power of God unto salvation, to the Jew first and also to the Greek" (Rom. 1:16 NKJV). Teach them that the Gospel message is for everyone in the world, that it is has one universal application: through faith. Teach them that the message has the potential to change every life and every eternity that falls under the power and grace of Jesus Christ (John 1:11-12 NKJV).

We are not just simply fishers of men but we are fishers of men making fishers of men by behaving as followers of Jesus Christ through the power that has been given Him by God the Father who has place that power in the heart of every child of God in the person of the Holy Spirit. My evangelism is not complete when I simply win a person to Christ on a street corner. I am to stay by that person, come along side that person until that person makes a public display of profession of faith by being baptized. But that is when my discipleship duty kicks in. Now I am to stay with that person, to love on that person, to edify that person, and teach them until that person becomes a fisher of men as well. Then I have fulfilled the Great Commission when I have taught that person what He commanded me. Then Christianity has begun to take off in such an incredible way. Who is your one? Who is someone that you can go after and complete the Great Commission? But don't stop there once you complete the Great Commission in one then go after another one.

We Have a Divine Mentor

We are living in perilous times but to sit there and think that even though we are living in the last days, that there is no power to fulfill the Great Commission! Jesus said, "and lo, I am with you always, even to the end of the age" (Matt. 28:20b NKJV). God is not dead! God is not old! God is not sick! God is not quarantined! His power is not and will not diminish! He still has the power to "rescue the perishing, care for the dying, snatch them in pity from sin and the grave" (Crosby 1991). I believe that these perilous days in which we live are the greatest days for evangelism the world has ever seen. Therefore, Jesus doesn't send us out in this world, without any resources. He doesn't expect us to accomplish this Great Commission in our own power. In fact, Jesus' statement here in verse 20 gives us two of the greatest resources we have as fishers of men.

First, we are promised His presence. Think about the entire Great Commission statement. The "lo" and "go" are linked together. "You go, and lo, I am with you". Jesus Christ will never be more near to you than when you are out in the mission field serving the Lord. When you are standing there sharing the Gospel with that friend, that family member, even that total stranger, the Lord Himself is right there with you. He will help you, enable you, encourage you, and use you if you will simply obey Him and share the Gospel. You will find that you have incredible faith and strength to share the Gospel, and all you have to do is open your mouth and let the Holy Spirit put the words in your mouth. God says, "So shall My word be that goes forth from My mouth; it shall not return to Me void, but it shall accomplish what I please, and it shall proper in the thing for which I sent it" (Isa. 55:11 NKJV). He will help with what to say when the witnessing opportunity presents itself. Jesus said, "But when they deliver you up, do not worry about how or what you should speak. For it will be given to you in that hour what you should speak; for it is not you who speak, but the Spirit of your Father who speaks in you" (Matt. 10:19-20 NKJV). If you think about it, when we are sharing the Gospel with someone we are on trial for our faith. And He will give us the words we need when the time comes.

Second, we are promised His power. If you have not picked up on it in this chapter, let me remind you again, "All power in heaven and earth is given unto Me" (Matt. 28:18 NKJV). Then later He says, "But you shall receive power when the Holy Spirit has come upon you; and you shall be my witnesses to Me" (Acts 1:8 NKJV). When we are faithful to share His Gospel message, we can behave in confidence as fisher of men, because God will use His message for His glory. He will take our feeble words and He will attach His power to them. The Holy Spirit will take our efforts and He will use the words we share to convict the hearts of the lost (John 16:7-8 NKJV). You are going to find that you have a sense of anointing because He is with you. He moves alongside of those who will follow Him and obey Him. His authority, His power is behind you. His Spirit will be within you as you carry out the Great Commission, and you are given your marching to "Go" behave as a fisher of men.

CHAPTER TWO

Seeing the Harvest Through His Eyes

But when He saw the multitudes, He was moved with compassion for them, because they were weary and scattered, like sheep having no shepherd. (Matthew 9:36 NKJV)

ON A DANGEROUS SEACOAST WHERE SHIPWRECKS OFTEN OCCUR, THERE was once a little-saving station. The building was primitive, and there was just one boat, but the members of the life-saving station were committed and kept a constant watch over the sea. When a ship went down, they unselfishly went out day or night to save the lost. Because so many lives were saved by that station, it became famous. Consequently, many people want to be associated with the station to give their time, talent, and money to support its important work. New boats were bought, new crews were recruited, and a formal training session was offered. As the membership in the life-saving station grew, some of the members became unhappy that the building was so primitive, and that the equipment was so outdated. They wanted a better place to welcome the survivors pulled from the sea. So, they replaced the emergency cot with beds and put better furniture in the enlarged and newly decorated building.

Now the life-saving station became a popular gathering place for its members. They met regularly and when they did, it was apparent how they loved one another. They greeted each other, hugged each other, and shared with one another the events that had been going on in their lives. But fewer members were now interested in going to sea on life-saving missions; so, they hired lifeboat crews to do this for them. About this time, a large ship was wrecked off the coast, and the hired crews brought into the life-saving station boatloads of cold, wet, dirty, sick, and half-drowned people. Some of them had black skin, some had yellow skin; some spoke English, and some could hardly speak it at all; some were first-class cabin passengers of the ship and some were the deck hands. The beautiful meeting place became a place of chaos. The plush carpets got dirty. Some of the exquisite furniture got scratched. So, the property committee immediately had a shower built outside the house where the victims of shipwrecks could be cleaned up before coming inside.

At the next meeting there was a rift in the membership. Most of the members wanted to stop the club's life-saving activities, for they were unpleasant and a hindrance to the normal fellowship of the members. Other members insisted that lifesaving was their primary purpose and pointed out that they were still called a life-saving station. But they were finally voted down and told that it if they wanted to save the lives all those various kinds of people who would be shipwrecked, they could begin their own life-saving station down the coast. And do you know what? That is what they did.

As the years passed, the new station experienced the same changes that had occurred in the old station. It evolved into a place to meet regularly for fellowship, for committee meetings, and for special training sessions about their mission, but few went out to the drowning people. The drowning people were no longer welcomed in that new life-saving station. So, another life-saving station was founded further down the coast. History continued to repeat itself. And if you visit that seacoast today, you will find several adequate meeting places with ample parking and plush carpeting. Shipwrecks are frequent in those waters, but most of the people drown.

This is a parable of the conditions of the modern church. I do not want to hurt anyone's feelings, but here are the facts. We have become more concerned about buildings than about people. We are more interested in having our meetings than we are in fulfilling our mission. We are more interested in our personal comfort than we are about who is drowning in the sea of sin just beyond our walls. We are more concerned about the condition of our budget than we are the right kind of people. I am afraid that The Great Commission has become a scab over our eyes, and we are no longer looking through the eyes of Jesus. Therefore, we need as individual fishers of men and as cooperate fishers of men to have a fresh vision for those who are lost and dying and going to a place called Hell.

That is why Jesus said, "The harvest truly is plentiful" (Matt. 9: 37 NKJV). There are people to reach; there is "work" to be done, and one of the greatest dangers of modern-day fisher of men is that we don't see this as the most important work. Most everything else comes before the work of reaching the lost with the Word of God. As Jesus ministered to the needs of the people around Him, He met their physical needs, but He was able to see beyond that. Jesus was able to see the deepest needs of their hearts. As Jesus looked at the multitudes around Him, He was moved with compassion for them. This word "compassion" literally means "to be moved in the heart" (Dictionary 1828). He saw the reality of the need of the people all around Him. He saw them as they were, and He sought to share this insight with His disciples. He still wants to share that insight with you and me as He continues to help us behave as fishers of men. He wants us to see the dilemma of humanity as He does. He wants us to see people as they really are. He wants us to be moved in the heart just as He was. He wants us to be able to see the harvest through His eyes. So, perhaps this pandemic, the rioting, and the mudslinging that surrounds the 2020 election is His way of opening our eyes to all that. In Matthew's account, the words of Jesus will help see the new vision if we are going to behave as fishers of men.

He Saw the Pity of the Harvest

When Jesus looked at the lost people around Him, He saw them as they really were (Matt. 9:36 NKJV). He was able to look beyond their self-sufficiency, self-righteousness, and self-confidence. He saw the pain, the loneliness, and the misery they felt in their hearts! Jesus saw a people who "fainted", that "grew weary" under the load of their sins and the unrealistic expectations forces upon them by the religious leaders. He saw a people who were "scattered". People who were wondering aimlessly through life with no direction and planned destination, people who lived life with no shepherd for their souls. He saw a people who were utterly and hopelessly lost.

What do we see when we look at people today? Can we see the multitudes like Jesus saw them? There could be a family in your community that seems happy. They have good jobs, plenty of money, a nice house, and all the thing this world can offer them. There are plenty of people like that live in our community. However, if you could look into their hearts, you would be able to see turmoil, fear, loneliness, and desperation. They have no answers to their questions. They need the Lord Jesus Christ! There is another family. They don't have much as the first family, but they do work, and they have a place to live. Their lives are driven by alcohol and drugs. They seem hard hearted towards the Gospel and are hostile toward those who try to tell them about Jesus. But, if you could rip aside the layers of their lives and peer into their souls, you would see people who are afraid to die and even afraid to life. They are people without hope, and they need someone to see them as they really are. Someone who can see them as they are and still love them, that is the person who can reach them for Jesus!

Then there are the youth and young children of our community. They seem happy without a care in this world. But if you could see their lives and know their hearts you would find that most of them are lonely because mom and dad doesn't love them; doesn't care about their health. You would find fear; afraid that mom and dad are going to fight again, or worse get a divorce; afraid that their parents may abuse them again. Then as you look at their souls you would find hatred toward a God who is supposed to love them but seems to allow bad things to happen to them. Let me give you some information that can be discovered from The Children's Defense Fund reports that takes place every single day in America. Every day 1 young person under the age of 25 dies from HIV infection. Every day 5 children or youth under the age of 20 commit suicide. Every day 9 children or youth under the age of 20 are homicide victims. Every day 34 children or youth under 20 die in accidents. Every day in America, 180 children are arrested for violent crimes; 367 children are arrested for drug abuse; 437 are arrested for drinking or drunk driving. Every day in America, 2,861 high school students drop out; 3,288 children run away from home. Every day in America, 7,883 children are reported abused or neglected. (The Children Defense Fund 2019) That is every day in our country. These youth and young children need hope, love, and joy that they have never experience. Oh, if we could only behave as fishers of men and see the harvest though His eyes!

I could go on and on with scenario after scenario, but what Jesus really saw was the end of those people's existence. He knew that without a relationship with Him, they were all doomed to perish in Hell. That is the fresh vision we need to see if we are going to behave as fishers of men. Our friends, family, neighbors may look like they have it all together, but if they are lost and they die lost the are going to a place called Hell, and they need to be saved before it is everlasting too late!

He Saw the Potential of the Harvest

Jesus looked up at the crowd around Him and He saw a "plentiful" harvest (Matt. 9:37 NKJV). I am sure all the disciples saw were people pushing and shoving to get close to their leader. But Jesus saw more! He saw men who needed to be saved by grace. He saw a harvest that was ripe for the picking! He looked beyond their condition and their destination and He saw a people that could be delivered, changed, and saved! He did not see the problems, only the potential!

What do we see when we look at all the people around us? Do we see sinners lost in their filthiness and vileness? Do we see people who live like dogs and don't care? Do we want people to go to Hell? Or do we see them as someone the Lord could make new when they came to Him? That is the view Jesus had of lost men. He saw them not as they were, but as they could be by grace! We need that same kind of vision if we are going to behave as fishers of men.

One day Jesus stood with His disciples outside the city of the Samaritans. Now the Samaritans were a people who were despised by the Jews of Jesus' day. The Samaritans came about through the intermarriage of Jews with colonist sent to live in Israel by the Babylonians. Jesus went to a city of the Samaritans and spoke to a sinful woman. He saw her not just as she was, but as she could be through grace. He saved her and many other Samaritans because Jesus looked at the harvest as being everywhere and plentiful. Now His words to His disciples immediately after this event is interesting as John 4:27-28 (NKJV) records it for us.

HE WANTED TO TEACH THEM ABOUT THEIR FARMING

Notice the phrase in John 4:35 (NKJV), "Do you not say, 'There are still four months and then comes the harvest?'" Now it is possible that as they traveled back to Galilee (John 4:3 NKJV) via Samaria (John 4:4 NKJV) they went through some fields and the disciples started talking about the harvest. Which reminded Jesus of a common farming statement, "Four months between seed time and harvest". This being fresh on His mind knew that the Samaritan woman was going to bring a vast multitude out to Jesus us their conversation and the farming statement to teach them the vision of His ministry and wanted them to be able to see the harvest through His eyes.

Think about the illustration that Jesus is using. When the farmer sows his seed, he must wait before it produces crops. He is encouraged that when he sows the seed he can expect fruit. Plus, it gives him encouragement that his labor is not in vain by that expectation. But no matter how hard he tries the fruit will not be "immediate". This is just the opposite when it comes to preaching, teaching, and sharing the Gospel because there are times when you can see the fruit spring up "immediately". However, the sad fact is that we have scarcely sown the Gospel seed. We go out and share the Gospel and see no fruit and therefore we back off. We have a revival meeting and get pumped up to go out and share the Gospel. We see some fruit but not enough to keep us going. Apparently we have sown in the wrong places. Jeremiah says, "They have sown wheat but reaped thorns; they have put themselves to pain but do not profit. But be ashamed of your harvest because of the fierce anger of the Lord" (Jer. 12:13 NKJV).

The farming statement is a common expression that says, "Hey, there is plenty of time until the hard work of the harvest comes". Since this was just a common expression that these disciples had heard all their life, they were unmotivated to the ministry they were being trained. Therefore, Jesus was giving them a vision to motivate them to behave as fishers of men. Today we have become unmotivated about sowing the Gospel seed and behaving as fishers of men because it seems like we have lost the ability to see the harvest through His eyes.

How much do you like fresh tomatoes, green beans, okra, cucumbers, and other fresh veggies? To have all those fresh veggies you must plant a garden. Would it be great if the garden spot tilled itself? Would it be great if the seeds of those vegetables went out and planted themselves in the newly tilled garden? Would you even have a garden if all you did was look at the seeds of these vegetables and wished you had fresh veggies? No, no you would not! The "Gospel" seed was just preached and planted in the woman at the well, but how many of the Samaritans came to hear it As well? The disciples had no reason to think that harvest time was still in the distance. They could not afford to spend their lives in quest of food or clothing, with the thought that God's work could be done later. We cannot afford to sit around on our seat of do nothing, while the harvest is white! We need to be about behaving as fishers of men and evangelizing the lost! Oh sure, you can have this event or that event going on at your church for inviting people to come to church, but if your event is not centered around sharing the Gospel and using that opportunity to disciple children of God how to be fishers of men then your event is not good enough. For all you will be doing is nothing more than "scratching itchy ears" (2 Tim. 4:3 NKJV). Our farming is to be about planting the seed of the Gospel.

HE WANTED TO TEACH THEM ABOUT THEIR FOCUS

Notice what Jesus says, "lift up your eyes and look at the fields" (John 4:35 NKJV). For Jesus to say lift up your eyes or to look implies that their focus was not in the right place. Where had the disciples been? According to John 4:8, they had gone into the city to buy food. When the disciples got back from getting food, they were shocked to find Jesus talking to a Samaritan woman. Once she left, they urged Jesus to share the meal with them because they knew He was hungry. However, Jesus told them, "I have food to eat of which you do not know" (John 4:32 NKJV). This shows us that their focus was not where it should have been, because they did not understand where in the world did He get the food to eat, (John 4:33 NKJV). Jesus was trying to turn their attention from the material things of this world to the spiritual. His food was to do the will of God, and to finish the work which God the Father had given Him to do. The disciples were satisfied with bread, but He was satisfied with accomplishing the Father's work.

Now don't be too hard on the disciples because we do the same thing; our focus is not where it should be. We are creatures of sight and habit. We will put our focus on material things (ex. Statistics, baptisms, budget, building size, children's events, youth programs, type of music we sing during worship, which version of the Bible is better, does the preacher preach expository or topical, color of pews or carpet, etc.). All these things are fine for the purpose they are intended but these material things can take our focus off the main thing behaving as fishers of men and sharing the Gospel with a lost and dying world. We need to revive the vision of seeing the harvest through his eyes. Because indifference on the part of our church members can bring a cold, compassionless, and complacent ministry to the pulpit, to the Sunday School class, to youth program, and children's ministry. Lack of concern for souls is often the result of poor farming preparation and a focus that is preoccupied with private interests. Many permits themselves are lulled to sleep by the promises and comforts of materialism. Consequently, in many instances evangelism has been on the sidetrack instead of the main track because we sit in our pews. Today many so-called Disciples of Christ have joined another movement called the "Sitting Squad". They found themselves a comfortable cushion instead behaving like fishers of men. We have made our church cold storage plants instead of power stations. When we sow the seed from our chairs and place our focus on the material instead of the spiritual, we will reap thorns and thistles instead of bringing in the sheaves, (Jer. 12:13 NKJV).

HE WANTED TO TEACH THEM ABOUT THEIR FIELD

Notice the last phrase that Jesus says, "for they are already white for the harvest" (John 4:35 NKJV)! At the very moment Jesus is speaking these words, He and His disciples were in the midst of a harvest field containing the souls of the Samaritans. He was telling them that it did not matter what type of human beings they were all lives matter to Jesus. He was telling them that a great work of the fishers of men lay before them, and they should give themselves to it immediately and diligently.

As we sit around in our chairs contemplating the great needs of the world and the answers to the pandemic, the rioting, and/or the election, there are human beings dying lost and going to a place called Hell. God has given us the Great Commission, but where does it say that we can bring in the harvest by sitting in our pews. It doesn't; but it says just the opposite, "Go" and "make". "Lift up your eyes, and look at the fields, for they are already white" (John 4:35 NKJV). Think about what Jesus is saying. Wheat fields, ready for the harvest are a beautiful golden color. That is why we sang, "for amber waves of grain" (Bates 1991). Now, if the harvest is delayed that kernel of wheat will swell and split wide open and give the field a white appearance rather than a golden appearance. If it is not harvested immediately, it spoils and is LOST. If we don't behave as fishers of men, people all around us are endanger of being lost forever, unless we reap them immediately. And these fields that Jesus spoke of were farmed by someone else. John the Baptist had planted a seed for six months and now the disciples come on the scene and they hear Jesus talking about these fields that needed to be harvested. They talked to others about it, who then talked to others about it, so what happened? According to the Book of Acts 2:41 (NKJV), 3,000 people are won to the Lord. In Acts 4:4 (NKJV), 5,000 more are won to the Lord, and in Acts 5:14 (NKJV) multitudes are won to the Lord. So, they went about doing that which Jesus taught them to do, behaving as fishers of men, because Jesus had shared the vision that we need to have and that is seeing the harvest through the eyes of Jesus. There are fields out there for us today!

He Saw the Problem of the Harvest

Matthew records what Jesus thinks the problem is about the harvest, Jesus says, "The harvest truly is plentiful, but the laborers are few" (Matt. 9:37 NKJV). As Jesus looked at the harvest, He acknowledged the fact that it was plentiful and that it was pitiful, for He saw lost men all around. Then He recognized a problem: there were not enough fishers of men working in the Father's fields. This is still a major problem today! Reaping the soul harvest is hard work and few, it seems are willing to roll up their sleeves, and get involved in the work. There are even some who know the vision, and have seen the vision that they have either determined to close their eyes to keep from looking at the field or they have determined which fields are only the ones that they want in their church.

My dad was sitting in a Sunday School classroom along with a pulpit committee of a church in Middle Tennessee one Sunday evening. They were going around and asking question to get to know my dad and the type of pastor he was. One question was asked, "If you come here to be our pastor what kind of ministries can we expect from you?" One of the things my dad said to them was he would like to start a van ministry to pick up the neighborhood kids from around the town and bring them to Sunday School and Church Training. One little old lady that happen to be on the Search Committee spoke up quick and I quote, "We do not want them snotty nose little kids running around in our church messing things up". Dad did not get the church. Now fast forward today, because of the location of the town which was about five miles from a city that growing with leaps and bounds due to the major college, the overflow began to move towards this town of that church. There are now three churches in that town that run well over 200 people. But this little church because they did not catch the vision or was unwilling to go out and bring in the harvest is now closed.

Jesus called His men to follow Him, promising to make them "fishers of men" (Matt. 4:18-22 NKJV). Of course, to fish, requires the fishermen to go where the fish are to the water! If you want those fresh vegetables, you know that they won't just gather themselves. You must go out to the garden, get down where the vegetables are, and do the dirty work of harvesting them. The same is true in bringing men to Jesus. We can sit in our pews if we want to, but we will not see the harvest unto we go where the lost men, women, boys, and girls are living. "Is the seed still in the barn? As yet the vine, the fig tree, the pomegranate, and the olive tree have not yielded fruit. But from this day I will bless you" (Hag. 2:19 NKJV). Haggai was telling them if they would resume the work of building the temple God would bless them. Listen if we would just catch the vision and "Go" and "make" God is going to bless. Behaving as fishers of men is dirty work, but it must be done, or the harvest will never be reaped!

Surely, we can see that people are in sad shape today, spiritually speaking. Surely, we care about them and want to see them saved by grace. May we come to the place where we are not content to just see the harvest through His eyes, but may we come to a place where we become willing to go into the harvest and reap it for Jesus' sake, behaving the fishers of men that we were discipled to be.

CHAPTER THREE

Mission Impossible: Reaching Out to the Dead

Where there is no vision, the people perish. (Proverbs 29:18 NKJV)

WHAT DOES IT MEAN TO BE A CHRISTIAN? THAT QUESTION WAS ASKED to one thousand people. Some of them gave multiple answers, while the response was astonishing with answers like: "Living different from other people"; "Loving and helping each other"; "Believing in God"; "Going to church"; and "Being good". There were some who just did not know what it means to be a Christian. The sad thing is that the lowest answer was "accepting Jesus Christ as Savior and having a personal relationship with Him". Now from this survey, it is obvious that the world doesn't know what it means to be Christian. It is also obvious that the world doesn't know what it means to be lost.

If we are going to see the harvest through the eyes of Jesus, then we must remember what it was like to be lost. Let me share with you eleven characteristics of a lost person, starting in the Book of Matthew and continuing through the New Testament. Matthew 12:30 (NKJV) tells us that the lost person is an enemy of God. Luke 15:11 (NKJV) and following refers to the lost son, simply meaning he is away from the Father. John 3:16 (NKJV) indicates that the lost person is perishing and heading towards an eternal torment. John 3:18 (NKJV) states that the lost person is under condemnation, which means he is already judged because of sin in his life. In John 8:44 (NKJV), Jesus tells some people they are children of the devil. Romans 3:9 (NKJV) states that the lost person is under sin, which simply means the he or she is born into sin. 2 Corinthians 4:3-4 (NKJV) states that a lost person is blind, which means that he or she cannot understand spiritual things. Ephesians 2:1 (NKJV) states, that a lost person is dead, which means that the lost person is spiritually dead. Ephesians 2:12 (NKJV) states that a lost person is without God, without hope, and without Jesus.

In the book of Ezekiel, Ezekiel's ministry was marked by a series of visions. One of those visions is the "Vision of the Valley of the Dry Bones" which has become a very familiar passage of Scripture. I have heard this vision used many times to preach about the need for revival in the church, and it is a valid use of Ezekiel 37:1-14 (NKJV). Yet, we must understand that God is not speaking to the church in those verses. He is speaking to the nation of Israel (Ezek. 37:11 NKJV). He sees them as a dead nation, and He promises that there will come a day when He will raise them from the dead and use them again for His glory.

Let me give some information on Ezekiel. He was a twenty-five-year-old priest from the family of Zadok, he, along with the king and 10,000 Jews were taken to Babylon in 598 BC. Five years later, in 593 BC, Ezekiel was called in to the ministry by God. Ezekiel's name means "strengthened by God" (Strong's Concordance 1984) and there can be little doubt that the visions he was given during his twenty plus years of faithful ministry were used to challenge and strengthen his fellow brethren. You see, that is what a vision is supposed to do, strengthen the one it is given to. Solomon knew this when he wrote Proverbs 29:18 (NKJV) which says, "Where there is no vision the people perish". If we do not keep the vision of the harvest of lost souls in front of us, we will let things like a pandemic, riots, persecution, an election, or other worldly issues over shadow the need to "go" and "make" because we have given up.

When Ezekiel received the vision of the dry bones, he found himself surrounded by the bones of the dead. Everywhere he looked he saw dead people. He was commanded to preach to them. And he was commanded to pray over them. When He obeyed the Lord's command, Ezekiel saw those dead bodies brought back to life. He saw the Lord's grace on display in that graveyard, and that is the thought I want to magnify from Ezekiel 37:1-4 (NKJV) for us today. Because even though this is written to Israel, we can draw from the it a vision to go out and behave as fishers of men. We can also learn and remember what it is like to be a lost soul. Like Ezekiel, we are surrounded by the dead. Everywhere we look there is evidence of the spiritual death that dominates our world. And like Ezekiel, we have been sent out to tell the dead that they can live. Now, from Ezekiel's position, staring at those dry bones, his task must have seemed like an impossible mission. Yet, he obeyed God and God blessed his efforts. From where we stand today, the task of reaching out to the dead in sin also may seem like an impossible task. However, we must remember who it is that is building the church and building His kingdom: it's Jesus!

A Shocking Revelation

If we are going to get a sense of the great need of the lostness of the world around us, then we are going to need to understand and get a clear grasp on the condition of the lost souls around us. The vision Ezekiel saw was a valley full of dry, scattered bones. It depicted the desolation, destitution, and devastation of Israel. Until we have a similar vision of the world in which we live we will not be stirred to action. We need to see what Ezekiel saw when he looked out over that valley of dry bones.

HE SAW DEATH

"The hand of the Lord came upon me and brought me out in the Spirit of the Lord and set me down in the midst of the valley; and it was full of bones" (Ezek. 37:1 NKJV). The bones speak of death. Since so many bones were in one place, it may be that Ezekiel saw the aftermath of a great battle. If that is the case, it must have broken his heart. One of the worst insults Jews could suffer was to be denied a proper burial. Here is a valley filled with the bones of the dead. They were defeated by their enemy and left to rot where they fell. Ezekiel saw a vision of death on a massive scale. What do you see when you look at the world around you, or on television? Although the people around us may be living lives, working jobs, enjoying their hobbies, raising their families, they may be charming, intellectual, reasonable, and physically fit; if they do not know Jesus Christ as their personal Lord and Savior, they are dead. Paul tells us that until the Holy Spirit quickens men and women to spiritual life they are "dead in trespasses and in sin" (Eph 2:1 NKJV). This can be true for your husband, your wife, your parents, your children, your friends, your neighbors, and your coworkers. While they may be full of life physically, they can be dead spiritually. We should pray and ask God to open our eyes and help us see the world around us as it really is (John 4:35 NKJV).

Paul gives us another description of the dead lost soul as he writes to the church at Corinth and tells them the lost is blind, "whose minds the gods of the age has blinded, who do not believe" (2 Cor. 4:4 NKJV). This simply means that lost people are blind to spiritual things by the god(s) of this world. They cannot see that they are without Christ. Spiritual things are as if they are covered and not seen at all by lost people. Although lost people can read the Bible and not understand it because God's Spirit does not live in them, they can understand enough to be saved. John 1:5 (NKJV) says, "and the light shine in the darkness, and the darkness did not comprehend it". John was saying that, although lost people may not understand spiritual things, they have received enough understanding to recognize that they are sinners and in need of a Savior in their life.

The great detriment to the church today is that we do not believe every person is lost. We draw the conclusion that if a man or woman is a good person, he or she must be saved. We draw our conclusion by what we see in this world of sin, drunks, adulterers, drug addicts, homosexuals, abortionist. We forget that those things don't make us sinners. Those things just reveal that we have sin in our lives. That sin was born in us when we were born physically. The Bible still teaches us that we are sinners by nature, then by choice. When we come to the place of choosing to be a sinner, we are no longer a sinner by nature, but by choice. The only thing it takes be lost is to refuse to accept Jesus Christ as your personal Lord and Savior. Good people are lost just like bad people are lost. Our outward lives do not make us sinners. The devil has led us to believe that if we are good, law-abiding citizens, everything is all right. Obviously, the church believes that also, because we lack the motivation and vision to share Jesus Christ with lost people.

HE SAW DEVASTATION

Then Ezekiel says, "Then He caused me to pass by them all around and behold, there were very many in the open valley; and indeed, they were dry" (Ezek. 37:2 NKJV). The bones Ezekiel saw were "very dry." They had been on that valley floor, under the merciless heat of the sun, until they were zapped of all moisture. In that dead, dry condition, they were fit for nothing but to be gathered and buried. They were absolutely useless. We need to recognize that this is the very condition of the lost around us. In Romans 3:12 (NKJV), Paul writes, "They have all turned aside; they have together become unprofitable; there is none who does good, no, not one." The word "unprofitable" means, "to be useless." (Dictionary 1828). This verse reminds us that the lost sinner is useless to God, they are unprofitable in the sense that He cannot use them for His glory. We should ask the Lord to open our eyes so that we can see the vision of the lost around and see the devastation of the world around us. The lost are trapped in a quagmire of sin, and they cannot escape. They are spiritually dead and devasted in their sins. In a real sense they are perishing, Paul writes, "But even if our gospel is veiled, it is veiled to those who are perishing" (2 Cor. 4:3 NKJV). The word "perishing" comes from the Greek word which means "taking away and being destroyed" (Strong's Concordance 1984). What this implies is that individuals are born into the world as sinners, and throughout their life they are in the process of being destroyed, without ever being destroyed. When they come to that time of dying physically, that destruction process will continue. Yet, even in the afterlife, they are never destroyed.

This is a picture of Hell. The Bible teaches that lost people begin to die the moment they are born, yet that death is never complete. They enter a place called Hell and continue the process but are never destroyed. Now, we don't like to think about this, but the vision of lost souls through the eyes of Jesus is teaching us about eternal separation from God in a place called Hell. I am not sure if we really believe it, because if we did, we would constantly be speaking to people we encounter about the need for salvation in their life. Pray, fishers of men, that God will open your eyes to the perishing. Look upon that family that is ruined by drugs and alcohol. They need someone to tell them about a way out. Look at the family destroyed by sexual sin. They need someone to tell them about a better way. Look at the family that seems so happy, yet they are headed to Hell. They need someone to warn them and to point them to the Lord Jesus Christ. Until we see the harvest through the eyes of Jesus we will never understand where they are, we will not be moved to reach out to them with the Gospel and behave as fishers of men.

HE SAW DEFEAT

Ezekiel says, "Then He said to me, "Son of man, these bones are the whole house of Israel. They indeed say, 'Our bones are dry, our hope is lost, and we ourselves are cut off!'"" (Ezek. 37:11 NKJV). The nation of Israel was defeated and had reached a place where they saw no way out of their captivity and no hope for their future. In a sense, they were not living; they were just existing. Ezekiel saw their hopelessness and he was moved by it. The Bible describes lost around us as "having no hope and without God in the world" (Eph. 2:12 NKJV). The hopelessness in the world is easy to see. The restlessness of the nations, the riots in our culture, the horrible condition of our economy, and the constant threat of war, all speak to the fact that people feel hopeless. When there is peace in the heart, there is rest in the life. When peace is missing, hopelessness reigns. Again, we need to ask the Lord to help us see the hopelessness of the lost that is living around us.

A Solemn Responsibility

As Ezekiel looked over that valley of dry bones, God spoke to the prophet and told him what to do. Ezekiel was shown that he had a personal responsibility to that valley of dead, dry bones. If we are going to behave as fishers of men, then we must understand that we have the same responsibility that rested on Ezekiel's shoulder. We have been planted where we are by God, and our responsibility is to reach out to the lost sinners that are in our communities, city, or town.

HE WAS COMMANCED TO PREACH

God said to Ezekiel, "Prophesy upon these bones, and say unto them, 'O dry bones, hear the word of the Lord!'" (Ezek. 37:4 NKJV). The Greek word for "prophesy" signifies two ideas: one is that of "forth-telling; speaking for God" or in other words preaching (Strong's Concordance 1984). The other idea of "prophesy" is that "foretelling" or predicting future events". To behave as a fisher of men you need to be able to do both: preach the word and foretell about the Second Coming of Christ. We will discuss the latter in another chapter. But just know, according to Paul, the primary purpose of prophecy is to build up the church. In 1 Corinthians 14:3-4 (NKJV) he says, "But he who prophesies speaks edification and exhortation and comfort to men…but he who prophesies edifies the church."

Ezekiel was commanded to preach to a valley filled with skeletons! Nothing could be more foolish or ridiculous than to preach to a bunch of dry bones. When God asked the question, "…Son of man, can these bones live…" (Ezek. 37:3 NKJV). Ezekiel answer was "O Lord God, thou know" (Ezek. 37:3 NKJV). You can almost hear the hesitation on the part of the prophet as he considered the utter uselessness of his assignment. And yet we hesitate to go, tell, and make followers of Jesus Christ to living people. There can be little doubt that Ezekiel was overwhelmed by the sight of all the death, devastation, and the defeat he saw represented by those dry bones. Any true child of God who sees the true condition of a lost world can understand Ezekiel's response because it is difficult to confront a world of lifeless, useless, and hopeless men and women with the Gospel seed. We have a clear mandate, and while God did not promise to bless our theological systems, our superficial interpretations, or our philosophical theorizing, He did promise to commit Himself to bless the preaching of the untainted Word of God. God says, "So shall My word be that goes forth from My mouth; it shall not return to Me void, but it shall accomplish what I please, and it shall prosper in the thing for which I sent it" (Isa. 55:11 NKJV). You see, only through the preaching of God's Word will there be "…a noise…a shaking…bones coming together, bone to his bone" (Ezek. 37:7 NKJV). It was only the Word of God which can produce such miracles, "for the Word of God is quick, and powerful, and sharper than any two-edge sword, piercing even to the dividing asunder of soul and spirit, and of the joints and marrow, and is a discerner of the thoughts and intents of the heart" (Heb. 4:12 NKJV). The Gospel of our Lord Jesus Christ "…is the power of God unto salvation to everyone that believes, for the Jew first and also for the Greek" (Rom. 1:16 NKJV).

So, what do we need to preach to lost sinners? What do lost sinners need to hear? They don't need to hear about our church, our denomination, our preachers, our opinions, and they certainly don't need to hear about our problems. They need to hear the Gospel of our Lord and Savior Jesus Christ. They need to hear that Jesus Christ died on the cross to save sinners. They need to hear that He rose again from the dead to save all who will call upon the name of the Lord (Rom. 10:13 NKJV). They need to hear that there is hope, love, life, and salvation in the only "name under heaven given among men by which we must be saved" (Acts 4:12 NKJV). They need to hear about Jesus, and it is our responsibility to behave as fishers of men and go and make followers of Jesus Christ (Mark 16:15 NKJV).

HE WAS COMMANDED TO PRAY

As Jesus was teaching his disciples about the harvest, He saw the power of the harvest through the avenue of prayer. He said, "Therefore pray the Lord of the harvest to send out laborers into His harvest" (Matt. 9:38 NKJV). The first thing that Jesus told his disciples to do was: pray. Why pray? Because seeing the harvest brought into the barn, because breathing upon a lost soul, saving a lost soul is the work of God, not yours! God must till the soil of the heart preparing the lost soul's heart to receive the Gospel seed. He must water the Gospel seed that you have planted, through the preaching of the Gospel. And He must cast the light of His grace upon the heart that lost soul or there will never be a harvest. You see, the new birth, salvation, is a miracle that is performed by God. Therefore, we must pray.

God told Ezekiel to "Prophesy to the breath", that is he was to speak through prayer to the Holy Spirit; "prophesy son of man, and say to the breath, 'Thus says the Lord God: "Come from the four winds, O breath, and breathe on these slain, that they may live"'" (Ezek. 37:9 NKJV). Now think, with the preaching there was a noise, a shaking, a coming together of bone to bone, and even the appearance of sinews (muscles) and skin, but Ezekiel said that "there was no breath in them" (Ezek. 37:8 NKJV). Understand, that Ezekiel had preached the Word of God to the bones, and they had the appearance of life, but they were still dead. They needed the touch of God before they could live. We are commanded to preach, share, be a witness of the Gospel to lost sinners, but we are not commanded to save them. We lack the power to perform the miracle of salvation, which is reserved for God. Though the preaching to people may convict them of the truth that they need a Savior, they will remain mere corpses until the Holy Spirit breathes upon them.

Undoubtedly, that is why Jesus told His disciples to wait in Jerusalem until they were spiritually equipped with power from on high (Luke 24:49 NKJV). Then came the day of Pentecost when there was "a sound from heaven as of a rushing mighty wind" (Acts 2:2 NKJV), at once their preaching ministry was vitalized. As they spoke, dead men and women came to life. This is still God's method of bringing the purpose of the gospel to fulfillment. It is our obligation to see that we not only preach with divine urgency but pray with divine fervency. We must be satisfied with nothing less than the outpouring of the Holy Spirit. The world of lifeless, useless, and hopeless men and women will never be changed unless the Holy Spirit breathes upon our preaching, sharing, and witnessing as fishers of men we must behave. Let us pray that the Lord of the harvest will send out the Gospel through empowered preachers, teachers, churches, missionaries, and witnesses. Let us pray with fervency that God will honor His Word, breath on the lost and draw many to the Lord Jesus Christ for salvation. It is our responsibility to tell them, and it is our responsibility to pray with urgency that they might be saved. May God give us the eyes to see the condition of the lost. May He give us ears to hear their cries. May He give us a heart that feels their pain. May He help us to see them like He sees them, so that we will develop the kind of burden for them that dwells in Him.

A Supernatural Resurrection

In response to the preaching and praying of Ezekiel, the Lord moves in power. There are several amazing things that take place when God moves in power upon the dead bones. First, they are activated, brought back to life! Ezekiel said, "So, I prophesied as He commanded me, and breath came into them, and they lived, and they stood upon their feet, and exceedingly great army" (Ezek. 37:10 NKJV). He said that the first thing these dead bones did after he preached, and the Holy Spirit moved was that "they lived" (Ezek. 37:10 NKJV). The same thing can happen today as we share the gospel in the power of the Holy Spirit. Jesus assures us that "it is the Spirit who gives life; the flesh profits nothing. The words that I speak to you are spirit, and they are life" (John 6:63 NKJV). The new birth is a supernatural event. It is a time when God raises those who were spiritually dead to new life in Jesus Christ. It is a sovereign event, and it is amazing to experience it for yourself and to witness it in the life of others.

Second, they were animated. Ezekiel said that the dead bones "stood upon their feet" (Ezek. 37:10 NKJV). God brought them to life, and then He caused them to stand before Him. The children of God can behave as fishers of men because we have been given the ability to stand and behave as a follower of Jesus as we put on the whole armor of God (Eph. 6:10-18 NKJV). And because we have that ability to stand, we should have a burden to see dead men, women, boys, and girls quicken to life; we should be concerned that they are strengthened (discipled) to stand for Christ and His church. Paul expresses this burden when writing to the Ephesian church. He says, "For this reason I bow my knees to the Father of our Lord Jesus Christ, from whom the whole family in heaven and earth is named, that He would grant you, according to the riches of His glory, to be strengthened with might through His Spirit in the inner man, the Christ may dwell in your hearts through faith; that you, being rooted and grounded in love" (Eph. 3:14-17 NKJV). If we are going to behave as fishers of men then we need to pray this prayer earnestly for those who are lost to come to faith in Christ Jesus, that they may be strengthened with might by His Spirit to stand and withstand the "the wiles of the devil" (Eph. 6:10 NKJV). After all, God saves people to serve him, "For we are His workmanship, created in Christ Jesus for good works, which God prepared beforehand that we should walk in them" (Eph. 2:10 NKJV). Speaking to His disciples the Lord Jesus said, "But you shall receive power when the Holy Spirit has come upon you; and you shall be witnesses to Me in Jerusalem, and in all Judea and Samaria, and to the end of the earth" (Acts 1:8 NKJV). You see, it would be foolish to try and stand against the devil, or to behave as a fisher of men without the power of the Holy Spirit.

Third, they were associated because Ezekiel said that they were transformed into "an exceeding great army" (Ezek. 37:10 NKJV). One moment they are dead bones filling a valley, the next they are a mighty, living army, ready for the Lord's use. Understand, it is the work of the Holy Spirit to bring individual units to a whole. Paul informs us that "for by one Spirit we are all baptized into one body" (1 Cor. 12:13 NKJV). Furthermore, we are encouraged "to keep the unity of the Spirit in the bond of peace" (Eph. 4:3 NKJV). God brings people out of deadness of sin to a new life in Jesus Christ. He saves them, gives them spiritual gifts, and then places them in a local church where they can work alongside other resurrected sinners saved by grace for the glory of God. May the Lord help us to see that we are not to be isolated units, but that we are to "stand fast in one spirit, with one mind striving together for the faith of the gospel" (Phil. 1:27 NKJV).

Then the last amazing thing that took place was they were assured. God said, "I will put My spirit in you, and you shall live, and I will place you in your own land. Then you shall know that I, the Lord, have spoken it and performed it" (Ezek. 37:14 NKJV). Remember that this is a promise to the nation of Israel that they will be restored to their land, and that they will receive His blessing again. God wants Israel to know that what He is about to do is a sovereign work. He is going to do something big in them, and through them. All they must do is believe Him, and go with Him, and they will see it come to pass. The same is true as we behave as fishers of men. The days of God's blessings for His church and His children are not over. The times of refreshing have not passed us forever. God is still the same God He has always been, and he is still working in supernatural, sovereign ways to accomplish His will in the world. We need to seek the Lord today, to ask Him to give us a vision of seeing the lost through His eyes, seeing the lost as they really are; asking Him to give us a burden to reach them with the Gospel, to fill us with His spirit which is already in us, and send us out into the world to tell them about Jesus Christ. God will still honor His Word, and He will still bless those who behave as fishers of men.

When you look at the world, what do you see? I must confess that I sometimes become angry when I look at the world. I see the things people do; I hear the things people say, I notice the way they live their lives; and I see the hatred they have for God and the Gospel. Those things bother me. Then I remember if it were not for the grace of God that could be me. But somebody cared enough to pray for me. Somebody cared enough to tell me about Jesus. The Lord reached out to me in grace and mercy and saved my soul. The least I can do is ask the Lord to give me the same compassion toward others that was shown to me. Can these bones live? Yes, they can! The mission that has been given to the church and to us as children of God seems impossible at times. But we can fulfill the Great Commission if we look to the Lord for the help and strength we need. Can these bones live? Yes, they can! They only need a witness to tell them, a warrior to pray for them, and a wonderful God who draws them to Jesus. They can live, and God can use us to reach them for Jesus.

CHAPTER FOUR

Courage to Go

For whoever is ashamed of Me and My words, of him the Son of Man will be ashamed when He comes in His own glory, and in His Father's, and of the holy angels. (Luke 9:26 NKJV)

IF WE ARE GOING TO BEHAVE AS FISHERS OF MEN, THEN IT IS GOING to take some courage. Paul wrote to a young pastor who was a little discouraged by the things going on around him and in the life of his friends. Paul must have sensed that Timothy was growing ashamed of the Gospel because of the affliction, persecutions, and trials that accompanied being a follower of Jesus Christ. Paul writes, "Therefore do not be ashamed of the testimony of our Lord, nor of me His prisoner, but share with me in the sufferings for the gospel according to the power of God, who has saved us and called us with a holy calling, not according to our works, but according to His own purpose and grace which was given to us in Christ Jesus before time began, but has now been revealed by the appearing of our Savior Jesus Christ, who has abolished death and brought life and immortality to light through the gospel, to which I was appointed a preacher, an apostle, and a teacher of the Gentiles" (2 Tim. 1:8-11 NKJV). Paul wants Timothy to know that there are some things in life of which we must never be ashamed.

There was this girl named Anna that grew up during the depression, but her family, despite its poverty, was rich in love and happiness. Here dad and mom were caring and tender parents, and laughter filled their home. Her father always whistled, and her mother always sang while doing her housework. Her father was a baker, but he lost his bakery in the first years of the depression. He had to take any job he could so he could pay the rent and keep food on the table. He worked at the local YMCA for a while and when that job ran out, he found a job as a janitor. Anna knew that her dad had taken a job as a janitor, but she did not know where. Until one day, during lunch at school Anna and her friends sat down at the lunch table to eat, when she heard a teacher call her father's name in a loud voice. Someone had dropped their tray, and food and milk covered the table and floor. She saw him walk toward the table carrying a mob and old rags. One of the girls said to Anna, "That janitor has the same last name as yours. Do you know him?"

Anna slowly raised her head and looked at the little gray head man cleaning up the spill. She hesitated, and then said, "I have never seen him before in my life." A wave of intense embarrassment swept over her, and she instantly felt ashamed of denying her dearest friend on earth. She hated herself for those words and tried to make up for what she had done by showing her father that she loved him more than ever. He loved for someone to brush his hair as he sat in his easy chair. She would do that. She sang to him and read to him and spent time with him. But regardless of how hard she tried; nothing made her feel better.

The years passed, and her father developed Alzheimer's disease. One day when he was ill and she was sitting with him, she started crying. Her mother asked her what was wrong, and Anna poured out her heart and told her what had been bothering her for more than fifteen years. She said, "I have been asking God to forgive me, but I can't get over what I had done". Her mother drew her close and held her tight as she wept. "Honey", she said, "your daddy knew you loved him, and he would have loved you even if he had known about you being ashamed of him when you were so young. You know Simon Peter denied that he knew our beloved Jesus before He was crucified on the cross, and Jesus loved him just the same." Suddenly Anna felt at peace with herself for the first time since she was in junior high. She felt that because of the love of Christ, it was time to turn the corner.

We have all been ashamed of things as we have passed through this life. Perhaps it was something we did, something we said, how we behaved in a certain situation or how we reacted to a certain situation. We have all experienced shame! As believers we have a tendency from time to time to be ashamed of who we are and what we have as Christians. There are times when we will hope that no one finds out that we are a believer. Maybe we are ashamed to admit that we love the Lord, and we trust Him to save our souls. Maybe we are ashamed to speak up in a discussion about doctrinal matter because the truth from the Bible differs from what those around us believe. Maybe we are ashamed to sell out completely to the Lord, like He wants us to. Maybe there is shame over some failure in the past that haunts us and prevents us from being all the Lord wants us to be. Whatever the reason, God's people often find themselves ashamed of the Gospel, the Lord, and our relationship to Him.

Jesus Gives Encouragement

Jesus gives the courage to go behave as fishers of men when He explains what it cost to follow Him. Jesus says, "If anyone desires to come after Me, let him deny himself, and take up his cross daily, and follow Me" (Luke 9:23 NKJV). Now this sounds like Jesus is pushing followers away, however, this encouragement that Jesus is giving is because Jesus wants people to know the truth. He wanted them to know that it would not be cheap or easy to be His disciples and it would not be easy behaving like fishers of men. There are requirements if you are going to have the courage to go.

First, Jesus said, "come after me" (Luke 9:23 NKJV). When Jesus said these words, His men surely remembered when He first called them to follow Him. Some two and a half years ago, they had left everything to follow Jesus. They had left family, friends, occupations, and everything else in their lives to follow Jesus. To the rest of the crowd that day, this was a call to the new birth. It was a call to make a personal commitment to Jesus. It was a call for them to turn their backs on everything else to go after Jesus. Being born again, getting saved, or whatever you want to call it, is far more than just praying a prayer at the altar, and accepting Jesus into your heart. Being born again is about being made a "new creation" (2 Cor. 5:17 NKJV) and behaving as a follower of Jesus. Which means you are now to fulfill the Great Commission by going out and behaving as fishers of men. True salvation is not some form of "easy believing" that leaves you unchanged. True salvation will make you behave as a different person. You will have different desires and habits. Your interests and commitments will be changed. When you come to know Jesus as your personal Lord and Savior you will be encouraged through the power of the Holy Spirit that is in you to behave as fishers of men.

Second, Jesus says, "deny himself" (Luke 9:23 NKJV). This phrase literally means, "to completely disown, to utterly separate oneself from someone." (Dictionary 1828). It is the same word used to describe Peter's denial of Jesus outside the high priest's home (Matt. 26:34 NKJV). Denying self is far more intense than self-denial. Denying self implies that I stop listening to my own voice, that I stop leaning on my own power, and I stop fulfilling my own desires. This is a foreign concept for us today because most religions and some popular ministries are focused on catering to self. They want people to feel good about themselves. Jesus, on the other hand, wants to encourage His follower to "go" by reminding them that they are nothing and can do nothing without Him (John 15:5 NKJV). Denying oneself is a call to action, an encouragement to go and make more fishers of men.

Next, Jesus says, "Take up his cross daily." (Luke 9:23 NKJV). This is perhaps the best encouragement that should encourage us to go. When Jesus tells His disciples to take up their cross and follow Him, He is calling us to die to ourselves. He is calling us to commit to a lifestyle of living death (Gal. 2:20 NKJV). He is calling us to willingly bear the shame, the reproach, the humiliation, the suffering, the hatred, the alienation, and even the death that may come to those who are associated with Him. We take up our cross when we choose the narrow way over the way of the world, regardless the cost. We take up our cross when we live out biblical ethics in our personal lives and in our business relationships, regardless the cost. We take up our cross when we are willing to suffer any attack for Jesus' sake. To take up your cross means that you are willing to identify yourself with Jesus Christ, His death, and His word, regardless of what it costs you personally, publicly, or financially! That may not be an encouragement you want to hear but if you are going to behave as fishers of men it is true, nonetheless. There are no cheap seats, but there is a high price to pay for being a genuine disciple of the Lord Jesus Christ.

Then the last requirement if you are to have the courage to go; follow Jesus. The true fisher of men turns his back on his self and his old life. The fisher of men takes up his cross and is willing to lay down everything for the glory of God daily. The fisher of men takes his place behind the Lord and he follows Jesus wherever He leads. The fisher of men walks in total obedience and submission to the Lord Jesus Christ! This phrase suggests an ongoing action. Jesus is calling His followers to be constant followers. Some people follow on Sunday but take a different path on Monday. Some people follow the Lord when they need help, but take another path when things get better. That is not what the Lord is looking for! Jesus is calling His people to make a radical commitment to follow Him all the time, all the way to the end of their lives.

Now as difficult of encouragement that Jesus gave in Luke 9:23 (NKJV), His warning is an even stronger encouragement for us to go. He says in Luke 9:26 (NKJV), "For whoever is ashamed of Me and My words, of him the Son of Man will be ashamed when He comes in His own glory, and in His Father's, and of the holy angels." The word "ashamed" in this context, means "unwilling or restrained because of fear of shame, ridicule, or disapproval" (Strong's Concordance 1984). It refers to the true disciple who should be glorifying the Lord in everything they do. Any fisher of men who is ashamed of Jesus will never take up his cross and follow Him. But if we are ashamed of Him now, He will be ashamed of us when He comes again (2 Tim. 2:11-13 NKJV), and we will be ashamed before Him (1 John 2:28 NKJV).

Be Not Ashamed of Your Savior

Now, while, Paul is tries to encourage the young Timothy, he also teaches us that there are some blessings that God's children should never be ashamed of, which should give us the courage to go and behave like fishers of men. Paul begins with reminding us about the Savior. He says, "Therefore, do not be ashamed of the testimony of our Lord, nor of me His prisoner, but share with me in the sufferings for the gospel according to the power of God" (2 Tim. 1:8 NKJV). Paul is telling Timothy, do not be ashamed to identify yourself with the cross of Jesus, for it was the cross that purchased salvation! It is the cross that stands as the dividing line between the saint and the sinner (1 Cor. 1:18, 21 NKJV)! It is what happened on the that cross that day at Calvary that makes all the differences in life. The cross is why the child of God is not in the gutter! Instead of being ashamed, let us find glory in His sufferings (Gal. 6:14 NKJV).

Paul also reminds us not to be ashamed to identify yourself with the Gospel message. It may bring division, it may bring affliction, it may bring persecution, but it is that very message that penetrated your heart and brought you to the feet of a risen, saving Lord! The Gospel is the power of God unto salvation (Rom. 1:16 NKJV)! The Gospel of the Lord Jesus Christ is the only message that delivers that which it promises, salvation (John 14:6 NKJV). Paul warns Timothy to not be ashamed of the people of God, including those like Paul who were imprisoned for the cause of Jesus Christ. We should never be ashamed to identify ourselves with the crowd that is serving the Lord! There is no finer group of people in the world than those who have left all to follow Him. Hey may be strange, they may be weird, but they are saved, and they are family! The best thing a believer can do is jump in with a bunch of folks who love the Lord! Because that's the crowd Jesus has chosen to hang out with (Matt. 18:20 NKJV). If He is going to be there, then that is where I want to be also! Remember Thomas missed a meeting, and he was absent when Jesus showed up (John 20:24 NKJV). Don't be ashamed of that, worshiping, praising, crowd. That is His crowd, and it should be your crowd as well!

Be Not Ashamed of His Salvation

Paul encourages Timothy not to be ashamed of His salvation. He says, "who saved us" (2 Tim. 1:9 NKJV). The word "saved" is in a tense that mean it is a completed action (Strong's Concordance 1984). We are saved and will remain saved forever! We have been delivered from the depths of sin and are saved from the wrath of God. His salvation is precious because it is complete, perfect, and eternal. It delivers the soul, changes the life, alters the courses, defines their destiny, and perfects the saints! Why would anyone be ashamed of that? If you are saved you owe God a debt of praise and gratitude!

Then Timothy is reminded that our salvation has nothing to do with who we are, or with anything we have done. Paul writes, "not according to our works, but according to His own purpose and grace" (2 Tim. 1:9 NKJV). We are saved by "grace through faith" (Eph. 2:8 NKJV). The unmerited love and favor of God for sinners was manifested toward us even before the world was ever formed! Before you and I were ever conceived, before Adam was even formed, grace had already been extended to you and me through Jesus Christ. Even though God knew all about us and all about the things we would do, He still extended His saving grace toward us. It was His grace that loved us, sought us, "called us with a holy calling" (2 Tim. 1:9 NKJV), and saved us, keeps us saved, and one day will take us home to heaven. Who we are has nothing to do with our salvation and calling (Eph. 2:8-9; Titus 3:5 NKJV)! Salvation is pure grace from start to finish! "But demonstrates His own love toward us, in that while we were still sinners, Christ died for us" (Rom. 5:8 NKJV). When we attempt to add anything to the grace of God, we have nullified salvation! Grace comes when we believe in the Lord Jesus Christ. And God counts it as righteousness to us. And you don't add works to it. If you think baptism, giving money, witnessing, Bible study, prayer, or anything else saves you, or helps save your, you have destroyed the concept of grace. "And if by grace, then it is no longer of works; otherwise, grace is no longer grace. But if it is of works, it is no longer grace; otherwise, work is no longer work" (Rom. 11:6 NKJV).

Paul tells Timothy that through His sufferings on the cross, that Jesus "abolished death" (2 Tim. 1:10 NKJV). The word "abolish" means "to render inoperative." (Dictionary 1828). The most dreaded enemy of mankind was rendered ineffective when Jesus came, died, and rose again. This is what Paul meant when he referred to the "sting of death" being taken away (1 Cor. 15:55 NKJV). For those who came to Christ, death is rendered inoperative! It is taken out of the picture and the spotlight of grace shines on life and immortality! These are the great gifts of Jesus Christ to those who trust Him by faith for the salvation of the souls (Rom. 6:23 NKJV)! Fishers of men are to behave as though they are not ashamed of their salvation!

Be Not Ashamed of Your Service

Paul continues his encouragement to Timothy by reminding him not to be ashamed of his service. He states that the positions we occupy in the Lord's kingdom work are not of our own choosing, they are appointed. Paul writes, "to which I was appointed a preacher, an apostle, and a teacher of the Gentiles" (2 Tim. 1:11 NKJV). The word "appointed" is in the passive voice (Strong's Concordance 1984). God chose Paul to be a preacher; one who conveys the message of the King, one who tells others about the King's glory". God chose Paul to be an apostle: "one sent out with orders on behalf of the King". God chose Paul to be a teacher to the Gentiles: "one who shows men the way of salvation or own who tells men about how to come to know the King". The whole point here is this: The Lord chooses when, where, and how we are to serve Him! The question is do you have the courage to go? Wherever? Whenever? And Whatever? Do you have the courage to go now? Do you have the courage to behave as a fisher of men? You see, our duty as we behave as a follower is be available, willing, yielded, usable, and faithful! Let us not be ashamed of the appointment of the Lord to serve Him as fishers of men, but let us be determined that, by His grace, we will fulfill His call on our lives for His glory! Whatever the Lord has appointed you to do, consider it a great privilege, consider it a high calling, and fulfill it completely and faithfully so that He receives the glory due His great Name. David puts it like this, "For a day in Your courts is better than a thousand. I would rather be a doorkeeper in the house of my God than dwell in the tents of wickedness" (Ps. 84:10 NKJV).

Paul reminds Timothy that he is not a lone as a fisher of men. Paul says, "For this reason I also suffer these things; nevertheless, I am not ashamed" (2 Tim. 1:12 NKJV). Paul was suffering for his testimony. He was in prison because he had faithfully served the Lord. This is the sobering truth about service to the Lord, that we are not alone. There have been others that have been tested, tried, and afflicted (2 Tim. 3:12; John 16:33 NKJV). However, this is what Jesus uses to mold us into His image! He uses it to help us behave as fishers of men! Have you ever heard about the story of the Potter and the clay? To mold the clay, the Potter must exert pressure on the clay. As He does, the clay is formed into a shape that pleases Him. This molding process may be painful and it may cause us to wonder about the Potter's wisdom, but we must always remember this: The Potter is never closer to the clay than when He is in the process of molding it into a vessel of honor! Don't be surprised or ashamed when suffering comes your way as a fisher of men. We must never forget that suffering is a part of His plan for us and that it merely allows God a fresh canvas upon which to paint the glorious colors of His grace!

Paul closes with a profound statement of faith and encouragement that still causes the people of the Lord to rejoice. Paul writes, "For I know whom I have believed and am persuaded that He is able to keep what I have committed to Him until that Day" (2 Tim. 1:12 NKJV). Paul says that he is "persuaded" which means that Paul is at a state that all is well with his soul. He is confident that the Lord is "able", mighty, powerful, strong. That the Lord is able to "keep": to guard, to watch, to keep an eye on. He is confident that the Lord is able to keep that which He has committed to Him. The Lord is well able to "keep" all thing we commit to His safekeeping! He will not lose a single soul committed to Him He will not forget our sacrifices for His sake. He will not forget the service rendered for His name's sake. He will see to it that these things are kept safe for His children. Left to ourselves, we would lose our salvation, but He is able to keep us (1 Pet. 1:5 NKJV). Left to ourselves, our sacrifices for Him would go unnoticed, but He is able to see and remember them all. Left to ourselves, our service to Him would die when we did, but He knows our service and He will reward His children when they stand before Him one day! Nobody else may see or care, but He does! The courage to go depends upon your determination to keep your eyes on the author and finisher of our faith, seeing the harvest through His eyes.

THE WATER BEARER AND THE POT

A water bearer in India had two large pots, hung on each end of a pole which he carried across his neck. One of the pots had a crack in it, while the other pot was perfect and always delivered a full portion of water at the end of the long walk from the stream to the master's house; the crack pot arrived only half full. For a full two years this went on daily, with the bearer delivering only one and a half pots full of water to his master's house. Of course, the perfect pot was proud of its accomplishments, perfect to the end for which it was made. But poor cracked pot was ashamed of its own imperfection, and miserable that it was able to accomplish only half of what it had been made to do.

After two years of what it perceived to be a bitter failure, it spoke to the water bearer. "I am ashamed of myself, and I want to apologize to you." "Why?" asked the bearer. "What are you ashamed of?" "I have been able for these past two years, to deliver only halve my load because this crack in my side causes water to leak out all the way back to your master's house. Because of my flaw, you must do all this work, and you don't get full value from your efforts," the pot said. The water bearer felt sorry, and said, "As we return to the master's house, I want you to notice the beautiful flowers along the path." Indeed, as they went up the hill, the crack pot took notice of the sun warming beautiful flowers on the side of the path, and this cheered it some. But at the end of the trail, it still felt bad because it had leaked out half its load, and so again it apologized to the bearer for its failure.

The bearer said to the pot, "Did you notice there were flowers only on your side of the path, but not on the other pot's side? I have always known about your flaw, and I planted flower seeds on your side of the path. Every day while we walk back from the stream, you water them. For two years I have been able to pick these beautiful flowers to decorate my master's table. Without you being just the way you are, my master would not have this beauty to grace his house." (Anonymous n.d.)

Each of us has our own unique flaws. We are all cracked pots. But if we will allow it, the Lord will use our flaws to grace His Father's table. As we seek to minister together, and as God calls you to the tasks, He has appointed you, don't be ashamed of your flaws. Go on boldly, knowing that in our weakness we find His strength. You too, can bring beauty to His pathway! I know that there are areas of your life that make you ashamed, but the good news is that He can and will still use you despite them! We are all just a bunch of cracked pots, but that is the kind He uses for His glory. So, what is holding you back from behaving as a fisher of men? Bring the things that you are ashamed of to Him and let Him give you the courage to "Go" and "Make"!

CHAPTER FIVE

Courage to Go After One

What man of you, having a hundred sheep, if he loses one of them,
does not leave the ninety-nine in the wilderness, and go after the
one which is lost until he finds it? (Luke 15:4 NKJV)

WHEN YOU ARE BUILDING UP YOUR COURAGE TO GO, A FISHER OF MEN should not overwhelm himself or herself with trying to bring everyone in the world to Jesus Christ. Even though that would be totally awesome, it would be a burdensome task for just one child of God. Probably the best place to start behaving as a fisher of men is going after one. As a fisherman, I am always looking to catch the biggest fish in the lake, river, or pond. When fishing with my parents, my wife, and daughter, I especially enjoy bringing home the biggest fish of that day's fishing trip. Now, I had one fish in mind the biggest. I went after just one at a time. I was not overwhelmed by trying to bring them all in at once.

The North American Mission Board of the Southern Baptist Convention has an evangelistic theme called "Who's Your One" (Who's Your One 2021). It is a theme that emphasized the need of going after just one. In Jesus' parable of the lost sheep (Luke 15:4-7 NKJV), He talks about a shepherd who was responsible for each sheep. By leaving the ninety-nine does not mean that they were not important, but that they were safe, and the lost sheep was in danger. The fact that the shepherd left the other to go after one proves that each sheep was dear to him. If we are going to behave as fishers of men, then we need the courage to go after one and to do that you need to count each lost soul as dear to Jesus Christ. A well-dressed man in a tie was handing out gospel tracts to people. However, while he was handing out tracts, he was talking to one of his friends while he tried to get people to take a booklet. While he was joking around with his buddy, he didn't even appear to be looking at the people passing by. While I admired his courage for doing this, his heart didn't seem in it. I wonder if his seeming lack of interest in individuals was getting the good news he was attempting to get out. Please understand our evangelism will only be as effective as the love and respect we have for people. Let me say it a bit stronger than that: Evangelism will have little effect if we don't love the lost.

To behave as a fisher of men there are two compelling forces that gives you the courage to go after one. They are the "want to" and the "how to". If you don't care about rescuing the dying then all the outreach sermons, seminars, evangelism rallies, or this book will not move you to go. Let's be honest, most believers don't have the "want to". Pastors and leaders can plan evangelism outreach programs, teach classes where they explain how to share the Gospel at these events, all the while there are only a hand full of believers; it is as though we are offering the "how to" to believer who don't have the "want to". As God grows in your heart the desire to help lost soul come to know Jesus Christ as their personal Lord and Savior, your courage to go will grow which in turn will cause a desire to know more how to effectively communicate the Gospel of our Lord and Savior Jesus Christ. Just think of the greatest example of evangelism, Jesus. Jesus reached out to people no one else cared for! That was why He came to the world (Luke 19:10; Mark 2:17 NKJV)! Sinners and outcasts were drawn to Jesus, and He gladly received them. He shared meals with them and as a matter of fact, Jesus spent much of His life around lost sinners. What an example! If we do not spend time with lost souls how can we expect to reach them with the Gospel? Who are the lost souls that you are spending time with? Who's your one?

Let me give a list of ideas about "how to" which I pray will give you the "want to" as you seek for the courage to go after one:

1. Love them in their language: or in other words, random acts of kindness (1 Pet. 2:15 NKJV).
2. Be there in the bad times and in the good times (Rom. 12:15 NKJV).
3. Show real interest in them (Jam. 1:19 NKJV).
4. Pray for them (Col. 4:3-4 NKJV).
5. Prepare your testimony (John 9:25; 1 Cor. 9:20-22 NKJV).
6. Lend the person something Christian
7. Invite the person to an outreach event.

Behaving as fishers of men involves getting involved in the person's life that you are going after. That is why "the Word became flesh and dwelt among us" (John 1:14 NKJV). Jesus got involved with those He was seeking to save (Luke 19:10 NKJV).

Paul's Ministry

In Acts 28:30 (NKJV), Luke closes his book by telling us what Paul's ministry looked like. He writes, "Then Paul dwelt two whole years in his own rented house and received all who came to him" (Acts 28:30 NKJV). Paul's example of evangelism should give us the courage to go after our one. Luke said that in Paul's ministry that he received "all" who came to him. He didn't discriminate, but shared Christ with all who he encountered. Paul was a fisher of men for Jesus, he shared the Gospel with both great and small that he might win some to Christ. For example: he shared the gospel with the Jews in the synagogue (Acts 9:20 NKJV); the Greeks (Acts 9:29 NKJV); to both Jews and Gentiles in Antioch (Acts 13:14-19 NKJV); To Lydia in Philippi (Acts 16:12-15 NKJV); to the Philippian jailer and his family (Acts 16:23-33 NKJV); to the Greeks in Athens (Acts 17:22-34 NKJV); to Felix the governor (Acts 24:22-25 NKJV); to King Agrippa (Acts 26:1-32 NKJV); to some sailors on a ship (Acts 27:22-29 NKJV); and to those of Caesar's household (Phil. 4:22 NKJV).

Paul realized that every person he met was a candidate for salvation, therefore, he did not discriminate and reached out to all in the awesome love of God. What a lesson for us today! Red and yellow, black, and white they are precious in His sight Jesus loves the little children of the world! We must never forget that the fields are white for harvest (John 4:35 NKJV), and that Jesus desires to save all men (2 Pet. 3:9; 2 Cor. 5:14; 1 Tim. 2:4 NKJV). The door of salvation is open to whosoever will (Rom. 10:13 NKJV). Therefore, we must reach out to all who cross our path. No human is beyond the reach of God's great love for sinners! They all need to hear, but they will need someone to tell them about Jesus. "How then shall they call on Him in whom they have not believed? And how shall they believe in Him of whom they have not heard? And how shall they hear without a preacher? And how shall they preach unless they are sent? As it is written: "How beautiful are the feet of those who preach the gospel of peace, who bring glad tidings of good things!" But they have not all obeyed the gospel. For Isaiah says, "Lord, who has believed our report?" So, then faith comes by hearing, and hearing by the word of God" (Rom. 10:13-17 NKJV).

Imagine being a salesman with a product that every person in the world needed. No matter who you met, they needed what you were selling. Not all would buy, but just knowing that everyone needed your product would give you the courage and the confidence in going and presenting it. That is what it is like with the Gospel of our Lord and Savior Jesus Christ. Everyone, even if it is not the one you are going after, needs to hear the message of salvation. Not all will receive it, but some will. Those who do, make it worth the effort. Whether they receive it or not, it still helps to know that they need it anyway. It isn't always easy to witness and the people we meet don't make it any easier, but they all need Jesus, and they all need to hear the Gospel. Start by going after one, look for ways to share the Gospel, and the more you practice with one at a time the easier it will be when you come in contact with one you had not planned on sharing the Gospel with. Making yourself available to Him is all He needs to bring or place one in front of you.

Sinners are all around us, so finding people to witness to isn't the problem. You never know where God is working, so tell all you meet about the wonderful savior. There was this leading newspaper executive who was visited by a local pastor. The man of God came right to the point as they shook hands. "My friend," he said, "I'm here to ask you to become a Christian." The editor walked over to a window and for several minutes stood looking down into the street. The minister thought he had offended him. Finally, the man turned, his face wet with tears. Taking his visitor's hand again, he said, "Thank you for your concern. Since I was a young boy at my mother's knee, not a single relative or business associate has ever taken an interest in my soul. I thought no one care!" Understand, no one cares how much you know till they know how much you care. If people don't believe that we care about them, they are not going to care much about what we believe. Or to say it another way, we will never lead people to Jesus until we learn to love people like Jesus does.

The Plan of Paul's Ministry

Paul spent his days pointing men to Jesus! He knew that the greatest need of their soul was for a personal relationship with the Lord Jesus Christ. Therefore, he didn't spend time talking about Paul's opinions; he just pointed them to Jesus, the place where real help can be found! As fishers of men our message isn't about the church to which you belong, it is not to the denomination, neither is it about our personal opinions Our message is about Jesus, His death, burial, resurrection, and love for sinners. After all, it isn't about our persuasiveness, our wit, our wisdom, or our familiarity with the Southern Baptist doctrine or whatever denomination you are associated with that saves, but it is the Gospel of Christ for it alone has the power of salvation. Paul said, "For I am not ashamed of the Gospel of Christ, for it is the power of God to salvation, for everyone who believes, for the Jew first and also for the Greek" (Rom. 1:16 NKJV). There are times when you may have to be ashamed of your denomination or of your church, but you never have to be ashamed of the Gospel of Christ. It never changes, never compromises, never weakens, and never fails (Isa. 55:11 NKJV)!

Over in Romans 9 (NKJV), Paul takes a pause in his teaching to let all his readers know that God wasn't finished with the Jews! They still figured prominently in God's plan for the future, therefore, Paul reveals his plan for ministry by revealing His heart for his people, the Jew. You see, up to this point Paul had been about the task of proving that salvation is a sovereign work of God brought about through grace by faith. He has been telling his readers that men are saved by trusting the finished work of Christ on Calvary, apart from any rituals or works. Any Jew reading Romans, might get the idea that salvation by faith was for Gentiles only. He might conclude that there was no hope for those who were descendants of Abraham. So, as Paul reveals his heart, it teaches us a lesson about the kind of courage we should have and the kind of heart we should have for the lost around us.

Paul says, "I tell the truth in Christ, I am not lying, my conscience also bearing witness in the Holy Spirit" (Rom. 9:1 NKJV). Just think, all lost people, especially the Jew, have looked with distrust and doubt at the message of the cross. Paul has shared a lot of truth. Truth that if taken literally proved that outside of a personal relationship with Jesus Christ there was no hope of salvation. Some people, hearing the message of Paul, may have been tempted to think that Paul was lying. After such a scalding condemnation of Judaism, some Jews may have felt that they were utterly outcast, hopelessly written off by God forever. Yet, Paul wants these people to know that he has a heart for them. He wants them to see that he is sincere about what he is saying and that he really does care. That is why he calls on the Holy Spirit, and his own heart to testify to his honesty. Paul wants them to know that his message is absolutely true.

Many people today are skeptical of Christians because they have either been conned or have watched a parade of holy hypocrites come and go in their lives. That's why it is so important for us to be sincere and authentic fishers of men. A study showed that between ages 16 to 29 they are showing more hostility, doubt, frustration, and skepticism towards Christianity. That their perception of Christians is filled with the image of being judge, hypocrites, lifestyle, and political activists. They have concluded that Christianity is out of date, boring, unintelligent, and that Christians are insincere and too focused on getting numbers. Paul says, "that I have great sorrow and continual grief in my heart" (Rom. 9:2 NKJV). To think that this is the type of behavior that breaks his heart, especially among the Jews. Paul is telling his readers in this verse that his life is paralyzed by this grief. The word "grief" here refers to those who are overcome by mourning. If you have ever seen people from the Middle East mourn, you know that they are very vocal about their grief. To listen to them wail it almost makes you feel as though they think they are being ripped apart. Paul wants his readers to know that he is operating under a heavy burden for the lost! Like a mother who has lost a child, Paul's heart is broken over the condition of the lost sinner. He lives under the constant burden of the reality that they are headed to Hell. The fact that they are perishing lies on his shoulders like a weight that is nearly impossible to carry.

Did you know that this is the kind of burden that we should be under for the sinner as fishers of men? We are surrounded by millions of people who are headed to Hell and often the church or we as individuals act like we don't care. We live our lives and attend worship services and never give them a second thought! When is the last time you shared the Gospel of the Lord and Savior Jesus Christ? When was the last time you tried? When was the last time you were burdened to pray for a lost sinner? When was the last time God woke you up in the middle of the night so you could seek His face for a person who was lost in sin? When was the last time that it moved you to think that men were going to Hell?

Listen Paul's heart, he says, "For I could wish that I myself were accursed from Christ for my brethren, my countrymen according to the flesh" (Rom. 9:3 NKJV). He says, if it were possible, he would allow himself to be separated from God and sentence to Hell if it would save the lost Jews! That is an amazing statement! Paul isn't joking! He meant what he said! He knew it was impossible. He knew that he was eternally secure in the Lord Jesus Christ, but he was willing in his heart to go to Hell that others might be saved. What a burden must have gripped this man's heart. I wonder if we have ever been to the place that we would be willing to pray a similar prayer? I wonder if we are burdened enough for the lost sinner that we would pray for the Lord to save them regardless of what it took to do it. When we get that serious, that means that we have the courage to go and share the Gospel of our Lord Jesus Christ!

A MISSED OPPORTUNITY

God had given Israel many gifts. Paul lists some of them: "who are Israelites, to who pertain the adoption, the glory, the covenants, the giving of the law, the service of God, and the promises; of who are the fathers and from whom, according to the flesh, Christ came" (Rom. 9:4-5b NKJV). Just think, they had been given truth and revelation. They were in a special covenant relationship with Him and were His people. All the Old Testament prophets and prophecies were given to them. All the promises concerning the Messiah and the coming kingdom were given to them. The people of Israel had been given more spiritual light than any people group in their world. Yet they became so bogged down in keeping the letter of the Law and the religious rituals that they missed their Messiah when He came!

When the Messiah did come; He was born from among them as one of their own. No other people had ever had such a privilege! God became a man and was born among the Jewish people, yet when He manifested Himself to them, they refused to have Him rule over them (John 1:11 NKJV). For them to come to that place where they outright refuse their Messiah, they had to ignore every prophecy concerning Him. They had to disregard every miracle and every proof that Jesus was the Messiah. How did they explain away bringing Lazarus back to life? What did they do with Zacchaeus who was a changed man? How could they keep Bartimaeus, (who was once blind), or the Gadarene Demoniac quiet? How did they silence five thousand people who were fed by Jesus? What did they do with the testimony of five hundred people who saw Him alive after He had risen from the dead? Do you see that they had to climb over many high hurdles to get passed the truth about Jesus? What they did was sin away their season of grace and missed a wonderful opportunity!

Since you have the power of the Holy Spirit in you don't quench the Holy Spirit (1 Thess. 5:19 NKJV) and miss your opportunity to go and make fishers of me. You have great courage inside you just waiting to be released, but the longer and more often you say no to Him, the more you sin against God.

A MAGNIFICENT OBSERVATION

So as a part of Paul's ministry plan, he would point men, women, boys, and girls to Jesus Christ. In Romans 9:5 (NKJV), he calls Him "Christ." This is a word that means "Anointed" (Strong's Concordance 1984). Paul is simply reminding us that Jesus is the fulfillment of the Old Testament prophecies concerning the Messiah. He is the Messiah God the Father promised to send. He is the One who came to take away the sins of the world (John 1:29 NKJV). He is worthy of our faith, our love, our service, and our worship. He is the Christ! He is Lord and He is Savior! May we never forget to love Him and honor Him as such!

Another observation that Paul makes as a part of his ministry plan is to show the power of Jesus. Paul says that He "over all" (Rom. 9:5 NKJV). We can draw strength and courage as we remember that Jesus is the agent of creation. "All things were made through Him, and without Him nothing was made that was made" (John 1:3 NKJV). We must remember that He possesses "all power in heaven and in earth" (Matt. 19:18 NKJV). We must remember that He is "King of kings and Lord of lords" (Rev. 19:16 NKJV). We must remember that Jesus is the One who holds all things together (Heb. 1:3 NKJV). Since Jesus has that kind of awesome power, we can trust Him to be able to do everything He has promised us He can and will do, then we can take great courage that when we go after just one, He is right there in the person and the power of the Holy Spirit. He is "able to do exceedingly abundantly above all that we ask or think, according to the power that works in us" (Eph. 3:20 NKJV)! Jesus is not the God who was, He is still the Great

I AM (Ex. 3:14 NKJV) and simply stated, Jesus is all you need to have the courage to go after one.

The success of Paul's ministry did not lie in the number of conversions he obtained. He was successful because he was faithful carrying out the Great Commission. Again, the Great Commission is a call and a command that lies upon the shoulders of every Christian. As a pastor was preaching one day, he noticed a young lawyer in his audience to whom he had often presented claims of the Gospel. At the close of the service, he greeted the man and inquired if he had yet received the Lord. "Yes," said the lawyer. "I now consider myself a full-fledged Christian." The pastor was delighted, but then he added, "I suppose you are seeking to bring others to Christ?" "No, I am not," he replied. "I don't believe that's my business, it's yours. I feel called to practice law, not to preach." The pastor sat down with him and opened his Bible to Acts 8. Pointing to verse 4, he said, "Here, see what is said about the early Christians." His lawyer friend read aloud, "They that were scattered abroad went everywhere preaching the word." Stopping abruptly, he objected, "Oh, but those were just the apostles." "Please look at the first verse of the chapter." The lawyer was amazed to read, "…and they were all scattered abroad throughout the regions of Judea and Samaria, except the apostles." The pastor reminded him that the Lord expects ALL His children in some way to tell other of His grace. No matter what your regular work may be, you should be engaged in witnessing.

We may not see people saved every day. We may go months or years and never personally lead a soul to Jesus. However, we are successful in the work if we are faithful to witness at every opportunity. Not all Christians are reapers. Some are planters, some are sent to water, but all are essential to the work of soul winning. Ultimately, it is God who decides who is a planter or a reaper (1 Cor. 3:6-8 NKJV). Our duty is to have the courage to go after one by being available and faithful to share the gospel. Opportunities for witnessing are everywhere! Our duty as fishers of men is to be ready when one presents itself to us. Peter writes, "But sanctify the Lord God in your hearts, and always be ready to give a defense to everyone who asks you a reason for the hope that is in you, with meekness and fear" (1 Pet.3:15 NKJV). Never feel that you cannot witness. Remember that all of Christ's disciples were just ordinary men until He called them and changed them. Jesus took them as they were, saved them and placed them into His harvest. By His power, Jesus made them something they had not formerly been. By the way, He has done the same thing for every child of God (Acts 1:8 NKJV). The Holy Spirit is your source of courage; He is your source of soul winning power. Who's your one?

CHAPTER SIX

Can God Really use Your Life?

For the Son of Man has come to seek and to save that
which was lost. (Luke 19:10 NKJV)

WHY DID JESUS COME? THE PERSONAL MISSION STATEMENT OF THE SON of God is summed up in Luke 19:10 NKJV. The word "save" that Jesus uses when He says He came to "save that which was lost" (Luke 19:10 NKJV), means to rescue from danger, to save from death. Peter uses the same word when he was about to drown and cried out desperately, "Lord, save me" (Matt. 14:30 NKJV). And the word Jesus uses for the "lost" means "ruined, destroyed, perishing" (Dictionary 1828). In John 3:16 (NKJV), when God announces He loved the us so much that He gave His one and only Son "that whosoever believes in Him shall not perish"; the word "perish" is that same word for ruin and destruction (Strong's Concordance 1984). The mission statement of Jesus is one that is a relentless, passionate, whatever it takes effort to "seek and to save" those who are dying."

But why are we here on Earth? Can God really use our life? There are three examples that shows us that "Yes, God can" use your life. All three examples are recorded for us in Scripture: The salvation of Saul, also known as Paul (Acts 9:1-6, 10-16 NKJV); the shepherds who watched their flocks by night (Luke 2:8-20 NKJV); and the watchman

(Isa. 21:6-10 NKJV). These are three types of people in unique settings that God uses to inspire us to behave as fishers of men. May we realize that there is hope and courage for people like you and me to be used of the Lord.

The Salvation of Saul

In the salvation of Saul, the Lord takes him, saves him by grace, and transforms him into the great apostle to the Gentiles. In all truth, Saul would be an unlikely candidate for the service of the Lord. Here was a man who was feared and hated by Christians and one who did everything in his power to destroy the name of the Lord Jesus Christ. Yet, God reached down in grace and took this man from where he was and used him to change the world. God used him in such a great manner that Paul's ministry is still reaping fruit today. Just the fact that we are talking about his life and the impact he had on the world is a testimony to the way God used him then and is using him now.

Now, don't sit there and think that Paul, (Saul's new name), is some sort of super saint. Neither should you think that there is no possible way that the Lord could use you like he did Paul nor that he could use you at all. But God can! I suppose that we may feel inferior and unworthy to be used of the Lord in His kingdom work, but I can tell you that Jesus can and will use you if you will make yourself available to Him. Let's look at Paul's salvation experience and see that the obstacles that may seem to be in the way of us behaving as fishers of men are no match for the Lord Jesus Christ.

YOUR PAST CONDITION IS NO OBSTACLE

Paul's past was one that was in opposition against the disciples of the Lord. "Then Saul, still breathing threats and murder against the disciples of the Lord, went to the high priest" (Acts 9:1 NKJV). Even Paul's own testimony, he said that he was guilty of doing everything in his power to put Christianity to death (Acts 22:4; 26:10 NKJV). In 1

Timothy 1:13-15 (NKJV), Paul tells us something about his past; that he was a murder and a rebel against the Lord Jesus Christ. Religiously, he was a man to be envied, but internally, he was as wicked as any other many who had ever walked the face of the earth. In Acts 7:58 (NKJV), the Bible indicates that Saul/Paul gave his approval to the murder of Stephen, since he guarded the clothes of those who stoned the preaching deacon to death. Paul was a wicked man, but this proved to be no obstacle to the grace and saving power of the Lord. When Paul received Jesus into his heart, he was changed forever by the grace of God.

Your past is no obstacle to your future work as a fisher of men! Regardless of what you did before you received Jesus as your Savior, it matters no longer! When He saved your soul, He washed your past away forever! It is just as though you got a brand-new start at that precious moment. In fact, the Bible refers to that event as a "new birth" (John 3:3 NKJV). There are three records of your past in the world today. First, there is the record you carry in your mind. Secondly, there is the record carried by all those who knew what you were before. Third, there is the record carried by Satan, and he will throw your past up to you all the time to keep you from behaving as a fisher of men. But may I remind you? That even though I may remember my past, my friends and family may remember my past, and even though Satan surely remembers my past, God in Heaven has forgotten my past and it is no obstacle to Him for using me now or into the future as a fisher of men!

YOUR PRESENT CIRCUMSTANCES ARE NO OBSTACLE

Paul was on his way to Damascus to find Christians to arrest and to take them to their deaths. He was filled with hatred and wanted nothing more than to completely destroy anyone or anything connected with the name of Jesus Christ. Yet, despite all of this, the Lord was able to change the man and to use him for the glory of God as a fisher of men. He can do the same thing in your life and mine. He can take us, with all the baggage that we carry, and He can use us for His glory. We all bring certain liabilities to the table. Some are uneducated; other have few resources; some are weak in faith; others are arrogant and filled with pride. However, I would like to remind you that the Lord is able to take us exactly where we are, change what needs to be changed and then use us greatly!

Your present circumstance did not catch the Lord by surprise! He knows everything there is to know about you (Heb. 4:13 NKJV). He knows where you are, and He still can use your life if it is yielded to Him for His glory. The secret lies in behaving as a follower of Christ. "I beseech you therefore, brethren, by the mercies of God, that you present your bodies a living sacrifice, holy, acceptable to God, which is your reasonable service. And do not be conformed to this world, but be transformed by the renewing of your mind, that you may prove what is that good and acceptable and perfect will of God" (Rom. 12:1-2 NKJV). When you do this now you can behave as a fisher of men.

YOUR PERSONAL CHARACTERISTICS ARE NO OBSTACLES

Paul was feared by the followers of the Lord Jesus. His conversion was seen by many to be nothing more than some sort of trap designed to find them and their leaders. In fact, when he went to Jerusalem to meet the Apostles, Barnabas had to go with him and introduce Paul to the leaders. Yet, God was able to overcome this hurdle and still use Paul in a great fashion. If you take the time to look at Paul's life, you will find that he was a man with many personal characteristics that seemed to be unfavorable to his success. Paul had many personal hurdles to get over to be used by the Lord, but God was able to use him despite of what was wrong with him physically.

If we get into the business of comparing ourselves with others, then we are in for a rough ride! Many of us have personal characteristics that may make us feel that we cannot be used by God effectively. Some Christians fight depression, other battle loneliness, some fight against feelings of inferiority, some keep their wickedness of days gone by constantly before their eyes; some keep worldlines in their lives; just feel inadequate to do the Lord's work; and some just flat out refuse which is sin against God. Listen, whatever weakness you may carry, it can be an obstacle to you if you allow it to be. However, to the Lord, your problem is nothing! He can take you amid your weakness and still use you to confound the strongest of those about you. He can take your life and make it an inspiration to everyone who meets you. The secret lies in one word, surrender! God can use your life to be a fisher of men!

The Shepherds

Another of example of God using people who behave as fishers of men is the shepherd on the night that Holy night that Christ was born. According to Luke 2:8-20 (NKJV), this passage reveals God's love for the most common and most sinful of men. These shepherds were just living their lives, doing what they needed to do to survive, and they experienced a life-changing, eternity-altering grace. They were visited by the heavenly messengers, they met Jesus, and their lives were never the same again. They came away with a new occupation they behaved as fishers of men. Now we might not all be shepherds, but we, the children of God, have the same occupational call; to be fishers of men. As you study this passage of Scripture, I want to point out a few similarities we share with these shepherds which should be a great encouragement for us to behave as fishers of men.

OUR OCCUPATIONS

These men were engaged in the business of life. They were doing what they felt they needed to do to provide for their families and for themselves. They were shepherds and their duties included: leading a flock, feeding, watering, protecting, etc. They probably were raising sheep to be used in the Temple services. They were just busy living their lives. That describes most people as well. We work, we live our lives, and days blend into days. We carry out various duties and spend the bulk of our days laboring. We give little thought about what awaits us after this life, little alone about the eternity of others (Heb. 9:27 NKJV).

OUR OFFENSIVES

These men are shepherds, and it did not matter that they were raising lambs to be sacrificed in the Temple, they themselves were social outcasts. Their work kept them away from the Temple for weeks at a time. Their nature of their work caused them to be ceremonially unclean. As they moved about the country tending to their flocks, they were often accused of being thieves. Shepherds were considered unreliable and were not allowed to give a testimony in court. These men were just dirty, defiled sinners. These men had no hope. No one, not even the religious elite, to care for them. They were lost and destined to Hell. Dear child of God we were once all defiled sinners in the eyes of God (Gal. 5:22; Rom. 3:10-23; 5:12; Eph. 2:1-3, 13 NKJV). In that lost condition, humanity has a common destination: Hell (Rom. 6:23 NKJV).

OUR OPPORTUNITIES

Even though these men were social outcasts, even though they were considered defiled by organized religion (Ps. 142:4 NKJV), and even though they were the kind of men you would never trust with anything of value; these men were the very men who received the good news of the Savior's birth, "For there is born to you this day in the city of David a Savior, who is Christ the Lord" (Luke 2:11 NKJV). The shepherds received an invitation from Heaven to go meet a Savior. They accepted that invitation and they were saved. Religion had no place for them. Society had no place for them. But God put them into His plan! God had a place in His grace and in His love for these dirty, defiled sinners. We have that same opportunity. The Gospel, or the Good News of Salvation, has been given to us to just as it was given to those shepherds. He loved us despite of what we are (Rom. 5:8 NKJV).

OUR OBLIGATION

The shepherds met Jesus. They were saved and they were changed forever (Luke 2:16-20 NKJV)! They went back to their sheep, but as they went, they told everyone they met what they had heard, what they had seen, and what the Lord had done for them. They had an experience, and they shared it with everybody. These men had been saved just a short time, and they already had the courage to share the good news with everybody. They returned to their flocks and resumed their lives, but these men had a new language, a new song, a new purpose, a new way of living, behaving as fishers of men. They were altered forever by that one encounter with the Lord Jesus Christ.

That is how it works! Jesus changes every life He saves (2 Cor. 5:17 NKJV). He gives us a new song (Ps. 40:1-3 NKJV). He makes us fishers of men by His saving grace (Acts 1:8) NKJV. He gives us a new life and a new purpose in that life. Meeting Him changes everything (Eph. 2:4-10 NKJV)! After we meet Him, like the shepherds, we will have a desire to tell other about Him. We will keep on living; will keep on working, but now we will do things with a new purpose of heart and behave as a fisher of men.

The Watchman

The last example of a life that God uses to be a fisher of men can be seen in the watchman that is discussed by the prophet Isaiah in Isaiah 21:6-10 (NKJV). The year is 689 BC, the world is in turmoil. The Babylonian Empire is under attack by the Assyrian Empire. All the nations in that area hoped against hope that Babylon would be able to defeat the Assyrian aggressors to their north. However, it was not to be! Babylon fell to the Assyrians and everyone knew they would not be stopped until the entire region was under domination. So, against this backdrop of war and a certain attack upon the nation of Israel, God commanded the prophet Isaiah to assume the role of a watchman.

Isaiah is to look to the prophetic future and tell the people what he sees approaching. This is just what Isaiah does.

The message might have been given nearly 2,700 years ago, but it is as timely as today's headlines: Pandemic claiming lives, political war, people losing their jobs, wildfires, natural disasters, and even persecution of the church. On a spiritual level, the pandemic of sin in our world continues to rise. People calling good evil and evil good; and people doing what is right in their own eyes. Old conviction and standards of living are being swept away right before our very eyes. The winds of change are blowing hard upon the world and around us, and there is even the threat of fearful things just over the horizon. Today, just as there was in Isaiah's day, there is a need for the people of God to assume the role of watchman and behave as fishers of men. There is a need for us to take a stand, look at that which is approaching and open our mouths and sound the alarm by sharing the Gospel of our Lord and Savior Jesus Christ. In this example of people that God can use to share the Gospel, please take courage, and be determined to behave as fisher of men by being a watchman in these perilous times we live in.

HIS MISSION

In ancient times, those who lived in walled cities were considered blessed individuals. By being inside a city with walls, they had two forms of protection. One was the wall itself. It stood as a barrier between the citizens and their enemies. The wall was a formidable barrier to trouble. The city of Jericho was an ancient city that placed great value in the defensive nature of its vast thick walls (Josh. 6:1 NKJV). A second form of protection the citizens had was the watchman. He is mentioned in Isaiah 21:6 (NKJV), "For thus has the Lord said to me: "Go, set a watchman, Let him declare what he sees."" The watchman was essential to the proper function of the wall. He stood upon that wall and kept watch over the surrounding countryside. When invading armies or other dangers came into his view, he sounded the warning and those inside the wall knew to prepare. Both the watchman and the wall were essential to the survival of the city itself. Without the watchman, those inside the wall were blind and without the wall the watchman would have been unnecessary.

There are two duties that the watchman was to do. First, and the most important duty the watchman had to do was for him to watch! He was to stand in the towers or upon the wall and his eyes was to scant the countryside for any signs of trouble. From his high and lofty perch, he could see the glistening of armor, swords, and spear; he could see banners of war as they waved; and he could see the clouds of dust raised by the drumming of thousands of feet upon the desert sands. He was to be in his place, with his eyes open to watch! The second duty the watchman had to do was to warn. Whether he saw anything approaching or not, he was to give his report to the people within the walls when they asked him of conditions outside. When trouble arose in the distance, he was to lift up his voice and sound the warning so that the people within the walls could prepare themselves and so that those who lived outside the city could run in and find refuge.

If there was ever a time when watchmen were needed around the church, the home, the family, the schoolhouse, and the community, the day is now! We need fishers of men who can discern God's Word, who know the enemy and his tactics (1 Pet. 5:8 NKJV) and are willing to watch and warn others of what they see coming. Whether it is good news or bad, we need men and women who will raise the warning the lost souls need a savior!

HIS METHODS

The watchman was to be "listening earnestly with great care" (Isa. 21:7 NKJV) in his watching. He was to be diligent in watching and noting everything he saw. In verse 8, he compares himself to a "lion." Lions have noticeably short eyelids. Even when they are asleep, they have the appearance that their eyes are open and watching. He tells us that he was in his place, both day and night. He did not leave his post but remained there to make sure that nothing occurred on his watch that he did not see.

The watchman sets a great example for those who would be watchman in our day. In 1 Peter 5:8 (NKJV), we are told to "Be sober, be vigilant; because your adversary the devil, as a roaring lion, walks about seeking who he may devour." The word "sober" means "to be calm and collected in spirit". The word "vigilant" means "to be watchful." (Strong's Concordance 1984) The idea here is that the Lord's watchmen are not to get caught up in the excitement of the times. We are not to be disturbed by the events around us, but we are to be ever watching. We know how things appear when there is calm. When we see trouble on the horizon, we are to sound the warning!

The watchman is to be vigorous in sounding the alarm! Notice the example that Isaiah gives: "and look, here comes a chariot of men with a pair of horsemen!' then he answered and said, "Babylon is fallen, is fallen! And all the carved images of her gods he has broken to the ground""" (Isa. 21:9 NKJV). You see, this watchman saw trouble approaching and he did not keep the message to himself. Instead, he opened his mouth and shouted out the warning for all to hear. He told everyone within earshot that trouble was coming. Again, there is a lesson for the watchmen in our day as well. As we watch the enemy approaching ever nearer towards the walls of the church, our homes, our families, and our communities, we have a responsibility to sound the alarm! Some say, "God can't use me." Yes, He can if you make yourself available to him. Some say, "What's the use? No one is listening to us!" Let me remind you that one of these days we are going to face our Savior at the Judgment Seat of Christ, and on that day, we will give an account of how well we raised the alarm to sinner that needed a Savior. Therefore, let us take heed to the certain signs of the enemy's approaching and let us warn them by inviting them to Jesus as we behave as fishers of men.

HIS MESSAGE

Notice the message that Isaiah gives as a watchman. "The burden against Dumah. He calls to me out of Seir, "Watchman, what of the night? Watchman, what of the night?" The watchman said, "The morning comes, and also the night. If you will inquire, inquire, Return! Come back!"" (Isa. 21:11-12 NKJV). The watchman speaks about the dawning of a new day, the watchman says, "the morning comes!" He sounds out the glad note that the night is nearly spent, and that dawn is about to break. You see, the night was the most frightening time of all. The watchman could not see as well, and the enemy had a better chance of sneaking in for the attack. In the daytime, the enemy would be far more easily exposed. The news was that dawn was coming brought comfort to the hearts of the people in the city. I'm not sure how great a watchman I am, but I am glad that I can tell you as we live in these perilous times that "the morning comes!" It won't be long brothers and sisters until the Lord comes to take us home to heaven. He promised He would come back (John 14:1-3; 1 Thess. 4:15-16 NKJV), and rest assure He will! In fact, His last recorded words are "Surely I come quickly" (Rev. 22:20 NKJV). Hang on fishers of men, it may be dark now, but morning is about to break, and there is a new day dawning.

But until then, we need to be about sharing not only dawning of hope of the Gospel message, but the other part of the message and that is the doom. The watchman tells the people that after the morning passes, night is coming back again! For the people of God, there is a bright and happy morning on the horizon; but for the lost sinner, there is nothing but the dark night of eternal separation and eternal punishment in Hell. Things are looking up for the people of God; but the lost man has nothing to look forward to but the undiluted wrath of Almighty God (John 3:36; Eph. 2:3; Heb. 10:31; Heb. 12:29 NKJV).

Now, when the watchman gives a message like this, that means now there is a decision that needs to be made. The watchman tells those who hear him to inquire, return, and come. He is calling the wayward ones back to God. He is saying to them, "There is great danger on the horizon, but there is still time to make a change. Come to God! Return to Him!" That was the message they needed to hear in that day and that is the message that still needs to be trumpeted by the watchmen of our day! Danger, great danger, looms on the near horizon, but it is not too late. God is still saving souls. He is still changing lives. He is still receiving all who will come to Him by faith. That is the message we need to share with a lost and dying world. They need to hear the news that there is still hope. All is not lost! They can be saved if they will come if they will return to God.

Where are the watchmen who are gazing out over the horizon? Where are the watchmen who see the danger of approaching judgment? Where are the watchmen who see the enemy creeping ever closer to the walls of our churches, our families, our homes, and our communities? Where are the watchmen who will set the trumpet to their lips and sound the warning? Are you behaving as a fisher of men? God can use your life to bring in the lost.

CHAPTER SEVEN

God's Response to Man's Sin

Therefore, just as through one mand sin entered the world, and death through sin, and thus death spread to all men, because all sinned. (Romans 5:12 NKJV)

As a fisher of men how important is it to study sin? In sharing the Gospel of Jesus Christ, if you do not include sin in the presentation then your presentation is inadequate. It is important to study sin because sin is a dominant fact of the human experience, not to mention sin is a major theme of the Bible. Therefore, understanding sin is elementary to understanding the need and the method that God applies for the purchase of your freedom from sin so that way you can give an account of the hope within you. Sin has been the subject of endless discussion. The Bible says that "for all have sinned and fall short of the glory of God" (Rom. 3:23 NKJV). And because of sin is the reason why Jesus went to the cross to die. The entire Bible is a revelation of our sin and our need to be redeemed by the shed blood of the Lord Jesus Christ. If there is no sin, there is no need for a Savior! Those who reject the Bible have frequently provided inadequate concepts of sin. Everyone seems to be an expert when it comes to sin. Everyone thinks they know what sin is and for most sin is what everyone else is doing.

Sin can be used to sell all kinds of products. The word sin is used in movie titles, advertisements for products, and the goal is to catch the eye of the people. Most people, at least those who attend some kind of worship service occasionally, want to feel they are bad enough to be fun, but they are good enough to get to heaven. The problem is that people don't read God's Holy Word and they shy away from the truth. And if there is ever an age where the people need to hear about sin, it is our sophisticated, electronic, and knowledge at your fingertip world today. We have almost done away the idea of sin. The word "sin" has become something that is old-fashion, and we have taken it away from our vocabulary. We now use words like error, mistake, misjudgment, weakness, psychological maladjustment, glandular malfunction, a stumble upward, anything but sin. And we have gone through the medicine cabinet and we have put new labels on the old bottles of poison, so that we have new terminology for an old fashion word. No longer is a man a drunkard; today, he is an alcoholic. No longer is a woman a harlot or a prostitute; today she is called a call girl or lady of the evening. No longer is man thief; today he is a politician. And we have just somehow tried to change things. But they have not really changed sin at all.

God Responds to Sin by Illumination

Do you know what darkness is? Well in theology, darkness is the absence of God's influence in our lives or the absence of God Himself in our lives. 1 John 1:5 (NKJV) says this about God, "That God is light and in Him is no darkness." Sin is defined as nonconformity to the will of God, which leads to physical and spiritual death, and an eternal separation from a God in a physical Hell that will one day deliver its inhabitants up for the final judgment and ultimately into the Lake of Fire. So, God responds to our darkness in sin with truth and illumination. God is proactive, all-knowing, and He has had a plan for our redemption since before the world began. Now the scientific answer to darkness is this: "Darkness is the absence of light." Today it appears that there is a great deal of dark light in the world and if you are going to behave as a fisher of men then you are going must understand that this dark light is robbing God's people of peace and power that God intends for us to enjoy.

What is dark light? Simply put it is false teaching that is disguised as light. It is often being offered by people who offer new meanings to our otherwise dull existence and tries to make sin out of date. And the Bible warns us about these false teachings, as a matter of fact the Bible calls them wells without waters (Jude 12-13 NKJV). There is a school of behavioristic psychology, which says that man is but the sum total of his environment and of his body chemistry, and if he does wrong it's because he's like a computer that has been programmed wrongly. And he's not to be blamed if he was raised in a bad neighborhood if he breaks into stores or smokes dope; after all, he was raised in that kind of neighborhood. There are many people who believe this about today's society, calling good evil and evil good (Isa. 5:20 NKJV).

Then you take the behavioristic psychologist, and you compound that with the idea of the evolutionist. And the evolutionist just tells us that we came into being by chance, by the unexpected concurrence of atoms, that we are the product of an impersonal force, an accident of nature, and an orphan of the ape. And when man believes that he is an orphan of the ape, he generally ends up making a monkey of himself. If man is the product of blind chance, then there is no God. And if there is no God, there is no ultimate standard of right or wrong. Now compound that thought with that of the humanists today. The humanists are these people who come along, and they are trying to remodel our education system in America. And they are telling our young people, "Don't get all hung up about this thing called sin, because, after all, sin is the invention of the church. It is something that some people have conjured up to whip everybody into line". Please understand, this fuzzy feeling preaching and teaching stuff, this dark light, is not really light at all; so be warned. If anyone offers to bring you out of darkness and into light be very careful. Because if their teaching does not involve putting your faith into the Lord Jesus Christ as your personal Lord and Savior, then it is a lie. Listen, sin is a reality and God responds to our sin by illumination.

The Explanation of Sin

Romans 5:12 (NKJV) says, "Therefore, just as through one man sin entered the world, and death through sin, and thus death spread to all men, because all sinned." The Greek word for sin here means "missing the mark, wondering from the path, going wrong or violating God's Law". That is the reason the Bible says, "For all have sinned, and come short of the glory of God" (Rom. 3:23 NKJV). The teaching of the Bible is that men do not sin and then become a sinner, rather men sin because they have a sin nature. Though sin is hereditary, every individual is still responsible for his or her own sin. Man cannot choose to reform his life or improve himself/herself to be acceptable to God. We cannot conform to the will of God because we are out of the will of God. No amount of self-reform or self-improvement, no matter how sincere, no matter how dedicated will atone for a single sin. Sometimes people will say, "Well, I am just as good as those folks down at the church." A church is but a society of sinners who finally realized it. The Bible says, "all have sinned, and come short of the glory of God" (Rom. 3:23 NKJV), so sin is just simply missing the mark. God's standard is perfection, and none of us live up to it.

Therefore, God give us the definition of sin or the explanation of sin in 1 John 3:4 which says, "Sin is the transgression of the law." James writes it this way, "Whoever shall keep the whole law, and yet offend in one point, he is guilty of all" (Jam. 2:10 NKJV). And what James is saying is that you don't have to break all ten of God's commandments to be a sinner in the sight of a righteous and holy God. Sin is the transgression of the law (1 John 3:4 NKJV). Another definition of sin; is that sin is the failure to do good; "Therefore, to him that knows to do good, and does not do it, to him it is sin" (Jam. 4:17 NKJV).

The Entrance of Sin

Did God create sin? That is a question I have been asked a lot as a pastor. Listen, sin originated with a created being in the form of an angel named Lucifer; whose name means "light bearer" (Ezek. 28:11-12 NKJV) (Strong's Concordance 1984). This anointed Cherub rebelled against God in Heaven and led a rebellion to dethrone God and take over (Rev. 12:4 NKJV). After being knocked out of heaven Lucifer is given a new name. He is no longer "light bearer" he is now "the adversary." Satan means "adversary" (Strong's Concordance 1984). He has become totally contrary to the will of God and is depraved beyond redemption. There is no salvation for Satan. Satan and all the demons that follow him are full of bitterness and they are looking for revenge.

Jesus described Satan in John 8:44 (NKJV), "You are your father the devil, and the desires of your father, you want to do. He was a murderer from the beginning, and does not stand in the truth, because there is no truth in him. When he speaks a lie, he speaks from his own resources, for he is a liar and the father of it." Here Jesus tells us two things about Satan: his motives and his methods. His motive is murder; his method is the lie. Satan is a liar, and he is a murderer; therefore, Satan came to the Garden of Eden, and enticed Eve, and tempted Adam, and both sinned and rebelled against God. Where did sin originate for man? Sin entered the human family by the action of the first man Adam. He had been created in the very image of God. He had been placed in a perfect environment, with a perfect companion, as the master of a perfect world, with only one restriction. He was forbidden to eat the fruit of one tree in the Garden of Eden (Gen. 2:15-17 NKJV). The penalty for eating from this tree was death! You would think that Adam would be content in that perfect paradise, but the Bible tells us that Adam broke the one Law that had been given by God (Gen. 3:1-7 NKJV).

That moment Adam sinned has been termed by theologians as "The Fall". Sadly, Adam's fall did not just effect Adam, but it effected the whole world. There is no way of explaining the things that go on in this world apart from the fall. There is only one way to explain things like: murder, abortion, theft, racism, hatred, fornication, adultery, idolatry, and other forms of wickedness. That is, "through one man sin entered the world" (Rom. 5:12 NKJV). How do you explain the hatred you see in politicians? How do you explain the hatred in the riots? How do you explain the abortion clinics? How do you explain homosexuality?

How do you explain the millions of crimes that are being committed against humanity? There is only one explanation: "Through one man sin entered the world". All sin and all the results of sin can be traced back to one moment in time. It can all be traced back to when Adam, the first man, sinned against God.

The Effects of Sin

The effects of sin can be summed up into one word: death. Remember, sin is the transgression of the law, and the law without a penalty is only advice and God is not giving advice when He give His Ten Commandments. Here is the penalty to breaking God's law: "For the wages of sin is death" (Rom. 6:23 NKJV). Death entered the world because man broke the specific Laws and commandments of God, but death entered the world through sin. Romans 5:13 (NKJV) says, "For until the law sin was in the world, but sin is not imputed when there is no law". So, even those who were not guilty of any specific violation of God's Law, because the Law had not yet been given, still died. You can see this effect of sin before the Law was given by reading Genesis 5, there you will see the terrible effect of sin in the human family, marked by the phrase "and he died." (Gen. 5:5, 8, 11, 14, 17, 20, 27, 31 NKJK).

But we need to understand what death Paul is talking about in Romans 5:12 (NKJV). He not talking about mere physical death. If you think just physical death is the only wage of sin, then that is awfully confusing, because all men die. The saved and the lost, physically die, and that's not what he's talking about. Don't think that death ends it all. Don't think that you can crawl up in the grave and pull the dirt over your face and hide from God because you cannot!

Remember, God told Adam in the Garden of Eden, "In the day that you eat you'll surely die" (Gen. 2:17 NKJV). When Adam disobeyed God, he died that day, however, he did not die physically; for he went on to live for hundreds of years. But he died spiritually. Death is not the separation of the soul from the body; death is the separation of the soul from God. That is the reason the Bible says, "He that has the Son

74

hath life; and he that hath not the Son of God hath not life" (1 John 5:12 NKJV).

Death is so certain that there are industries that are built around the truth that you will die. There is the mortuary and the life insurance industries that exist because people die. Death is as certain as is life (Heb. 9:27 NKJV). However, many do not fully understand that death is more than just laying this body in a grave. In truth, sin produces three kinds of death in humans. First, there is the spiritual death. This the natural state of all humanity as they are born into this world. Spiritual death is the reality of being separated from God (Eph 2:1-2; 4:18 NKJV). Second is the physical death. This is the place that all human come to, when these temporal, earthly bodies are laid aside (Heb. 9:27 NKJV). Third is the eternal death. This is known as "the second death". It refers not only to eternal separation from the presence of God (2 Thess. 1:8-9 NKJV); but also, of eternal torment in the Lake of Fire (Rev. 20;14-15 NKJV). It is the ultimate doom of every person who is not saved by the grace of God.

Every lost person needs to understand that you are spiritually dead and one day you will die physically, and then you will spend eternity enduring the second death if you do not accept Jesus as your personal Lord and Savior. Every child of God needs to behave as a fisher of men by knowing that we have already passed from death unto life (John 5:24 NKJV). Jesus said, he that "believes in me shall never die" (John 11:26 NKJV). The child of God can never die spiritually because the child of God can never be separated from God. Paul said that there is nothing can "separated us from the love of God, which is Christ Jesus our Lord" (Rom. 8:35-39 NKJV).

God Responds to Sin by Revelation

The other half of Romans 6: 23 (NKJV) says, "but the gift of God is eternal life in Christ Jesus our Lord." When it appeared that sin would completely take over and destroy mankind God stepped in to save a remnant. Through the true story and the events of Noah and his family, and the animals we can see a wonderful revelation that not only recorded for us in Scripture, but is a legend that is taught in many other religions in different ways. There is a lot of people who talk about the Great Flood from countries all over the world. Plus, there is evidence that the flood happened, because of the fossil record, as the bones of sea dwelling creatures are found in the desert and in the mountains. But the greatest proof that the flood happened is that Jesus believed it happened. Jesus said, "As it was in the days of Noah…" (Matt. 24:37 NKJV). What Jesus has to say about the flood means more to me than what any theological professor or professor of history, archeologist, paleontologist, or geologist would have to say. God could have destroyed everything and every human being and started all over again. But He didn't because He loves us and contrary to popular belief God is still in control over the world today.

In Genesis 6:5 NKJV, it tells us that in the days of Noah, that man was addicted to sin; it tells us what God saw in mankind and His view of mankind is sad. However, God had a plan. He would save a remnant and reveal His love and mercy through the most severe judgment that the world had ever seen. Over in Luke 17:22-29 (NKJV), when Jesus was asked by the Pharisees, "When would the kingdom of God come?" He tried to explain to them that it would not come gradually with the observation of man, but after His rejection it would come suddenly like the flood that came in the days of Noah, and like the fire that fell from Heaven to destroy Sodom and Gomorrah. The flood (water) represented God's judgment, but it also demonstrated God's grace, "But Noah found grace in the eyes of the Lord" (Gen. 6:8 NKJV). God required the obedience of Noah in building the ark. Noah had faith because he believed God and therefore, he built the ark.

The flood provided the purging of the demonic powers that were running ramped within humanity. If a world is left entirely to itself the devil will try to take over and this is clearly been seen in what is going on in our world today. The closer we get to the return of Jesus Christ, the more successful the devil it will be. While the ark is a picture of what will happened during the Great Tribulation, it is also a picture of Jesus and His completed work at Calvary. This can be useful if we are going to behave as fishers of men. You have a creative way of sharing the Gospel to children and to parents who have never heard the Gospel before.

Noah's Ark Pictures the Savior

There are four pictures of the Savior that we can see in Noah's ark. The first is the security of the ship. "Make yourself an ark of gopherwood; makes rooms in the ark and cover it inside and outside with pitch" (Gen. 6:14 NKJV). The ark that Noah built was made of gopher wood or as we know it, cypress. Cypress is almost indestructible; or incorruptible. The wood for this ship speaks of the humanity of Jesus. Isaiah says He will be like a shoot out of a dry ground (Isa. 53:2 NKJV). When the Bibles often speaks about a tree when it refers to a man it usually represents a righteous man. God has this to say about a righteous a man, "He shall be like a tree planted by the rivers of water" (Ps. 1:3 NKJV). The ark is a picture of Jesus and His righteous humanity and in order to provide salvation to man, Jesus had to be cut down (Isa. 53:3-8 NKJV) just as the gopher wood had be cut to make the ark.

Then Noah was instructed to put "pitch" on the inside and the outside of the ark (Gen. 6:14 NKJV). Pitch is a gummy tar, a rosin, made from an oily substance that was very much like goo and glue put together. The interesting thing about this word "pitch", it is the Hebrew word "*kopher*" (Strong's Concordance 1984). It is translated in the Bible more than seventy times as "atonement". Atonement and pitch are the same word. It all depends on how you use it. Over in the book of Leviticus 17:11 (NKJV), when the Bible speaks of the blood, it says it will be "atonement for your souls." You could also read it like this: "pitch for your souls." When you look at Noah's ark you can get a clear picture of the Lord Jesus Christ. The ark made from cypress wood, on the outside is atonement, and on the inside is atonement. The water from all the rain represents God's judgment, the wrath of God against sin. Therefore, you can plainly see what the atonement does, it keeps out every drop of wrath and judgment and keeps God's children safe with the arms of Christ. It covers those who are on the inside from the wrath of God. Thank God for the blood atonement of the Lord Jesus Christ, for God's judgment will not penetrate the atonement.

The second picture of Jesus that we can see in the ark is the sufficiency of the ship. God told Noah to build inside this ship "rooms" (Gen. 6:14 NKJV). We are not told how many rooms Noah was to build, however when you consider the instructions for the length X height X width plus the three decks there is plenty of square feet to put many rooms (Gen. 6:15-16 NKJV): three million cubic feet. It is an incredibly large ship. As a matter of fact, using the Biblical dimensions the ship was longer than a football field: 450 feet long. That just shows that there is plenty of space to put eight people plus two of every kind of animal into the ship. This reminds us of what Jesus said, "In My Father's house are many mansions" (John 14:2 NKJV). When you consider the vastness of Heaven there is plenty of room for anyone to come to Jesus. Listen,

if you are not saved, there is room at the cross for you. But think about this the ark was not pointed like we see boats today, but the ark that Noah built is square at both ends and is in the shape of a coffin. The ancient people used to make their coffins out of cypress wood, using the same shape as this ship. And Noah's ark represents for us, that Jesus is our coffin. You can see this in the picture of the Believer's Baptism, that you are buried with Christ. Standing there in the water you are being crucified with Christ, being submersed into the water you are buried with Christ, and then coming up out of the water you are resurrected with Jesus. You see, we die with Christ that we might live with Christ. The reason that the ship is not pointed at both ends is because it had no course of its own, therefore, it could not be guided by human hands. Neither was there a steering wheel where Noah could steer the ship. We are to be guide by the Holy Spirit that is within us as we read, meditate, and pray upon God's Holy Word. "Your word is a lamp to my feet and a light to my path. I have sworn and confirmed that I will keep your righteous judgments" (Ps. 119:105-106 NKJV). Noah was committed to that ship just as we should be committed to Jesus and committed to behave as fishers of men.

A third picture of Jesus that we can see in the ark is the structure of the ship. According to Genesis 6:16 (NKJV), not only were there three decks but there was one door in the side of the ship and one window on the roof of the ship. What this means is that Noah could control the window, but God was the only one in control of the door. Noah could go to the third story, look out the window, and look up into heaven. But Noah could not and should not open the door until the flood water were gone. So, Noah was closed in, in order that he might look up. Think, that simply reminds us that the only way to be close to Jehovah God is through Jesus Christ. If I want to look unto the face of God, then I must look at Him from my position in Christ Jesus. When God shut the door and locked the door, that tells us that God is the only one who sets the guideline or requirement to enter the ark. The only way of salvation is through the precious blood, the atonement, of Jesus Christ. You must admit to God you are a sinner (Rom. 3:23 NKJV); believe that Jesus is the Son of God (Rom. 10:9-10 NKJV); call upon Him as your Savior and Lord (Rom. 10:13 NKJV). The door represents Jesus, the door was the only way of salvation for Noah and His family. Jesus is the only way of salvation. Jesus said, "I am the way, the truth, and the life. No one comes to the Father except through Me" (John 14:6 NKJV). Peter said while addressing the Sanhedrin, "nor is there salvation in any other, for there is no other name under heaven given among men by which we must be saved" (Acts 4:12 NKJV). The window allowed light to come into the dark boat. Noah had to look up to the light, the sinner must look up to the light of Jesus to be saved (Eph. 2:8-9 NKJV).

The last picture of Jesus that we can see in the ark is the schedule of the ship. "Then the ark rested in the seventh month, the seventeenth day of the month, on the mountains of Ararat. And the waters decreased continually until the tenth month. In the tenth month, on the first day of the month, the tops of the mountains were seen" (Gen. 8:4-5 NKJV). The ship had a schedule, and it arrived right on time. According to the Jewish civil calendar, the first month is October and the seventh month is April. The seventeenth day of April is three days after the Passover (Ex. 12:6 NKJV). Therefore, the ark rested on the same day that Jesus would walk out of the tomb hundreds of years later! Jesus died on the fourteenth day of the month and rose on the seventeenth day! Is that a coincidence? Certainly not! You have here a wonderful picture of the Lord Jesus who passes through the water of judgment and stands in resurrection upon the earth the same day of the month that the ark rested on Mount Ararat.

Noah's Ark Pictures Our Salvation

Ephesians 2:8-10 (NKJV) says, "For by grace you have been saved through faith, and that not of yourselves; it is the gift of God, not of works, lest anyone should boast. For we are His workmanship, created in Christ Jesus for good works, which God prepared beforehand that we should walk in them." Noah was saved by grace through faith, "but Noah found grace in the eyes of the Lord" (Gen. 6:8 NKJV). This is the first time that we find the word grace in the Bible. Grace is what makes God love us when there is no loveliness about us. As a matter of fact, grace is what makes God love us when we were enemies and rebels to God (Rom. 3:22 NKJV). Grace comes when we believe in the Lord Jesus Christ. And God counts it to us as righteousness. And you don't add works to it. If you try to add works to it, then it is no longer grace by faith. Listen if you think that baptism is what saves a person or you think that giving money can deliver you to Heaven, or you think that witnessing, Bible study, and prayer can save your soul then you have destroyed the concept of grace (Rom. 11:6 NKJV).

Noah was saved by grace through faith. Think about it, the way was prepared for Noah to come to God by faith. How did Noah get on the ark? By a step of faith. God said to Noah, "Come into the ark, you and all your household because I have seen that you are righteous before Me in this generation" (Gen. 7:1 NKJV). How do we know that Noah came to God by the grace of the ark (Jesus) through faith? The Bible tells us, in Hebrews 11:7 (NKJV), "By faith Noah, being warned of God of things not seen as yet, moved with fear, prepared an ark to the saving of his house; by which he condemned the world, and became heir of the righteousness which is by faith." Jesus is our salvation by grace through faith.

Noah's Ark Pictures Our Security

Now it is clear that God said to him "come into the ark" (Gen. 7:1 NKJV). Can you see the difference? If it was told to Noah, go into the ark, that would imply that God was on the outside of the ark and sent Noah into the ark. However, God said to Noah "come into the ark" (Gen. 7:1 NKJV) which means that God was on the inside of the ark inviting Noah to come to Him. And once Noah receive the invitation from God to come, "and the Lord shut him in" (Gen. 7:16 NKJV). Catch that; it was God who shut the door. The Bible says, that after we believe, (upon the ark: Jesus; and we go through the door: Jesus) we are sealed with the Holy Spirit of promise (Eph. 1:13 NKJV). God was in the ark because the ark represents Jesus. Jesus is God's son and Jesus, and God are one. Had the ark gone down, Noah would have gone down, but God would have gone down also. God is in Christ and I am in Christ. And my security is in the Lord Jesus Christ. So many people have the idea that somehow, they are saved by grace and kept by works. But friend, if you are saved by grace, then you are kept by grace.

God put Noah in the ark with Himself, shut the door, kept the storm out, sealed the door, on the outside was atonement, on the inside was atonement; but just how safe was Noah? He was as safe as God was safe! Do you know when I will lose my salvation? I will lose my salvation when Jesus loses His relationship with the Heavenly Father, because I am in Christ Jesus! Some people have the idea that they're going to be secure when they get to Heaven. Please understand, that there were angels who fell from Heaven. Salvation is not in a place; security is not in a place. Salvation and security are in a person; God's response to man's sin is through revelation of a person and that person is Jesus Christ. Jesus said, "My sheep hear My voice, and I know them, and they follow Me. And I give them eternal life, and they shall never perish; neither shall anyone snatch them out of My hand" (John 10:27-28 NKJV).

Thank God for the ark. Praise God for the Lord Jesus Christ. And thank God that if you will come to Him by faith, your sins will be forgiven; you will be kept safe from the wrath of God, the flood water of His wrath. We the children of God need to behave as fishers of men by telling the world around us the good news of Jesus Christ that can be clearly seen in Noah's Ark.

CHAPTER EIGHT

Evangelism in the Hands of Sinners

*Go, stand in the temple, and speak to the people all
the word of this life. (Acts 5:20 NKJV)*

THE BOOK OF ACTS NOT ONLY SHOWS THE BIRTH OF THE CHURCH BUT
also describes the early church's evangelism. Contrary to the modern
notion that churches should strive to make unbelievers comfortable, the
church in Acts stressed purity. In fact, the biggest threat to evangelism
in the early church was not persecution, but tolerance of sin. While
the church's first recorded sin, (Ananias's lying to the Holy Spirit; Acts
5:1-11 NKJV), may have temporarily scared unbelievers away, the Lord
used it to return the church to its focus: outreach based on a testimony
of holiness, spurred on by persecution. Who knows this may have been
why God allowed the coronavirus pandemic to happen in 2020? It
might be that He used Covid-19 to temporarily shut down church for
a while or prune churches back so that the church can regain her focus
upon the Great Commission.

The New Testament presents a simple truth: those who love Jesus
Christ care about evangelism. Christians are called to continually
communicate the Gospel to the world, no matter the situation. When
Jesus ascended into Heaven, He left His disciples behind in Jerusalem.

His saving work on the cross was complete, and the penalty of sin was paid in full. But there was still more work to be done, and the disciples were left on earth to be hands and feet of Jesus by being fishers of men. Jesus commissioned His followers to go into the world and preach the Gospel to every creature, and to be His witnesses not only in Jerusalem but also in the uttermost part (Acts 1:8 NKJV).

However, there was going to be so much opposition to the evangelism of the church. The Jewish leaders, frustrated by Jesus' resurrection, were very much opposed to Christianity. The Apostles would be arrested, Stephen and James martyred, and converts hated. Beyond that, Gentiles would treat the message of the Gospel as foolishness, and Christians were to find themselves being treated like second class citizens. But the fact of the matter is, none of those obstacles halted evangelism, and on the contrary, the more opposition there was, the more the Gospel spread. Do you want to know what is wrong with the average church? Do you want to know why pastors, associate pastors, and/or leaders have been scrambling around and becoming discouraged and stressed out during this pandemic and the temporary closing of churches? It is because of two reasons. First, there are many church members who are not sharing their faith. Second, we failed to make disciples and show them how to share their faith. There are many church members who think that they have really served God when they just faithfully show up to church, live clean lives; some think if they have a job in the church like teaching Sunday School or singing in the choir, and if they give their money to God's work; then they are a pretty good Christian. Please understand, you may be serving God in those capacities, however, unless you are actively and vitally interested in behaving as a fisher of men then you are not right with God. There are even some church members who make the excuse why they are not sharing the Gospel, because they think it is the pastor's job. But the truth of the matter is that God has called all His children to be fishers of men, not just a select few. Let me clarify this: a pastor is not some hired gun that does all the praying, Bible Study, visiting, and the soul winning for us. He is to be the under shepherd guiding us, training us, teaching us, encouraging us to behave as fishers of men. So, using Acts 5 let me point out that there is an even more danger to evangelism in the church than Christians not evangelizing which is sin being tolerated inside the church.

The Enemy of Their Evangelism

The enemy of evangelism in the church is sin. It has the power to stop evangelism. Think about it, if persecution from outside the church propelled, advanced evangelism, then according to Acts 5, the opposite effect is that sin inside the church has the power to destroy evangelism. The church leadership had just endured arrests, beatings, and prohibition; none of which slowed the movement. But the moment sin entered the church; the Lord turned His attention to the reality that the church's biggest danger is not external persecution, but internal iniquity.

The story of Ananias and Sapphira is both a well-known and a tragic story (Acts 5:1-11 NKJV). A husband and wife sold their land for the purpose of giving the proceeds to the church to help the poor in the church. They publicly committed to give the whole amount to the Apostles, and they made that commitment voluntarily, not under compulsion. However, when the sale occurred, they kept half of the proceeds for themselves. In front of the church, they laid the money at the Apostles' feet in a dramatic fashion, while publicly declaring that they had donated the entire proceeds from the sale. It was lying pride cloaked in sinful and self-serving humility. For the first time, the focus of the church shifted from outside evangelism to inside hypocrisy.

Despite the sinful nature of this transaction, it began well enough. The church was compassionate, and Christians were demonstrating the love of Christ by taking care of one another. This selfless sacrifice was opening everything for evangelism. In addition to loving one another, they knew they could not expect to have an effective witness for Christ to those in need outside the church if those in need inside the church were being ignored. So, the early church made it a practice of sharing its wealth to meet its members' needs. The result was that "the multitude of those who believed were of one heart and one soul; neither did anyone say that any of the things he possessed was his own, but they had all things in common" (Acts 4:32 NKJV). The members of the church were generous to one another, and so their evangelism was particularly powerful. It was in this context that Ananias sold a piece of property and pretended to place all the money at the Apostles' feet. Their sin was not that they did not give everything to the church. God never commanded anyone to sell or give everything from a sale. The sin was deceit, rooted in pride. He wanted people to think that he gave everything to the church.

Notice, that since the demonically inspired persecution of the church from the outside clearly failed (Acts 3:11-26 NKJV), Satan shifted his approach. Rather than only attacking the church from the outside, he assaulted it from the inside. Hypocrisy became Satan's weapon of choice to corrupt the church. Because the early church was growing in large part based on the way Christians were meeting one another's needs, Satan move in to twist that sacrificial behavior. Not much has changed in the past 2,000 years. Satan is still doing the same thing today to the modern church, and it can clearly be seen in the pandemic of 2020. Satan is using fear on the outside to persecute the church while using hypocrisy inside the church to keep church members away. Church members who said, "we are committed to church", are now afraid to come back due to fear. Satan is still using hypocrisy against the Gospel, to him it is the best way to douse the flame of evangelism. God hates sin, but no sin is as ugly as the one that attempts to paint pride so that it looks like spiritual beauty. When such people get into the church, they corrupt it. When they get into leadership of the church, they can kill it.

The Sin of the Evangelism Exposed

"Peter said, "Ananias, why has Satan filled you heart to lie to the Holy Spirit and keep back part of the price of the land for yourself?"" (Acts 5:3 NKJV). True to what we would expect from God who hates sin, the deception of Ananias's hypocrisy gave way to the spiritual perception of Peter's leadership. Peter, who could only have known the truth behind

Ananias's actions by direct revelation from God, confronted him. Peter recognized that Satan was behind this sin, and he also recognized that an attack on the church of Jesus was also an attack on the Holy Spirit.

God publicly confirmed the truth of Peter's accusation by striking Ananias dead. Luke describes the fallout from this judgment with an understatement: "Then Ananias, hearing these words, fell down and breathed his last. So great fear came upon all those who heard these things" (Acts 5:5 NKJV). If there were any illusions about the nature of the Christian church, they were just shattered by this judgment. The church was not going to be about fun and games, because the God of the church is serious about sin. This was not exactly what you could call a seeker-friendly environment, and it certainly was not a sin-friendly environment. The message that Christians should be sending out to the world is not that the church sin and sinners, but that God hates sin. When the world understands that God will judge sin, people are prepared to appreciate that God also provided a means for complete forgiveness through His grace. Sapphira's death is further powerful illustration that God hates the sins of His saints, no matter how trivial those sins might be. The sins of Christians are the most heinous aspect of the church because they subtly allow Satan to destroy credibility and stifle evangelism. Because their sin was exposed, the Lord used this event to return the church's focus on being fishers of men.

The Source of their Evangelism was Purity

Effective evangelism is empowered by the Holy Spirit who has the freedom to move and work inside the lives of the members of a church. Therefore, a church needs to be pure and holy, not quenching the Holy Spirit (1 Thess. 4:19 NKJV). People might imagine that a church that deals with sin seriously would drive people away, not attract them. And to some extent that is true, however, Luke explains that despite the fact that the Apostles were performing signs and wonders publicly, "none of the rest dared join them, but the people esteemed them highly" (Acts 5:13 NKJV). The believers were meeting publicly; nobody was impulsively joining the church because they knew that they should not become Christians unless they were willing to have their lives exposed. The world knew that people were not genuine in church ran the risk of being struck dead by God, so no one joined them who was not ready for that kind of commitment.

A church that refuses to deal with sin, like so many churches today, becomes a breeding ground for both sinful believers and false converts. People make false professions of faith and are even allowed to live the lie because there is never any exposure to their sin. The most shocking part of the is entire story is that while the death of Ananias and Sapphira kept sinners from joining the church for the wrong reason, the end results of the whole event was that "believers were increasingly added to the Lord, multitudes of both men and women" (Acts 5:14 NKJV).

How to Recognize a Fisher of Men

Over in Romans 15:14-17 (NKJV), we can see another example of evangelism in the hands of sinners. In these verses Paul is a fisher of men and has a heart for soul winning. As you examine these verses think about the personal thoughts Paul shares with us, and the portrait of what a soul winner is. And then begin to examine your soul winning experience. Because I believe that within the heart oof every child of God, there should be a desire to see men saved!

THE CHARACTER OF A FISHER OF MEN

Paul writes, "Now I myself am confident concerning you, my brethren, that you also are full of goodness, filled with all knowledge, able also to admonish one another" (Rom. 15:14 NKJV). One characteristic that Paul had as a fisher of men is the fact that he has a heart for the lost. Paul was a great preacher, and writer for he wrote thirteen books of the twenty-seven books in the New Testament. Paul was a pioneer in the mission field as traveled place to place, starting churches and feeding the sheep of the Lord. Everywhere this man journeyed, he told men, women, boys, and girls about Jesus. When he was chained as a prisoner in Rome, or standing before kings and world rulers, or when he encountered a group of women praying by a river, he was busy telling people about Jesus. Paul's heart was full of the message of the Gospel. He wanted men to know the same Jesus he himself knew so well.

That is why he was confident that those who received Jesus as their Savior would be "full of the goodness" that could only come from a relationship with the Savior Jesus Christ. These Roman Christians were just like everyone else who has ever lived. They were born into this world as wicked sinners in need of a Savior, As members of the human race, there was no good dwelling in them at all; "There is none righteous, no, not one" (Rom. 3:10 NKJV). In fact, there is no good in the universe apart from the Person of God Himself! When Jesus was visited by the rich young ruler, the young man called Jesus good. Jesus replied, "Why do you call Me good? No one is good but One, that is, God" (Matt. 19:17 NKJV). Yet, Paul tells these Romans that they are filled with goodness. What does He mean? He is merely speaking of the goodness they received when they trusted Jesus by faith for salvation. When they were born again, they received the Holy Spirit, and along with Him, they received goodness from the Lord (Gal. 5:22; Eph. 5:9 NKJV). This new birth transformed their lives so that now they were able to do the things that were good in the sigh of God, and that showed those who were watching that there was life changing power in the Gospel of the Lord Jesus Christ (Matt. 5:16 NKJV).

Another characteristic of a fisher of men is that they possess a heavenly learning. Paul tells them that they are "filled with all knowledge" of spiritual things (Rom. 15:14 NKJV). The knowledge he is referring to has to do with know the Word of God, which is being taught to you through the power of the Holy Spirit which reside in your heart. This is a necessary ingredient in the life of a fisher of men. As we study the Word of God, the Holy Spirit uses Scripture to create a desire to see men saved! Why? Because the Bible is where we are going to learn that men are sinners in need of a savior. We learn that these lost men are headed to Hell without God. We learn that just as God loved us and saved us, He will do the same for them if they will trust Him to do it. It is there that we also learn how to tell men about Jesus. We learn that the most powerful witnessing tool we have is His Word. The Holy Living Word of God will speak to heart and it will bring men to Jesus (Rom. 10:17; Isa. 55:11 NKJV). Please understand, our study and increasing knowledge of the Bible out to birth a desire in our hearts to see people saved! If it doesn't then we should ask ourselves if we really believe the Word of God or not! I mean, how can we learn of men going to Hell and not be moved? How can we see their lost condition and it not break our hearts? There is something fundamentally wrong with people growing fat on the Word of God and not sharing the message with those who do not know Jesus!

Then one last character of a soul winner is that they possess a heavenly love. Paul moves deeper by telling them that their goodness and knowledge are to be used to "admonish" (Rom. 15:14 NKJV) one another. This is a word that means, "to rebuke, to warn, to exhort or encourage" (Dictionary 1828). In the New Testament, it often refers to the ministry of the pastor who is called upon "admonish" the church. That is, he is to warn them, encourage them, and from time to time rebuke them. The ideal is that of communicating the truth of God to someone to help them behave as a follower of Jesus Christ. There are times when Christians are to admonish one another (Col. 3:16 NKJV), however, this is a missing component in the modern church! Most believers don't have the love for their fellow believers or the courage to go up to them when they see error in their lives. Most believers don't have the grace to accept it either!

The idea is that we are to love one another enough to tell them the truth. When a pastor loves the church that he pastors, he will tell them the truth, even when it hurts! When believers love one another, they will speak to each other in truth (Col. 3:16 NKJV). Now, if we apply this to the realm of soul winning, Paul is telling us to love the sinner enough to tell them the truth! Instead of praying for a burden for the lost, I think the church needs to fall in love with Jesus all over again, because this will produce a love for the lost sinner with in us. When you fall in love with Christ there will be a burden for the lost. When we love Jesus more than anything, His love will reach out through us to reach this world for His glory!

THE BEHAVIOR OF THE FISHER OF MEN

Paul writes, "that I might be a minister of Jesus Christ to the Gentiles, ministering the gospel of God, that the offering of the Gentiles might be acceptable, sanctified by the Holy Spirit" (Rom. 15:16 NKJV). If you are going to behave as a fisher of men, then you need to be engaged in the proclaiming work. Paul says that he is a "minister". That means that he is busy with holy things. The word "minister" carries the idea of a person who is engaged in the public ministries of God (Dictionary 1828). Paul is letting us know that he has busied himself with spreading the Gospel to a lost and dying world. That what he means by using the phrase "ministering the Gospel." As we pass through this world, there is no greater calling than that of being a fisher of men! It greater than being the President of the United States. It overshadows that of a preacher. There is nothing as vital and wonderful as the ministry of sharing the Gospel of grace with a lost and dying world. What is so great about being a fisher of men is the fact that every child of God is called to be one! Only a few get to preach, but every child of God gets to be a soul winner (Acts 1:8 NKJV). Wherever you go in this life, the Lord has placed you there to tell others about Him and about His plan of salvation. That place where you work, that community where you live, that little Sunday School class, wherever it may be, God has placed you there as a minister of the Gospel.

Paul says that you are His priest in that place and He wants you to be busy with holy things. And there is nothing as holy and as sacred as being involved in telling a dying world about a living Lord! As a priest you are to go about doing your sacred duties. And one of the primary duties of the priest was that of intercession. The priest would enter the Tabernacle and place incense on the altar of incense and as the smoke rose before the Lord, he would place the names of the people, which he wore across his chest, before the Lord in prayer. This should speak to us a church and as individuals! One of the reasons we are so ineffective in bringing men to Jesus is that we have not gotten them in our hearts! We have not labored for them before the Lord, with a burden on our souls for their salvation. We have not become broken by their need and moved by their lost condition. We will never see souls saved in abundance until we learn to weep over them before the Lord, until we learn to carry then in our hearts, until we are consumed with a burden for their birth!

Another primary duty of the priest is that they must have a sacrifice that he can offer to the Lord. Of course, the first sacrifice we are to offer is for ourselves on the altar of service. "I beseech you therefore, brethren, by the mercies of God, that you present your bodies a living sacrifice, holy, acceptable to God, which is your reasonable service" (Rom. 12:1 NKJV). There are other sacrifices that we should offer to the Lord as well. For example: "Therefore by Him let us continually offer the sacrifice of praise to God, that is, the fruit of our lips, giving thanks to His name" (Heb. 13:15 NKJV). Paul says that his ministry sacrifice is the Gentiles. You see, the Lord placed them as a burden on Paul's heart and Paul says that he will offer them up to God as a sacrifice for the glory of the Lord. Here is how he did that; God laid them on Paul's heart, Paul interceded for them before the Lord, and then he went and told them about Jesus. Those who believed, he was able to lay on the altar as a redeemed sacrifice to the glory of God.

As hard as it may be for us to hear; the truth is this: You can tell how much a person loves Jesus by how much he shares the Gospel. You can tell how much a church loves Jesus by looking at the redeemed souls they lay on the altar for the glory of the Lord! Some might protest and say, "but, isn't it God that saves souls?" Absolutely! Salvation does not happen apart from His sovereign grace and will. However, He does allow His people the privilege of being involved. He burdens our hearts, fills us with the message, and uses us to tell the world about His saving grace. May the Lord help us to arrive at the place where we are willing to be used as fishers of men bring men, women, boys, and girls to Jesus!

THE COMPENSATION OF A FISHER OF MEN

Paul says, "Therefore I have reason to glory in Christ Jesus in the things which pertain to God" (Rom. 15:17 NKJV). Without a doubt, one of the secrets to a happy Christian life is that of being used of the Lord to bring men to faith in Christ Jesus. This can be seen in Psalm 126:6 (NKJV), "He that goes forth and weeps, bearing precious see, shall doubtless come again with rejoicing, bringing his sheaves with him." If you want to be happy in the Lord, then start telling people about Jesus! Nothing will transform a dead, dry church any quicker that souls being saved. Nothing will change your home more than a baby being born into it. It is one of the happiest and exciting times of life! So, it is in the church, there are million-dollar churches all around that are dead cemeteries because they do not bring men to Jesus. But there are little churches operating out of storefront buildings that are bubbling over with joy of the Lord because they are taking the message of salvation to a world that desperately needs to hear that good news. They are leading men to Jesus and it profoundly affects their level of joy in the Lord! That is the fisher of men needs in his life! May God help us to fall in love with Jesus once again so that we might love the world like He does. So that we might love them enough to tell them about Him!

Paul says that his rejoicing was on a profound level, or on a spiritual level with all the glory belonging to Jesus. Paul never won a soul; it was Jesus working through him. Therefore, all the glory must go to the Lord Jesus Christ and to Him alone! Therefore, when a soul is saved on visitation, or in worship service we need to slip off somewhere and thank the Lord for using us and for letting us see Him work in such a powerful manner. Beyond that, we need to be quick to give the Lord public glory for the work He has done as well.

When we are seeing folks saved, it means that He is pleased to be working among us. That's good! However, when we do not see people saved, what does that say about the church or about us? Does it mean that for whatever reason, the Lord has chosen not to work among us for the time being? I suppose it does! Therefore, when the well dries up, so to speak, and souls are not being saved, we need to get before Him and ask Him to show us our hearts. It may be that we are not in love with Him as we should be. It may mean that we have allowed our priorities to get out of line. It may mean that we need a revival, to confess our sins, and seek forgiveness. Because that is what it means when evangelism is in the hands of sinners.

CHAPTER NINE

Salvation Plain and Simple

Therefore, He is able to save to the uttermost those who come to God through Him, since He always lives to make intercession for them. (Hebrews 7:25 NKJV)

TO BEHAVE AS A FISHER OF MEN YOU MUST HAVE THE RIGHT TOOLS FOR the work of fulfilling the Great Commission. One of those tools is knowing the plan of salvation plain and simple. It has been said that the average person has around twenty thousand words in his or her vocabulary. Of course, most folks only use around two thousand different words in a normal conversation. In the English language there are around two hundred thousand words that are commonly used today. According to some estimates, the total number of English words of is over three million, which includes words used exclusively in the medical, technological, and scientific fields! That is a lot of words! As a pastor I use words when I preach, when I pray, when I witness, when I fellowship, when I write, etc. I use words in every area of my life. But it seems to me that of all the words that I use and encounter daily; the words of the Bible are the most precious to me.

If the Holy Spirit is the inspiration of the Word of God, and I believe He is, then I must also believe that He chose the precise words that He wanted to use. Therefore, when I read, study, and mediate on the Bible, it is imperative that I find out what the words in the text mean. To do this, the use of dictionaries, Hebrew and Greek dictionaries, and other reference materials are a big help. This way you can find what the word means in that society and time, then we can take that word and apply it to our lives today. However, depending on what stage you are in with your walk with Christ, depending upon how mature you are as a follower of Christ, there is going to be problems of understanding what the Bible says. You see, some people have been saved for years, and the Word of God is a blessing to you. While others are new believers and they are still learning the language of the church; plus, they are still trying to figure out how to understand the Bible. Still others who ready the Bible and hear the lingo of the church and it just does not make a lot sense to them.

In fact, one of the words that we hear in and around church is the word "saved", plus it is use in Hebrews 7:25 (NKJV). We talk about being saved. We sing about being saved. We preach about being saved. We testify about being saved. We shout about being saved. And it is fitting that we behave in this way, for salvation is a wonderful thing! But if you are going to behave as a fisher of men and you are a babe in Christ then you must learn what being saved means and what the plan of salvation is; so that you can share it with someone who does not know Jesus Christ as their personal Lord and Savior. And you can use words that will help you point them to Christ.

The simple definition of this word "save" means "to rescue somebody or something; to rescue someone or something form harm or danger" (Dictionary 1828) We use that word often and might speak of "saving someone from drowning"; "saving a person from a burning building"; "saving someone from certain spiritual death"; etc. The English word has the idea of "delivering another person from impending doom." The Greek word, which is translated "save" in Hebrews 7:25 (NKJV), is the word "*sozo*". It means "to save, to keep safe and sound, to rescue from danger or destruction; to make well, heal, restore to health" (Strong's Concordance 1984) In other words, nothing at all is lost in the translation. When we speak of "getting saved"; "being saved"; in the church, we are referring to God's ability to rescue us from death and Hell; and of His power to keep us in that safe and sound condition forever.

Salvation is about a Person

Hebrews 7:25 (NKJV) says, "Therefore, He is also able to save to the uttermost those who come to God through Him, since He always live to make intercession for them." The "He" in this verse is identified in verse 22 of this same chapter, which says, "by so much more Jesus has become a surety of a better covenant." Jesus is the "He". So, when you read the phrase "He is also able" it is talking about Jesus alone can and will provide salvation to those who call upon His name. That is the clear message of the New Testament: Jesus said, "I am the way, the truth, and the life. No one comes to the Father except through Me" (John 14:6 NKJV). "Nor is there salvation in any other, for there is no other name under heaven given among men by which we must be saved" (Acts 4:12 NKJV). "Believe on the Lord Jesus Christ, and you will be saved, you and your household" (Acts 16:31 NKJV). "He who has the Son has life; he who does not have the Son of God does not have life" (1 John 5:12 NKJV). Jesus said, "I am the door. If anyone enters by Me, he will be saved, and will go in and out and find pasture" (John 10:9 NKJV). It may seem narrow and sound narrow to our modern minds, but salvation will ONLY be found in a personal relationship with the Lord Jesus Christ!

Why? Because Jesus did what no other man has ever done or will ever do. He lived a sinless life, and then He went to on old rugged cross and died there in agony and shame. When He did, He shed His precious, sinless blood for the sin of all who will come to Him for salvation (1 Pet. 2:24 NKJV)! The church is not the answer. The preacher is not the answer. Only Jesus can rescue you from the danger that threatens your soul. Only Jesus can save!

In Romans 10 (NKJV), Paul wants the Jews to know that God is still working to bring them to faith in Christ Jesus. He shows them how God is bringing men to Himself through a person in the Lord Jesus

Christ. Paul gives them and us the crystal-clear picture of God's plan of salvation that centers upon only one way through the Jesus Christ. Unfortunately, one of the common misunderstandings in our day is that man somehow cooperates with God in bringing about salvation. People believe that they must be good to be accepted. Or, that they must do certain things to please the Lord and earn His good favor. However, nothing could be farther from the truth! Salvation is the work of God through His only begotten Son who died upon the cross for the entire world, and whosoever call upon His Son Jesus; will be saved (John 3:16 NKJV).

THE CONDITION OF ISRAEL

"Brethren, my heart's desire and prayer to God for Israel is that they be saved" (Rom. 10:1 NKJV). Paul begins with a clear statement concerning the condition of the Jew. Paul says that the Jew is lost in sin! He wants to see them saved. Earlier in this letter to the Romans Paul mentioned his burden for his kinsmen (Rom. 9:1-3 NKJV). He wants to see them come to know the Lord and to be delivered from the wrath of God that hangs over them. God would like to see that His people would get under such burden for the lost. When is the last time that you wept for someone who is lost and going to a place called hell? People today may appear well and healthy that are walking dead men (Eph. 2:1 NKJV), who live under the constant threat of divine wrath, (John 3:18, 36 NKJV). These are people who, at any moment of time, could be cut off and cast into Hell! They are not promised another moment. Do you have a burden for the lost? If you aren't fishing, you're not following. May we learn to love the lost and reach out to them in the name of Jesus with good news of salvation!

THE CONFUSION OF ISRAEL

"For I bear witness that they have a zeal for God, but not according to knowledge. For they being ignorant of God's righteousness, and seeking to establish their own righteousness, have not submitted to the righteousness of God" (Rom. 10:2-3 NKJV). The Jews, in their desire to please God by their works, totally missed the truth that God is pleased through faith alone (Heb. 11:6 NKJV). True righteousness can never be produced by the works of the flesh. Why? Because the flesh is totally corrupt and incapable of producing anything righteous that will be accepted by God (Isa. 64:6 NKJV). Israel thought they could please God by keeping His law. They failed to see that they could never keep the Law and that real righteousness is awarded to those who simply look to God by faith and trust Him and the finished work of Jesus on the cross!

Sadly, many followers of Jesus Christ behave the same way today. They are trying to be good so that they can please God and earn a place in Heaven. They hope God will weigh their good against their bad. Their hope is that the good will outweigh the bad and that God will let them into Heaven based on their good works. However, the Bible is clear when it tells us that this will never work (Eph. 2:8-9; Titus 3:5 NKJV). It is not about what we can do, it is about what Jesus has already done for us!

THE CONCLUSION OF PAUL

"For Christ is the end of the law for righteousness to everyone who believes" (Rom. 10:4 NKJV). What Paul is saying here is that Jesus did what the Law could never do. He makes those who trust Him by faith righteous! We could never keep the Law and please the Lord. However, Jesus lived a sinless life and died in the place of every sinner. He fulfilled the just demands of the Law and set us free from the Law! He provides righteousness full and free for everyone that will trust Him by faith (2 Cor. 5:21; Rom. 4:18-25 NKJV). Salvation and righteousness are given to all those who call upon the name of the Lord by faith (Rom. 10:13 NKJV). Paul's conclusion is that salvation can be found in the finished work of Jesus alone!

Salvation is about a Possibility

There is a little verb "is" in Hebrews 7:25 (NKJV) that is in the present tense. It speaks of something that is possible right now. When we speak of salvation, we are not talking about something that was or of something that will be later. We are speaking of something that can happen right now. In that verse it reads "He IS able to save" (Heb. 7:25 NKJV; *emphasis added*). Jesus did not operate in power just during Bible times, but He is still saving souls today. You who wonder about what will happen to you in eternity need not wonder or worry. If you will just come to Jesus and put your faith in His shed blood, then He IS able and IS willing to save your soul today! That is His call, "In an acceptable time I have heard you, and in the day of salvation I have helped you" (2 Cor. 6:2 NKJV). That is His promise, "All that the Father gives Me will come to Me, and the one who comes to Me I will by no means cast out" (John 6:37 NKJV). You do not have to live in your sins for one more minute! You can be free; you can be saved; you can be assured of Heaven today if you will come to Jesus!

As we behave as fishers of men, we need share this possibility of salvation with those we encounter. Being a fisher of men is about getting lost souls out of the darkness and into the light. It is about behaving with a sense of urgency, because while salvation is available right now, I am afraid that it will not always be available. There is coming a day when the Lord will speak to the lost heart no more (Gen. 6:3 NKJV) therefore it is not up to us to determine that as fishers of men, we need to be determined to share the Gospel as if God is still speaking to that lost person's heart. If you are reading this book and you are lost, do let time run out when God stops speaking to your heart. My advice to you is this: if the Lord is speaking to you about coming to Him, then you need to come and wait no longer. Put down the book and ask Jesus to come into your heart and save you from your sin. He IS able today, and if He is calling, He intends for you to come to Him today.

▌ Salvation is about a Power

The writer of Hebrews goes on to say in Hebrew 7:25 (NKJV) "He is able…" That word means, "to have the power to do something" (Dictionary 1828). Jesus has the power to do something about the lost condition of the sinner. He has the power and the ability to save a soul! The word "able" comes from the same word which we get the English words "dynamite" and "dynamic." It has the idea of explosive power. Jesus Christ has the power to invade your life and break the chains of sin that holds a lost sinner in bondage. He has the power to affect and give eternal freedom instantly the moment the lost sinner asks Jesus to come into his/her heart. He is ABLE to set the sinner free (John 8:36 NKJV).

The word "able" also has the idea of "competence." In other words, it refers to someone "who knows what He is doing." If my car is acting up and I need a mechanic, I want to take it to someone who is competent to get it fixed. If I have problem with my body, I want to take it to someone who is competent to get me the help I need. But when it comes to my soul, I want Someone Who is competent. You see, your soul is far more valuable than your car or even your body. Your soul is the most important and valuable possession you have "For what will it profit a man if he gains the whole world, and loses his own soul? Or what will a man give in exchange for his soul?" (Mark 8:36-37 NKJV). Please understand that Jesus is more than able; He is more than competent when it comes to saving souls. He can save anybody, anywhere, anytime, from any sin (John 6:37 NKJV). He has the power to save because He paid the ultimate price to save. He has the power to save because He lived a sinless life, died on the cross for sins and rose again from the dead. Jesus can save and will save all who come to Him by faith (Rom. 10:9-10 NKJV).

THE PROCEDURE TO RECEIVE THE SAVIOR

In Romans 10:5-10 (NKJV), Paul teaches us the true path to salvation. He shows what won't work, and then he shows us what will work to save man's soul. Paul first begins telling us that salvation is not found in keeping the statutes (Rom. 10:5 NKJV). Paul reminds us that righteousness is possible through the Law, but only if a person could keep every precept (Law) perfectly and not break even the smallest. According to James, "for whoever shall keep the whole law and yet stumble in one point, he is guilty of all" (Jam. 2:10 NKJV). Of course, even if a person were able to perfectly keep the Law, he would still have to deal with the problem of his sinful nature. You see, man isn't a sinner because he sins, man sins because he is a sinner. Paul points this out in Romans 3:23 (NKJV) when he says, "for all have sinned and fall short of the glory of God." We were born in sin; we just prove the reality of our sinful nature by the things we do.

The second thing that Paul says won't work is that salvation is not found in great signs (Rom. 10:6-8 NKJV). Paul quotes form Deuteronomy 30:12-14 (NKJV) telling his readers that no one needs to look to Heaven for signs or the earth for signs. Just as no one must search the seas to find the way, Jesus has come to make and be the way (John 14:6 NKJV). What Paul says seems to be confusion; however, his emphasis is on the fact that no personal effort is required to seek and find Jesus. That means the sinner does not have to perform some sort of mystical, fantastic scavenger hunt to find Jesus. He has already come and made the way clear. Jesus has already taken care of everything all the sinner has to is what Paul says will work.

Salvation is found in a simple surrender. Paul writes, "that if you confess with your mouth the Lord Jesus and believe in your heart that God has raised Him from the dead, you will be saved. For with the heart one believes unto righteousness, and with the mouth confession is made unto salvation" (Rom. 10:9-10 NKJV). Paul is telling us and his readers that their entrance into salvation is as close to them as their own hearts and their own mouth. They have everything they need to be saved present with them. All they need to do to receive Jesus Christ as their savior for salvation is surrender to Jesus and make Him your Lord and Savior. Paul tells us that the heart and the mouth are involved in this matter of our salvation. The mouth is used to confess the Lord Jesus. The word "confess" carries the idea of "saying the same thing about" (Dictionary 1828). God wants the lost sinner to come to the place where he can say the same thing about Jesus that God the Father has already said about God the Son: Jesus. God wants us to come to the place where we agree with everything the Bible says concerning the Person and work of the Lord Jesus Christ. The mouth is required to confess the truth about Who He is! So, the first step is agreement with God about the Person and work of the Lord Jesus Christ.

The second step is the heart. The ancients saw the heart as the center of all thought, the house of will, the deepest and most sacred part of man. Paul is saying that to be saved, a person must place his absolute trust in the finished work of Christ. Paul mentions the resurrection. However, a resurrection presupposes a death. So, Paul wants lost men to know that if they are going to be saved, they must believe in the complete work of Jesu with all their beings, that means His death, His burial, and His resurrection. The idea being that we are to trust what He did on the cross (shed His blood to atone for sins), in the tomb (conquering hell), and the resurrection (conquering death and the grave) for our salvation! Our faith should be in Christ Jesus and Christ Jesus alone! He must not be joined with anything else, but He must be trusted exclusively. Anything less than that total trust in the Lord Jesus will not produce salvation but will lead the sinner straight to hell. Sadly, many are trying to hold Jesus with one hand and other things with the other. This will not work! Salvation is Jesus plus nothing! That is made clear many times in the Word of God (Acts 16:31; John 3:16, John 6:47; Eph. 2:8-9 NKJV). The question we need to answer for ourselves is this "What am I trusting to get me to Heaven right now?" As a fisher of men, we need to be asking people this question.

Salvation is about Perfection

You see, not only does Jesus have the power to provide salvation, but the next part of Hebrews 7:25 (NKJV) says, "He is also about to save to the uttermost". This is a precious word! It means "completely, perfectly, utterly." When God saves a soul from sin, He does it right; He does it perfectly; He does it completely; He does it utterly! What does that mean for you? Listen, if you are saved to the uttermost, here is a little of what it means for you. First, it means that you are saved completely from your sins. All your sins, every single one, have been washed way through the precious blood of Jesus (Ps. 103:12; Isa. 38:17; Isa. 43:25; Jer. 50:20; Micah 7:19; and 1 John 1:7 NKJV). Second, it means you are saved form the power of your sins. Romans 6:6-14 tells us that we died with Jesus and have been raised to a new life in Him. As a result, He has forever broken the bondage of our sins and set us free from their power. Third, it means you are saved forever from your sins. Some people read Hebrew 7:25 (NKJV) and think that the word "uttermost" means that Jesus can save anyone. Well, He can, but that is not the emphasis of that word. This word has the idea that Jesus has the ability "to save us to the end" (Dictionary 1828). In other words, when Jesus saves a soul, He does it completely and He will keep you saved forever (John 10:28; John 6:37-40, 47; 1 Pet. 1:5 NKJV). For some say that you can lose your salvation is to say that Jesus does not have enough power to keep you saved and would make this verse null and void. Jesus can save you to the uttermost; He is able to keep you saved! That encourages me! I mess up a lot in life, but even I cannot mess up and lose my salvation! It is complete in Jesus and it is mine forever! Salvation will not wear out and it will not wear off! Those who are saved today will be saved forever!

THE PROMISE

When we come to faith is Christ Jesus the right way, God's way; we are given some precious promises. Notice what Paul writes, "For the Scripture says, "Whoever believes on Him will not be put to shame." For there is no distinction between Jew and Greek, for the same Lord over all is rich to all who call upon Him. For "whoever calls on the name of the Lord shall be saved" (Rom. 10:11-13 NKJV). Paul first pointed to the assurance of that we have in Christ Jesus and reminds us that according God's plan of salvation we will never be disappointed. When we call upon the name of the Lord for salvation, we will never hear Him say to us, "I'm sorry, but I can't save you." Instead, we will hear Him say, "Well done good and faithful servant." (Matt. 25:21, 23 NKJV). No one who puts their trust in Jesus for their soul's salvation needs never to fear that they will lose their salvation or never has to fear being shamed as they stand before God in the next life!

Paul then talks about acceptance. There in Romans 10:12 (NKJV) he tells us the precious truth that God does not play favorites. Anyone who hears His call and responds in faith will be saved by the grace of God. You see, there are many places here on earth where you and I would not be accepted. Yet, when we come to the Lord by faith, we can and will be saved and accepted by Him. Compared to that, what else really matters? Then finally, Paul points out the amnesty (the pardon) that has been promised in salvation. In Romans 10:13 (NKJV), he is reminding us that whosoever calls on the name of the Lord will be saved. However, to call upon the name of the Lord means to do so according to God's Way! Not on your terms, but His way! So, when someone says, "God and I have an arrangement." You can bank on the fact that they are lost. They may be calling on the lord, but they are not calling on the Lord Jesus! No one who comes to Jesus His way will be turned away (John 6:37 NKJV). We are granted eternal, divine amnesty, and will never be brought into judgment for our sins ever again!

You see, one of the primary reasons that Jesus is able to save so completely, perfectly, and utterly is because He is alive, in Heaven today. As we know from the Bible, Jesus died on the cross, but He also rose from the dead (Matt. 28:1-6 NKJV). After that, Jesus ascended back to Heaven and sat down at the right hand of God. He is present in Heaven today and He is there to make "intercession" (Heb. 7:25 NKJV) for us. He is our High Priest. If you go back and read the first part of Hebrews 7 you will see that it is about the superiority of Jesus to earthly priests. All other priests die, and their ministry ends forever. Jesus died and that is when His ministry began! He rose from the dead and now He prays for us in the very presence of God. When we fail as believers, and we often do, He is there to plead our case (1 John 2:1 NKJV). His presence in Heaven is our guarantee of eternal life and that our sins are forgiven! Jesus is there as the proof that sin had been conquered and that "the way" has been opened into God's presence. He is the Door (John 10:9

NKJV) and all who enter through Him have His presence in Heaven as their promise, as their hope, as their anchor.

Name any other religious figure that can make that claim. Every founder of every other major religion has a grave where their followers can go to mourn their deaths. Only Christians have an empty tomb! Our Leader, the Author and Finisher of our faith, rose from the dead, ascended back to Heaven, and is there today as our representative and the guarantee that we will be there one day as well. Listen to the great promise that Jesus made. "Let not your heart be troubled; you believe in God, believe also in Me. In My Father's house are many mansions, If it were not so, I would have told you. I go to prepare a place for you. And if I go and prepare a place for you, I will come again and receive you to Myself; that where I am, there you may be also" (John 14:1-3 NKJV). What a promise! What a guarantee! If there is anything that we can learn from these truths that we have just discussed is that God only has one plan of salvation. It is not a Jewish plan, nor is it a Southern Baptist plan. The plan of salvation is plain and simple, and all Jesus asks of His followers is just go and make. We are to behave as fishers of men by simply telling the plain and simple Gospel of our Lord and Savior Jesus Christ. Are you behaving?

CHAPTER TEN

The Rejection of the King

Then Pilate said to them, "Why, what evil has He done?" But they
cried out all the more, "Crucify Him!" (Mark 15:14 NKJV)

HOW WISE DO YOU CONSIDER YOURSELF? NOW, I AM NOT ASKING,
"How smart you are?" I am not even asking you, "Do you consider
yourself a successful person?" Do you consider yourself a wise person?
Let me ask you a different way. How wise does God consider you to
be? If you are not fishing for souls, then you are not wise. The Bibles
says, "He that wins souls is wise" (Prov. 11:30 NKJV). To behave
as a fisherman, you are to be about winning souls by sharing the
Gospel of Jesus Christ because souls are of great worth it costed the
life of Jesus When Jesus spoke of the great worth of a soul, said, "For
what will it profit a man if he gains the whole world, and loses his
own soul?" (Mark 8:36 NKJV). What this is saying is that one soul
is worth more than all the world, all the stocks, all the bonds, all the
rubies, all the diamonds, and the banks put together. The psalmist
makes the promise, "He who continually goes forth weeping, bearing
seed for sowing, shall doubtless come again with rejoicing, bringing
his sheaves with him" (Ps. 126:6 NKJV). But that doesn't mean that
everybody you witness to is going to get saved. Think about this, not
everyone that the Lord witnessed to was saved. The rich, young ruler

went away sorrowful. He could never have a better witness than the Lord Jesus.

In the Gospel of Mark, Jesus shared a parable about the sower who went forth to sow, and as he scattered the seed out of his basket, some fell by the wayside. That's the soil that is hard, and the seed couldn't get in. others fell on stony ground. The seed got in, but it couldn't get down, because beneath the soil in the subsurface was a rocky ledge. Other seed fell among thorns, and it sprouted. But then, the weeds and the briars came and choked it out. But some fell on good ground, and it brought forth fruit. Listen as you behave as a fisher of men it is not your job to analyze the soil; it's our job to sow the seed! The seed is the Gospel of Jesus Christ. And there is going to be some who accept the seed and some who reject the seed. The sower in Jesus' parable was Himself and it did not matter where the seed fell, He kept sowing the seed.

To behave as fisher of men you need to know about rejection of the seed, and there is no greater example to learn about rejection than to look at the rejection of the king. Before Mark 15 (NKJV) opens, Jesus has been arrested by His enemies. He been tried by the religious authorities and condemned. Jesus is the Messiah that was promised, and He offers Himself to Israel as their Messiah. However, they reject Him because they weren't not looking for the Messiah to come this way. So, the religious leaders condemned Him based on the testimony of false witnesses and wrongful accusations. You can see as you read Mark 15:1-15 (NKJV), the very heart of human nature. This text proves that man, in his natural state, is a totally wicked sinner, capable of intense hatred and evil. This text proves that man, in his natural state, is God's enemy, just as Paul points out in Romans 8:7 (NKJV) which says, "because the carnal mind is enmity against God; for it is not subject to the law of God nor indeed can be." Mark 15:1-15 (NKJV) is a mirror for the human heart, fully revealing its behavior and condition. This text is a mirror of our own souls. When we look at Jesus and what the people did to Him that day, we can see ourselves. We either see that we are walking with our faith in Jesus or we see that we are guilty of rejecting and crucifying the king.

❙ The King is Rejected by the Priest

The language of Mark 15:1 (NKJV) suggest that these events occurred exceedingly early in the morning, just as the sun was rising. The word "morning" translates from a Greed word that refers to a time between 3 AM and 6 AM, also known as the fourth watch of the night. So, as soon as dawn begins to break, the chief priest convenes all the rulers of Israel together to legalize the decision they reached during the night. Because according to Jewish custom a decision made at night was not binding. Mark 14:55-65 (NKJV) tells us that, after Jesus was arrested, He was subjected to an illegal trial before the chief priest. During this trial, Jesus was accused of blasphemy and condemned to death. He was then beaten and mistreated by the religious leaders and the temple police. This early morning meeting was held for just one purpose; these men wanted to add a sense of legitimacy to the illegal decision they had made during the night. During this phase of the trial, the Jews asked Jesus the same question they had asked Him during the night. Luke 22:66-71 (NKJV), tells us that they once again asked Jesus if He was the Son of God. Once again, Jesus answered that indeed He was the Son of God. Jesus was in way telling them that He was their prophesied Messiah and they rejected Him by accusing Him of blasphemy and therefore they reaffirmed the sentence of death.

Israel was under Roman domination. They were allowed a great measure of freedom to try cases and pronounce sentences, but they were not allowed to hand down a sentence of death. This right belonged to the Roman governor alone. The Jews had condemned Jesus to death, but they lacked the authority to carry out the sentence, so they bound Jesus like a common criminal and led Him away to Pontius Pilate, the Roman governor. When the Jews came before Pilate, they knew they could not accuse Jesus of blaspheme. They knew that Pilate would never intervene in a Jewish religious argument. So, when they brough Jesus to Pilate, they changed the charges against Him. Luke 23:2 (NKJV) says, "And they began to accuse Him, saying, we found this fellow perverting the nation, and forbidding to give tribute to Caesar, saying that He Himself is Christ a King." These wicked men knew that this would get Pilate's attention and help them accomplish their evil agenda of seeing Jesus crucified.

The actions of these religious men teach us an especially important truth: Religion has no place for Jesus Christ. The Jewish religious rulers had a good thing going. As far as daily life in Israel was concerned, they held all the power over the people. They were making vast amounts of money through the buying and selling that went on at the Temple. They were rich, powerful, and believed that they were right with God. These men thought they were justified in all their actions. They believed their religion was enough! The Jews rejected Jesus because religion has no room for Jesus Christ.

The fact is, no religious system has room for Jesus. Religion is all about human involvement and human activity. Religion is always based on the external work. Biblical Christianity, on the other hand, is always based in faith. Religion seeks to approach God based on what man can do. Biblical Christianity seeks to approach God based on what God has done for us through Jesus Christ. There is a vast difference between the two! The Bible is crystal clear on this issue: no one is saved by works, even religious works (Eph. 2:8-9; Rom. 3:20; Titus 3:3-5 NKJV). It is also crystal clear that salvation is based on faith in Christ alone (John 1:12; 3:15-16; 6:40, 47; Acts 16:31; Rom. 10:9; Mark 16:16; Rom. 5:1-5; 1 John 5:10-13 NKJV). Salvation is never about what man can do; it is always about what Jesus has already done. The Gospel is a plain and simple message. It can be summed up in two verses. Romans 4:25 (NKJV) says, "Who was delivered up because of our offenses, and was raised because of our justification." 1 Corinthians 14:1-4 (NKJV) says, "Moreover, brethren, I declare to you the gospel which I preached to you, which also you received and in which you stand, by which also you are saved, if you hold fast that word which I preached to you; unless you believe in vain. For I delivered to you first of all that which I also received: that Christ died for our sins according to the Scriptures, and that He was buried, and the He rose again the third day according to the Scriptures." What matter are these simple questions that we the fishers of men should be asking people: "Have you believed the Gospel message of Christ's death and resurrection? Are you trusting Jesus and Jesus alone for your soul's salvation?

Things like giving, praying, good works, baptism, church attendance, etc., are all good things, but none of them have the power to save the soul. Religion has the power to make people respectable and decent, but it does not have the power to make anyone right with God. On the other hand, biblical redemption has the power to make people holy. It has the power to save the souls, secure the soul, and alter one's eternal destiny. Seeking God man's way will always result in eternal damnation in Hell. Coming to God through faith in the Lord Jesus Christ will always result in the soul's salvation and eternal glory in Heaven!

The King is Rejected by Pilate

When Jesus arrives before Pilate, the governor asks Jesus about the accusation that He is the King of the Jews. The answer Jesus gives Pilate is somewhat different from the answer He gave the Jews. "Then Pilate asked Him, "Are you the King of the Jews?" He answered and said to him, "It is as you say" (Mark 15:2 NKJV). When the Jews asked Jesus about His identity as the Son of God and the Messiah, Jesus simply said, "I Am" (Mark 14:62 NKJV)! When Pilate askes Jesus if He is the King of the Jews, Jesus responds by saying, "It is as you say" (Mark 15:2 NKJV). This statement has three possible interpretations. First possible interpretation, "You got it exactly right! That's Who I Am." Second possible interpretation, "That's for you to decide." Third possible interpretation, "I Am the King of the Jews, but I Am not a king in any way you would understand. My Kingdom is not of this world. My authority comes from above and not from you or the men who have accused Me." The last one is confirmed by what John records in John 18:33-36 (NKJV).

So, why the difference? Why was Jesus, so clear with the Jews and why was He not so clear with Pilate? The Jews had every reason to believe that Jesus was Who He claimed to be. They had the Old Testament with its laws and prophecies that predicted the coming of the Messiah. Jesus fulfilled every one of them to the letter. He proved He was their Messiah. Pilate did not have this information. He was a Gentile, and he did not know Who Jesus was. He had not seen the miracles, nor had he heard His words. On that morning, Pilate was brought face to face with Jesus, and when he was, he had a decision to make. Pilate was given the opportunity to meet Jesus in a personal, faith relationship, and he failed! According to Mark 15:3 (NKJV), it tells us that the Jews made all manner of accusations against Jesus, but the Lord stood there in absolute silence. He refused to defend Himself against their lies. He was just as Isaiah said He would be, "He was oppressed and He was afflicted, yet He opened not His mouth; as a sheep before its shearer is silent, so He opened not His mouth" (Isa. 53:7 NKJV). In Mark 15:4-5 (NKJV), Pilate attempted to get Jesus to defend Himself. Again, Jesus simply stood there in regal silence. His refusal to answer left Pilate amazed. Pilate was amazed, but he was convinced that Jesus was innocent of the charges being leveled against Him.

This whole encounter between Jesus and Pilate comes down to what is said in John 18:37-38 (NKJV). In John 18:37 (NKJV), Jesus plainly declared His identity and offers to teach Pilate the truth. In John 18:38 (NKJV), Pilate flippantly says, "What is truth?" and walks out on Jesus, turning his back on truth and salvation. The question was a rhetorical question. In essence, he was telling Jesus, "What is true for you may not be true for me! You say 'to-may-to', I say, 'to-mah-toe'. Don't talk to me about truth, for truth cannot really be known!" So, Pilate threw away a glorious opportunity to come to know the truth for himself. He looked in the face of Jesus, refused to see it, and walked away, forever lost in his sins! So, let's ponder Pilates question for a minute.

THE PERCEPTION OF TRUTH

Pilate's question leads me to believe that he had no grasp of truth. Perhaps his thinking had been jaded by the empty philosophies of the day, that said truth was unknowable and unattainable. Evidently, Pilate had come to believe what many in his day believed: there is no absolute truth! The same is true for people living in America. We live in a day when almost no one believes in absolute truth. What is sad is that half of born-again Christians think that truth is relative. That is, they believe that what is true for one person may not be true for another. Let me just say, they can believe what they will, however, there is such a thing as absolute truth! Jesus Himself, in this passage, stated that He came to "bear witness to the truth." (John 18:37 NKJV). So, what is truth? The word from which "truth" is translated means, "That which is accurate or true in any matter under consideration. It is the opposite of that which is feigned, fictious, or false" (Strong's Concordance 1984). For instance, suppose I tell you that there is a truth called the Law of Gravity. This law states, "That whatever goes up must come down." Now, suppose that you reject that as being just "my truth." So, you decide to test your theory and leap from a building. It will not take you long to learn that there is such a thing as absolute truth, and that it can be known!

But, if there is truth and truth can be known, then how can we learn the truth? Well, for those who have placed their trust in the Lord Jesus Christ as their personal Lord and Savior, the task is made easier by the indwelling of the Holy Spirit. Jesus tells us three times in John's Gospel that the Spirit of God is the "Spirit of Truth" (John 14:17; 15:26; 16:23 NKJV). John 16:13 (NKJV) says, "However, when He, the Spirit of Truth, has come, He will guide you into all truth' for He will not speak of His own authority, but whatever He hears He will speak; and He will tell you things to come." This verse tells us that the Holy Spirit will reveal the things of God to us, thus teaching us the truth. Therefore, believers are in a far better position to learn the truth because of the Spirit of Truth Who lives within us. The world, on the other hand, has a spirit within them which blinds them to the truth (2 Cor. 4:4 NKJV). This accounts for the fact that they will consistently reject the truth and choose lies instead. This also demonstrates why they live their lives the way that they do and how they attempt to justify their sins before God and man (Eph. 2:1-3 NKJV). Jesus believed in absolute truth. He believed in absolute truth so strongly that He came to this world, lived, and died to bear witness to that truth. Yes, there is such a thing as truth, regardless of what society says about it.

THE POWER OF TRUTH

Truth, when it is perceived, touches the heart of a man, and draws him to God (John 3:21 NKJV). When they come to Him and embrace the truth, they can and will experience its power in their lives. Notice three things about the power contained in absolute truth. First, truth has the power to liberate. Jesus says, "And you shall know the truth, and the truth shall make you free" (John 8:32 NKJV). Jesus was telling His hearers that the truth has the power to deliver them from their bondage to sin and the Law. It would literally set them free in Christ Jesus When you come to know the truth, you come to know something that sets captives free, opens blinded eyes, heals broken hearts, transforms shattered and ruined lives, and fills men with the love of God, the peace of God, and the joy of God.

Second, truth has the power to separate. Jesus says, "Sanctify them by Your truth. Your word is truth" (John 17:17 NKJV). Here Jesus is praying for His disciples and for us today! The word "sanctify" means "to render something holy; to dedicate or consecrate something to God" (Dictionary 1828). Think about it, the truth of God has the power to cleanse us and make us more like our heavenly Father! I have heard it said, that "sin will either keep you from God's Word; or God's word will keep you from sin!" What is truth? When you yield yourself to the truth of God's Word, and walk as the Spirit directs you, you will find your life becoming clearer and more pleasing to God.

Third, truth has the power to invigorate. "God is Spirit, and those who worship Him must worship in spirit and truth" (John 4:24 NKJV). Here Jesus tells the woman at the well that the truth will make you want to worship! You see, real worship- is us acknowledging Him to be our everything! Real worship arises out of a heart that had been saturated with His truth. Real worship comes about when the Holy Spirit takes the truth of God's Word and makes it clear to us. When we comprehend Who Jesus is, what He has done for us and what He is doing; it will leave us at His feet in humble, simple worship of Him! But, if we do not understand the truth about Who God is and what He has done, then our worship will be warped. Until we know the truth about Him, we cannot truly worship Him There is nothing like the truth to put a fresh spark into your worship!

THE PERSONALITY OF TRUTH

Where can you find truth? Thankfully, the Holy Spirit led John to write plainly for us to know where to find truth. There are two places. First, the Holy Word of God is truth (John 17:17 NKJV). Everything either stands or falls right here! If the Bible is the inspired, infallible, inerrant Word of God as it claims (2 Tim. 3:16 NKJV) then the living Word of God and God's Word alone is the final authority and standard by which all living things live by. Not the opinions of men, not the musing of great philosophers, not the teachings of great theologians, but the Bible is the final word in all manners of life. However, if the Bible is wrong and cannot be believed, then our foundation is destroyed and we have no faith, no hope, and no rules (Ps. 11:3 NKJV). If the Bible is a lie, then there is no absolute truth! This is the way we are raising up the next generation. They have been taught to doubt the Word of God. When a child sits in a classroom and hears that the earth is billions of years old and that man evolved from a single-celled organism over millions of years, the foundation has been destroyed! If God did not make man in His own image, then it is not wrong to kill babies through abortion; then it is not wrong to rape and murder other people because we are all just animals. If man evolved, then there is no sin, there is no right and wrong, there are no absolutes. You might as well live like you want to because there is no Hell; there is no accountability to God; there is no after life.

If the first eleven chapters of the Book of Genesis are not true, then you might as well junk the whole book! If God lied in Genesis 1-11 (NKJV), then He is not worthy to be trusted anywhere else in the book! If I cannot trust Him in Genesis 1:1 (NKJV), then I cannot trust Him in John 3:16 (NKJV)! Think about this, when we take the Ten Commandments and say they are not relevant for today, we have undermined the foundations of faith. When we tell society that the Bible cannot be trusted, we undermine the foundations of the teaching of Christ. When we treat the Bible like a giant buffet and choose the parts we like and ignore the parts that bother us personally, then we undermine the foundation of what it takes to behave as a follower of Christ. When we ignore the Great Commission and disobey His command to "Go" and "Make", then we have undermined the foundation of Jesus making us to become fishers of men. There is a price to pay for our haughtiness; and that price is the absence of truth in America! Do you see why being able to trust the Bible is so important? In its pages, we learn about God, the creation of man, sin, salvation, good, evil, the family, etc. If that foundation is destroyed, then there is no basis for truth and if there is no truth then everybody is right, and nobody is wrong! Praise God, we can trust the Bible! It is God's Living Word! It is inspired! It is truth, without any errors. Praise God, it can be believed for it is forever settled in Heaven (Isa. 40:8; Ps. 119:89 NKJV).

The second place that we can find truth is in the Savior. Jesus said, "I am the way, the truth, and the life. No one comes to the Father except through Me" (John 14:6 NKJV). Jesus plainly calls attention to the fact that He and He alone is the real deal! Jesus was and is the embodiment of truth (John 1:14; 17 NKJV). All other would be saviors are merely pretenders. It doesn't matter who many followers they have or how sincere their followers are. Jesus alone is: "the WAY, the TRUTH, and the LIFE!" (John 14:6 NKJV; *emphasis added*). Jesus alone is the Lamb of God slain from the foundation of the world. Jesus alone is the truth! All other men are liars, and all other methods are lies; and they all lead down the broad road of destruction. They have their end in the fires of Hell! Jesus alone is the door into the narrow way that leads to life everlasting (John 14:6; Acts 4:12; 1 John 5:12 NKJV)! What is truth? It is the difference between saved and lost.

Ultimately, Pilate would allow the Jews to take Jesus away and crucify Him. Pilate ignored what he knew to be the truth. He ignored a clear warning from his wife (Matt. 27:19 NKJV). He ignored the fact that the Jews were lying and just wanted Jesus dead for their own purposes. Pilate ignores the truth because he wanted to hold on to his position with Rome and his power over the people. Pilate was a weak, cowardly man who was more concerned with maintaining his position and his power than he was with knowing the truth. He was more concerned with keeping the Jews happy than he was in protecting an innocent man. Pilate was a coward who place his position, his prosperity, his pride, and his person before his soul. Pilate could have been saved, but he was too much a coward to bow before Jesus and believe in Him for salvation. Pilate rejected Jesus because cowardice has no room for Christ.

I am afraid there are many people like Pilate in our world today. Not too many possess the position or power that Pilate enjoyed, but many are confronted with the truth of Who Jesus Christ is. Many are confronted with the sure knowledge that He is the only way to get to Heaven (John 14:6; Acts 4:12 NKJV). They come face to face with the truth, but they are too afraid to commit to a life of following Jesus. Instead, they cling to their sins, their empty lives, and their tragic eternities. Some reject Jesus because they are afraid, they cannot live for Him. Some reject Jesus because they are afraid of what other will say about them. Some reject Jesus because they love their sin more than they love the truth. At the end of the day, all those who reject Jesus do so for the very same reasons Pilate rejected Him. They reject Him because they are cowards. They reject Jesus because they are afraid!

It takes courage to come to Jesus! It takes courage to admit that you are a sinner. It takes courage to admit that you are helpless to save yourself. It takes courage to admit that you need the Lord Jesus Christ. It takes courage to bow before Him and call on Him for salvation. It takes courage to stand against the world and behave as a follower of Christ. It takes courage to be different in a world that demands that everyone behave the same way. It takes great courage to behave as a fisher of men and tell people that are controlled by the devil about Jesus Christ and His saving power. I salute every believer today who is living for Jesus Christ, who is behaving as follower of Christ. I salute every believer today who is "Going" and "Making" as fishers of men. I salute my brothers and my sister who are living as lights in this dark world.

▌ The King is Rejected by the People

Now that Pilate has examined Jesus and is convinced that He is innocent. He takes a gamble to try and free Jesus without any political backlash. According to Mark 15:6, it was Pilate's custom to release to the crowds a prisoner of their own choosing. He has, in his custody, a prisoner name Barabbas (Mark 15:7 NKJV). Barabbas was a political prisoner. He had been arrested for "insurrection" and "murder". He was a revolutionary trying to overthrow the Roman government. He had been caught and now he was headed for death on a Roman cross. (Let that picture sink in for a moment, because Jesus took his place on the Roman cross which symbolically represent that Jesus took the place of every sinner upon the Cross of Sacrifice to atone for mankind's sin.)

So, Pilate offers the crowd a choice between Jesus Christ and Barabbas (Mark15:8-10 NKJV). He thinks the people will choose the peace-loving Jesus over the violent Barabbas. He believes that people will choose the One Who has done good and right over the one who had only done evil. Pilate was wrong! Pilate rolled the dice and he lost. The Jewish leaders stirred up the crowds and caused them to choose Barabbas over Jesus (Mark 15:11 NKJV). When they made their choice, Pilate asks them what he should do with Jesus (Mark 15:12 NKJV). They cry out that He should be crucified (Mark 15:13 NKJV). Pilate again states his belief in Christ's innocence and asks the crowd why (Mark 15:14 NKJV). The people have been whipped into a state of near frenzy and they call for the death of Jesus by crucifixion (Mark 15:14 NKJV). They even called down a curse upon themselves (Matt. 7:25 NKJV). Pilate gives in to the will of the people and allows them to have their way with Him (Mark 15:15 NKJV).

Barabbas' full name was "Jesus Bar-Abbas." (*Strong's Concordance* 1984) This name means "Jesus the son of the fathers." On this day, the crowds had a choice between "Jesus son the fathers", or "Jesus the Son of God." Had they been acting in faith; Israel would have chosen Jesus the Son of God. However, being blinded by unbelief, they chose the way of the world over the Way to God. Many in our world are just like the crowd that condemned Jesus. All around this world are people who choose the world over the Lord every day. We see it in the elections. We see it in the actions of the government. We see it in our choices of entertainment. We see it in the way people live their lives. The majority is not always right! The majority rejected Jesus. The majority condemned Him to death. The majority stood against Him. The majority is still standing against Him today! The world rejects Him through sheer unbelief. The world ignores the Word of God. It ignores the changed lives of the redeemed. It ignores God's free offer of salvation. The lost multitude chooses its sin over God's salvation. The lost multitude chooses Hell over Heaven. The lost multitude refuses to believe in Jesus. Now if the is a lost multitude, then we are to behave as fishers of men and go and win souls. How wise are you?

CHAPTER ELEVEN

The Crucifixion of the King

Therefore, My Father loves Me, because I lay down My life that I may take it again. No one takes it from Me, but I lay it down of Myself. I have the power to lay it down, and I have the power to take it again. This command I have received from My Father. (John 10:17-18 NKJV)

BEHAVING AS FISHERS OF MEN BY SHARING THE GOSPEL OF JESUS Christ is one thing, however, to really know and fully understand the death, burial, and resurrection of Jesus Christ is another. Jesus taught His disciples about how to become fishers of men through the many sermons, commands, miracles, and private teachings of His parables. One of His lessons was to prepare them for His impending death. He taught them that His death was planned before the world began (1 Pet. 1:20 NKJV), and about how God the Father gave Him the power to lay His life down and to resurrect it again (John 10:17-18 NKJV). He probably even tied the Old Testament sacrifices into His death sacrifice, by telling them "Do not think that I came to destroy the Law or the Prophets. I did not come to destroy but to fulfill" (Matt. 5:17 NKJV). For these disciples, to have all this knowledge about what is going to take place is one thing, but to experience and not use that knowledge that was given to them is another. That is why after seeing Jesus in the upper room you see Peter and the other disciples standing there on the shore of the Sea of Galilee contemplating what they should do next. We have the completed Word of God, His love letter, His Revelation to us; it teaches us what we need to know, how to behave, how to worship Him, how to depend upon Him, and how to share the Gospel. We must get s grasp on what Jesus did for us on the cross, through His burial, and though His resurrection. We can know about the events that happened that day that Jesus laid down His life for a friend (John 15:13 NKJV), and we can experience it when we accept Jesus as our personal Lord and Savior. That will be the moment we fully know and understand what Jesus did on the cross in us, for us, and will do through us. Let's look at the events that surrounds the crucifixion of the King.

The Trip to His Crucifixion

John writes in his Gospel, "Then he delivered Him to them to be crucified. So, they took Jesus and led Him away" (John 19:16 NKJV). Pilate delivered his prisoner to the cross, but God was fulfilling an age-old plan by delivering up His Son "the Lamb slain from the foundation of the world" (Rev. 13:8 NKJV). "He indeed was foreordained before the foundation of the world but was manifest in these last times for you" (1 Pet. 1:20 NKJV). Calvary was no accident; it was a divine assignment. Remember God told the serpent, "and I will put enmity between you and the woman, and between your seed and her Seed; He shall bruise your head, and you shall bruise His heel" (Gen. 3:15 NKJV)? This assignment was designed to purchase salvation. John continues, "and He, bearing His cross, went to a place called the Place of a Skull, which is called in the Hebrew, Golgotha" (John 19:17 NKJV). John tells us that He carried His cross all the way to Golgotha, or as we know Calvary. The trip was about a mile long and He is already sleep deprived and He has been scourged and mocked by the Romans soldiers (John 19:1-5 NKJV). On the journey, according to the other Gospel writers, a man by the name of Simon of Cyrene carried the cross for Him. There is no reason as to why He was relieved of this burden for the Holy Scriptures are quiet. Nevertheless, one thing is most certain, for someone to carry a cross was a mark of guilt and Jesus was not guilty (Mark 15:20-21 NKJV). But as Jesus carried the burden of that cross you can see an excellent picture of what Jesus was going to the cross for. Jesus was bearing upon Him the sins of the world! That cross was more than wood. It represented the heartbreak, the pain, the slavery, and the debt of sin. That is what Jesus was carrying that day.

The Place of His Crucifixion

John reminds that when He arrives at Golgotha "they crucified Him" (John 19:18a NKJV). Golgotha in the Hebrew means "the place of the skull" (*Strong's Concordance* 1984), in the Greek language it means "Calvary". That place resembles the skull of a dead man. It is a place that is littered with the skulls of dead men. Golgotha sits just outside the gates of the city of Jerusalem and was well known to all the people who lived there. They had witnessed the deaths of thousands of criminals and others who were considered enemies of the Roman government. Since it was Roman practice to allow the bodies of the crucified to rot on their crosses, you can believe that the people of Israel knew this place very well.

Now, historically this mountain that was being defiled by Rome was a special place to the Jews. This mount was part of the same ridge upon which the Temple itself was built. It was also here that Abraham had brought his son Isaac many centuries before, to offer to God (Gen. 22:1-19 NKJV). The passage is one of the clearest pictures of the coming death of God's Son Jesus on the cross at Calvary. Think for a moment that as Abraham and Isaac ascended the mount with the necessary items to make an altar and worship God. Isaac asked Abraham, "Where is the lamb for a burnt offering" (Gen. 22:7 NKJV)? To which Abraham would answer "My son, God will provide for Himself the lamb for a burnt offering" (Gen. 22:8 NKJV). Little did they know that on the other side of the mount God was bring up a lamb for the burnt sacrifice that eventually got caught in the thicket by it horns (Gen.

22:13 NKJV). Symbolically, years later God did provide for Himself a Lamb for the sacrifice (Gen. 22:14 NKJV). This passage was a prophetic announcement that God would give His Lamb on this very mount which is called Golgotha (John 19:17 NKJV). This was a very prominent place for the Jewish people.

The Testimony of His Crucifixion

There are three testimonies that John records that took place a Calvary that day that speaks volumes. First, John records in John 19:18 (NKJV) that Jesus was crucified between two thieves. Luke 23:39-43 (NKJV) gives the details of that testimony that transpired that day. According to Luke that one man saw his sins (Luke 23:40-41 NKJV) while the other man did not. One man realized that he and his life offended a Holy God. The other could not have cared less! The difference in the is that one learned the fear of God before he died, and the other did not! One of these men had come to understand that he was facing more than death, that he had an appointment with God after death. Because he understood that it was appointed for once a man to die, then the judgment (Heb. 9:27 NKJV). While he grasped this truth, the other man did not. Understand, the person who does not fear God, will never fear the punishment he faces from God when he leaves this world. Until a sinner understands the fear of God, he will never experience the grace of God.

As the unbelieving thief hung on the cross, he heard the crowd, the rulers, and the soldiers question Christ's claim of being the Messiah (Luke 23:35-37 NKJV). In those verses you will notice that they all said the word "if". The unbelieving thief also knew who Jesus claimed to be, so when he opened his mouth to speak, he said, "If you are the Christ, save Yourself and us" (Luke 23:39 NKJV). He was merely echoing the rebuke everyone else was saying by using the word "if". That little word is filled with doubt. It calls into question everything that Jesus claimed: The Son of God, Savior of the world, His sinless nature, etc. When it comes to Jesus there is no room for the word "if". When this man said "if", he was throwing out everything about Jesus and rejecting Him. So, while one man was listening to the crowd, the rulers, and the soldiers; the other was listening to Jesus. While the one heard the "if's", the other heard Jesus say, "Father forgive them, for they do not know what they do" (Luke 23:34 NKJV). Now according to Matthew 27:41-44 (NKJV) this believing thief once was mocking Jesus along with the crowd. But something changed as he watched Jesus on the cross. Who knows what made the difference, but the testimony of His crucifixion is that it spoke to this dying thief and it was warmed and opened as he looked at Jesus with new eyes!

Can you see the difference in the way these two men responded to Jesus Christ? One saw Him as a liar to be ridiculed, the other saw Him as a Lord to be received. The thief who rejected Jesus is not mentioned again in Luke's account, but according to John 19:32 (NKJV), he is only mentioned when the soldiers came by to break his legs. The last thing he felt in this world was the crushing blows of the hammer against his shins. He felt the bones shatter and he was no longer able to push up against the nails in his feet so that he might breathe. When he drew his last breath, he entered a Christ-less, hopeless eternity and went to a place called Hell. The last thing he experienced was pain, rejection, and sorrow. The first thing he experienced was more pain and the endless torments of Hell and eternal separation from God. The dying thief that looked to Jesus by faith received one of the most wonderful promises ever recorded in the Bible. Jesus says to him, "Assuredly, I say to you, today you will be with Me in Paradise" (Luke 23:43 NKJV). This man was in the presence of the Lord in paradise before the soldiers ever pronounced him dead! He is a perfect illustration of "absent from the body and present with the Lord" (2 Cor. 5:8 NKJV). The last man this thief spoke with on earth was the Lord Jesus and the first person he saw in paradise was the Lord Jesus! What a testimony we have in His crucifixion.

The second testimony of His crucifixion is the testimony of the writing. "Pilate wrote a title and put it on the cross. And the writing was: JESUS OF NAZARETH, THE KING OF THE JEWS" (John 19:19 NKJV). Pilate's sign was written in Hebrew (the language of religion), Greek (the language of philosophy and culture), and Latin (the language of law and government). The sign told all who might have passed by that Jesus was the King of the Jews. The cross of Christ became a giant Gospel tract for all who were passing by. The importance of this is Jesus is pictured as a universal Savior. That does not mean He will automatically save everybody, but that He will save anyone who will come to Him by faith regardless of their social standing or background. He is the Savior of "whosoever will" (John 3:16; Rom. 10:13 NKJV).

The third testimony is the testimony of the wager. John says, "Then the soldiers, when they had crucified Jesus, took His garments and made four parts, to each solder a part, and also the tunic. Now the tunic was without seam, woven from the top in one piece. They said therefore among themselves, "Let us not tear it, but cast lots for it, whose it shall be," that the Scripture might be fulfilled which says: "they divided My garments among them, and for My clothing they cast lots." Therefore, the soldiers did these things" (John 19:23-24 NKJV). The soldiers gambled for the garments of Jesus, just as the Scripture had prophesied (Ps. 22:18 NKJV). The picture in this garment is special. First, the seamless garment of Jesus was to be worn by the High Priest of Israel as part of his ceremonial dress (Ex. 39:22-29 NKJV). This was to remind him that he was going into the presence of God without blemish and without flaw. This is a picture of the Lord Jesus Christ and what he did as our Great High Priest (Heb. 9:24-28; 10:12 NKJV). Second, just the night before, Israel's high priest had rent (tore) his own garments in the presence of Jesus. This was forbidden by the Law (Lev. 21:10 NKJV) and was a picture of the end of the high priestly system in Israel. Also, when Jesus died, we are told that the veil of the Temple was rent from top to bottom (Matt. 27:51 NKJV) which is also a picture of the end of the Old Testament system. When Christ died, He was the only one whose garments were not torn! This is God's way of picturing for us that the old system had forever passed away and that we now have a new High Priest! He alone is qualified for the Job! Thank God, He is in Heaven right now carrying out that job for you and me (Heb. 7:25 NKJV)!

▌ The Pain of His Crucifixion

When the Bible describes what they did to Jesus on the cross just simply says, "then they crucified Him" (Matt. 27:35a NKJV). Those words do not even begin to convey the horror of what Jesus Christ endured on that cross. Consider again the fact that before He arrived at Calvary Jesus had been awake all night. He had been through at least four trials. He had been beaten by the Jews. Beaten by the Roman Soldiers who scourged, mocked, ridiculed, spit upon, and made to carry His cross to Calvary, and then He is crucified! An act more horrible than anything you and I can imagine! Here is a brief description of what it must have been like taken from *The Expositor's Bible Commentary Vol. 8*, written by C. Truman Davis, M.D.

"The cross is placed on the ground and the exhausted man is quickly thrown backwards with his shoulders against the wood. The legionnaire feels for the depression at the front of the wrist. He drives a heavy, square wrought-iron nail through the wrist and deep into the wood. Quickly he moves to the other side and repeats the action, being careful not to pull the arms too tightly, but to allow some flex and movement. The cross is then lifted into place. The left foot is pressed backward against the right foot, and with both feet extended, toes downward, a nail is driven through the arch of each foot, leaving the knees flexed. The victim is now crucified. As he slowly sags down with more weight on the nails in the wrist, excruciating, fiery pain shoots along the fingers and up the arms to explode in the brain; the nails in the wrist are putting pressure on the median nerves. As he pushes himself upward to avoid this stretching torment, he places the full weight on the nail through his feet. Again, he feels the searing agony of the nail tearing through the nerves between the bones of his feet. As the arms fatigue, cramps sweep through the muscles, knotting them in deep, relentless, throbbing pain. With these cramps comes the inability to push himself upward to breathe. Air can be drawn into the lungs, but he cannot exhale. He fights to raise himself to get even one small breath. Finally, carbon dioxide builds up in the lungs and in the blood stream, and the cramps partially subside. Spasmodically he can push himself upward to exhale and bring in life-giving oxygen. Hours of this searing pain as tissue is torn from his lacerated back as he moves up and down against the rough timber. Then another agony begins: a deep, crushing pain deep in the chest as the pericardium slowly fills with serum and begins to compress the heart. It is now almost over; the loss of tissue fluids has reached a critical level; the compressed heart is struggling to pump heavy, thick, sluggish blood into the tissues; the tortured lungs are making a frantic effort to gasp in small gulps of air. He can feel the chill of death creeping through his tissues…Finally, he can allow his body to die." (*C. Truman Davis* n.d.). All this the Bible records with the simple words, "and they crucified Him" (Mark 15:24 NKJV). What wonderous love is this? That was what Jesus endured because of His love for you and me (Rom. 5:8 NKJV)! Let me remind you, He was still the Creator of the universe as He hung on that cross! He could have called for myriads of angels (Matt. 26:53 NKJV) but He endured His crucifixion in silence, just as the prophet has said He would (Isa. 53:7 NKJV) Why did He do this? Because He loves you!

While Jesus endured the agony of the cross; those who were at Calvary that day did everything in their power to enhance His suffering. The soldiers who had nailed Him to the cross are at His feet gambling over His clothes. The religious leaders ridicule this sad, broken figure hanging on the cross. Even two other men who are hanging there with Him that day joined in the mockery of the Lord Jesus Christ! The only compassion He received that day was from a tiny group of people gathered at the foot of His cross watching Him die. The group included His mother, an aunt, a beloved disciple, and a woman that had been delivered from a life of sin (John 19:25 NKJV). They were there to love Him and mourn His death! Again, I am reminded of just Who this was hanging there that day! One Word from Him and His tormentors would have been evaporated into nothingness! Yet, He did not return their tormenting and attacking words. When He did speak, it was to pray for them and to ask God the Father for forgiveness for them (Luke 23:34 NKJV). Oh, what grace! Why did He do this? Because He loves you and me!

The greatest pain of the crucifixion that Jesus endured for you and me was that amazing event that took place during the three hours of darkness. That moment in time when Jesus Christ, the Son of God, literally became "sin for us, that we might become the righteousness of God in Him" (2 Cor. 5:21 NKJV). I will never understand it, but I praise and thank my Lord and Savior every day for what He did for me and the world upon that cross. Somehow, all our sins were transferred to Him as He hung on that cross. He, the Last Adam, became our sins and He was judged by God in my place, in your place! The first Adam brough sin and death to the entire human race by his actions in the Garden of Eden. The Second Adam, the Lord Jesus, brough salvation and life to all who will receive Him by His actions on the cross of Calvary! God judged Him as if He were every sinner when He died. He paid the price for all of us that we might be saved! Why did He endure the full brunt of the wrath of God on the cross? Why did He take our Hell and feel our death? Simply because He loves you!

The Power of the Crucifixion

With all this this information the fisher of men has for sharing the Gospel, we must not think that Calvary was a place of death and suffering only. Jesus makes three statements that has great power in each statement but there is even more to what took place that proves that there is power in the blood!

THE POWER OF COMPASSION

Amid His dying hour, with His enemies reveling in His death, and with a little band of faithful followers at His feet, Jesus took the time to make provision for His mother. "When Jesus therefore saw His mother, and the disciple who He love standing by, we said to His mother, "Woman, behold your son!" Then He said to the disciple, "Behold your mother!" and from that hour that disciples took her to his own home." (John 19:26-27 NKJV). There are many truths here, but the one that stands out the most is that even in death, He did not forget others! He was dying to save men and He remembered His mother that day. He made sure that Mary would be taken care of for the rest of her life. His actions are symbolic of the fact that through his death, those who receive Him enter a new relationship with God. One in which they too are taken care of forever. "And I give them eternal life, and they shall never perish; neither shall any one snatch them out of My hand." (John 10:28 NKJV). He may not have mentioned our names, but as He was on the cross, we were on His mind that day!

THE POWER OF CONNECTION

The next statement from the Lord was "I thirst!" (John 19:28 NKJV). His agony and the conditions He had endured that day is ironic for the One Who created the streams, the creek, and the river; the One Who filled the oceans with water; the One Who said "he who believes in Me shall never thirst" (John 6:35 NKJV) and here He is saying "I thirst!" (John 19:28 NKJV). I am sure that His physical body was thirsty that day, but there is far more in view here! If you take all the conditions of Calvary into account, if you consider the darkness, the pain, the isolation, the separation from the Father and the physical thirst (Luke 16:24 NKJV), you get a clear picture of Hell. When Jesus was on the cross, He was enduring Hell on earth. He was suffering our Hell so that we might enjoy His Heaven! Don't misunderstand me, there is a literal burning Hell where the lost will experience pain, torment, thirst, isolation, and separation from God forever! And while that is true, it is also true, that Jesus endured all the torments of Hell while He hung on the cross for you and for me. He endured Hell for countless number of humans in His six hours on the cross that day! He took your Hell for you, so that you wouldn't have to! All you have to do is come, call upon the Name of the Lord, trust Him and you will be saved!

THE POWER OF REDEMPTION

When the Savior breathed His last on the cross; redemption had been secured for all those who will place their faith in Him! No greater words have ever been spoken than when Jesus, just before He died said, "It is finished" (John 19:30 NKJV). Through His death, He satisfied God's just demands for sin (Rom. 6:23 NKJV). The Greek word (*teleo*) means something that took place in the past which had present abiding results (Strong's Concordance 1984). It could be translated this way: "It stands finished and always will be finished!" That means that Jesus finished the assignment He was given! He applied the last strokes to the picture of salvation, it is finished. He paid the penalty for sin, it is finished! He took the place of the guilty before the judgment bar of God and secured redemption through His blood for all who will trust Him as their Savior (1 Pet. 1:18-19 NKJV)! His death on the cross forever satisfied God (1 John 2:2; Rom. 3:25 NKJV). His death on the cross liberates those trapped and victimized by sin! He sets us free when we receive Him by faith! Thank God, our salvation rest upon the finished work of Jesus on the cross! It is finished! It is done! To be saved, all I must do is nothing but lean on what He has already done for me! There is nothing left for me to do!

A young man, after a revival service, came up to the visiting evangelist as they were getting ready to put up everything for the night. The young man had left after the invitation, under conviction, he had returned at the conclusion of the service and went up to the evangelist and he said, "Sir, what can I do to be saved?" And the evangelist hardly even lifted his eyes form the work he was doing, he said, "I'm sorry, son, you're too late." And the boy said, "Surely, surely, that can't be. Surely, I'm not too late. You're still here. Won't you tell me what I must do to be saved?" And the evangelist stopped what he was doing, looked at him, and he said, "I'm sorry, son, you're too late. Jesus did everything necessary for you to be saved, two thousand years ago. All you need to do is just receive His finished work for your salvation". That is a major part of the good news of the Gospel and as a fisher of men that is what we need to be telling lost sinners. That all they need to do is just receive His finished work for their salvation, because redemption, salvation, and forgiveness of sin has been paid in full. It is finished!

THE POWER OF RESTORATION

Fishers of men must not get the power of restoration confused with that of the power of reconciliation. To get an understanding of restoration a fisher of men would have to refer to the Old Testament teachings. The prophets in the Old Testament had a foreknowledge of the impending exile that was going to take place for the nation of Israel. However, to bring about hope to the people they would also prophesy that God would restore his people to their own land (Jer. 27:22; Dan. 9:25 NKJV). When this exile took place, men begin to look for and long for the restoration of the nation to the land. Over time the people of Israel began to associate this restoration with the coming Messiah. They believe that the Messiah, when He came would restore their material prosperity, however, we know that John the Baptist fulfilled the prophecy of Malachi 4:5 and that John, the Baptist in the spirit of Elijah, will restore all things (Matt. 17:11; Mark 9:12 NKJV). In the fullest sense the restoration is still in the future. Even though they did not fully understand what Jesus was referring to, they still asked on the eve of His ascension, "Lord, will You at this time restore the kingdom to Israel?" (Acts 1:6 NKJV). Jesus answers and says, "It is not for you to know times or seasons which the Father has put in His own authority." (Acts 1:7 NKJV). His answer puts a halt to their speculation about matters for which they have no control, however, He did not deny that there will be a restoration.

Peter gives reference to the restoration in his message in Solomon's portico in Acts 3:11-26 (NKJV). There Peter is looking for "times of refreshing" which he associates with the return of the Lord Jesus Christ (Acts 3:20 NKJV), who is in Heaven "until the times of restoration of all things, which God has spoken by the mouth of all His holy prophets since the world began" (Acts 3:21 NKJV). Now, from one point of view Peter sees this as prophecy that the restoration waits the Second Coming of Jesus Christ. However, there is nothing wrong with associating that Peter is also referring to the restoration of fallen men. Just know that there is no biblical passage which says this in so many words.

THE POWER OF RECONCILIATION

Now the power of reconciliation is the proper term that refers to the state of men being reconciled back to the Lord. Reconciliation applies not to good relation in general but to the doing away of the enmity, or the bridging over of a separation because of a quarrel. Paul tells us that sinners are "enemies" of God (Rom. 5:10; Col. 1:21; Jas. 4:4 NKJV). Therefore, as fishers of men should not minimize the seriousness of reconciliation. To that reason Paul tells the Corinthians that as God's fishers of men we have been given the task or the ministry of reconciliation (2 Cor. 5:19 NKJV). Through the death of Jesus on the cross, the believer finds himself restored (reconciled) to a right relationship with God. Through His death, all those who receive Him by faith, are justified (Rom. 5:9 NKJV). The word "justified" means to be declared righteous; to render one righteous, or to make one as he ought to be (*Dictionary* 1828). What the blood of Jesus does for an individual, they could never do for themselves! It washes my sins away and renders me righteous in the sight of the Lord. It is the blood of Jesus that makes men worthy to go to Heaven (Phil. 3:9 NKJV).

So now notice this powerful message of the power of reconciliation. Matthew records, "Then, behold, the veil of the temple was torn in two from top to bottom; and the earth quaked, and the rocks were split." (Matt. 27:51 NKJV). When Jesus died on the cross, we are told that the veil of the Temple was torn in half, (by the Lord Himself), from the top to bottom. The veil stood as a barrier between the Holy Place and the Holy of Holies in the Temple. Behind this veil was the mercy seat. The high priest would enter behind that veil once each year on the Day of Atonement and place the blood of the sacrifice on the mercy seat to atone for the sins of the people. That veil had stood as a reminder that man was separated from God by his sins and was unworthy to approach God (Isa. 59:2 NKJV). However, when Jesus died on the cross, that veil was torn in two, signifying that the way of God had been opened. Mankind, no longer has a need to ever be separated from God by his sins any longer. He can be brought into the presence of God by placing his/her trust in the blood of Jesus Christ that was shed on the cross (Eph. 2:12-16 NKJV). The blood brings sinful man and a Holy God together as one!

The Treasure of His Crucifixion

Have you ever noticed that the death of Jesus took place just like the Old Testament Scriptures had predicted it would? His legs were not broken (Ps. 34:20 NKJV). His side was pierced (Zech. 12:10 NKJV). In fact, over three hundred precious prophecies were fulfilled to the letter during the birth, life, and death of Jesus. He accomplished the plan of God for the lost humanity so that we might be saved from the penalty, power, and presence of sin!

John 19:34 (NKJV) records a precious truth when Jesus died. It tells us that when they pierced His side blood and water both ran out. This indicates that He was dead before they pierced His side with the spear. Doctors who have studied the death of Jesus and the record of Scripture have concluded that His heart probably burst while He was on the cross. When it did, the platelets and the serum in His blood separated. When they thrust in the spear, blood and water came forth. Jesus literally died of a broken heart! Broken hearted for you!

Listen, the blood that flowed that day was precious blood! It was the blood of the atonement. That blood, and that blood alone, is the price that satisfies God and opens the door of Heaven to those to whom it is applied. There is only one means of salvation! You must be washed in the blood (1 Pet. 1:18-19 NKJV). Nothing else that you do in life matters until you are washed in the blood of the Lamb (Heb. 9:22 NKJV). How does one get washed in the blood? When you look to Jesus by faith for your soul's salvation, His blood is counted as the payment for your sins. In other words, the blood is applied, and you are saved by grace (Eph. 2:8-9 NKJV). The atonement we have through the blood of Jesus is a treasure that is priceless in its value to the human soul.

But also notice what John writes in John 19:30 (NKJV), "And bowing His head, He gave up His spirit." Now, when people die, they rarely bow their heads. In fact, it is far more common for people to raise their heads to try and get just one more breath. Not Jesus! When He knew that God the Father had been satisfied and that the price of salvation had forever been paid, He willingly allowed His spirit to leave His body (John 10:18 NKJV). He died only when He knew that He had opened a perfect way for you and me to be saved!

So, as a fisher of men does the truth of what Jesus did on the cross move you in your heart? Are you more motivated to "go" and "make" followers of Christ? The old-rugged cross can make a difference in the life of someone who is lost.

CHAPTER TWELVE

What a Difference a Day Makes

When Joseph had taken the body, he wrapped it in a clean linen cloth, and laid it in his new tomb which he had hewn out of the rock; and he rolled a large stone against the door of the tomb and departed. (Matthew 27:59-60 NKJV)

IF THAT HAD BEEN THE END OF JESUS, THEN THERE WOULD BE NO hope. If that was all there was to teaching of Jesus, then His promise to make His disciples fishers of men are for naught. If the death of Jesus was the end of His ministry, then there would not be a Kingdom of Heaven. Oh, how this world would be in such utter chaos if Jehovah God, in human form in the person of Jesus Christ, made the ultimate sacrifice by dying on the cross and was just buried in a tomb.

What a difference a day makes! As fishers of men, we have hope because "up from the ground He arose!" (*Lowery* 1991). Jesus rose from the dead! "He lives! Halleluiah! He lives!" (Ackley 1991). Just think, if there was not a resurrection, then Peter and the disciples would not have seen him in the upper room on that Sunday morning, and they would not be standing there on the shore of Galilee wondering what they should be doing while they waited for Jesus to meet them there. If Jesus had not rose from the dead, then they probably would have stayed hidden for they would have no need to go fishing for men. When the body of Jesus was place in the tomb by Joseph of Arimathea and Nicodemus (John 19:38-39 NKJV) the day He was crucified, it was a dark and terrible day. As the sun went down that night, so did the hopes and dreams of all the Lord's disciples and followers. Mark is the only Gospel writer to mention that a day that must have seemed like a dark, dreary, depressing day had passed between the day Jesus died and the day He rose again from the dead. "Now when the Sabbath was past" (Mark 16:1a NKJV). Matthew mentions the sabbath only to emphasize the first day of the week. "Now after the Sabbath, as the first day of the week began to dawn" (Matt. 28:1a NKJV). The point is that I am sure, that one day was a long, miserable day for all those who loved and followed Jesus.

But what a difference a day makes! Mark, as well as the other Gospel writers, moves us beyond that tragic Saturday to a glorious Sunday, when the world changed forever. If we are going to behave as fishers of men, then we need to know the events of that first resurrection. Why is this day so important? That day is important because the events of that day have made a difference in every day that has and will follow that day. That day makes a difference because what happened that day has influenced many fishers of men who have placed their faith and trust in the Lord Jesus Christ. That day is important because what happened on that day can make a difference in the men, women, boys, and girls that we have the privilege of talking about a Savior who died for their sin, who was buried, and who lives. Just FYI: the reason why the church holds worship on Sunday is to commemorate the resurrection of our Lord and Savior Jesus Christ! So, let's look in on the events that occurred at that tomb just outside Jerusalem the morning Jesus arose from the dead.

The Approach of the Women

Mark mentioned three women that had observed the long, dark Sabbath day. "Now when the Sabbath was past, Mary Magdalene, Mary the mother of James, and Salome bought spices that they might come and anoint Him" (Mark 16:1 NKJV). They rested in their homes as they were commanded by Law. Just the day before, they had witnessed the death of Jesus. They watched as His body was placed in a tomb and as a stone was rolled over the opening to seal His body inside (Mark 15:46-47 NKJV). At sundown, the Sabbath began, these women went to their homes to wait. When the Sabbath ended, on Saturday at sunset, they emerged from their homes, went into town, and purchased the spices to anoint the body of Jesus. Joseph of Arimathea and Nicodemus had already wrapped the body in linen strips and poured embalming spices on the body. The perfume these women were intending to use would have served the purpose of masking the smell of decomposition. Their intention is to go to the tomb the next morning and perform one final act of love and service to the Lord Jesus Christ. For them, it was a way to have closure concerning His death.

"Very early in the morning on the first day of the week, they came to the tomb when the sun had risen" (Mark 16:2 NKJV). In that society, most people arose just before dawn, at around 5:30 AM. These women must have got up earlier than that. They arose from their beds, gathered their spices together and made their way from Bethany, where they lived, to the tomb just outside the city of Jerusalem. It was a trip of some two miles. Their love and devotion to the Lord Jesus Christ is seen in their labor of love. They are broken hearted over His death and they are in a hurry to get to Him so that they might minister to Him one final time. Matthew records that it was two women came that morning while along with Mark; Luke and John reveal that other came also. Note: there is no contradiction; it is possible that they arrived as different groups. However, they came and were sad, defeated, and discouraged. Some had witnessed and others had heard of the death of Jesus on the cross and they were coming to pay their last respects to the body of the Lord. If you take notice of their motive for coming that morning you can see what they were doing early that Sunday morning.

Matthew tells us that these women came to "see the tomb" (Matt. 28:1 NKJV). Maybe they were coming to pray or to meditate near the place where His body had been. Maybe they were coming to make sure that everything was in order at the tomb. Mark and Luke tell us that these women came to perform one last labor of love for the Lord Jesus.

That they came to finish anointing His body for burial. John tells us that one came to linger at the tomb. "But Mary stood outside by the tomb weeping, and as she wept, she stooped down and looked into the tomb" (John 20:11 NKJV). Now according to verse 18 we know that this is Mary Magdalene. But here is a woman that owed so much to Jesus. There had been a time in her life when she had been possessed by seven demons (Mark 16:9 NKJV). Her life had been radically changed by Jesus and she loved Him more than life itself. She was one of the last people at the cross (Matt. 27:61 NKJV) and she was the first to see Him after He had risen from the dead (Mark 16:9 NKJV). She loved Him so much for what He had done for her. Surely her heart was broken that morning, but still she came to love Him and worship Him!

"And they said among themselves, "Who will roll away the stone from the door of the tomb for us?"" (Mark 16:3 NKJV). As they walked, they kept talking about the stone over the door of the tomb. It must have dawned on them after they purchased their spices that they might have trouble accessing the body of the Lord. After all, the tomb had been sealed by have a large stone rolled over the door. By some estimates, this stone could have weighed around one thousand pounds. These ladies could never have moved that stone by themselves, and they knew it. They are concerned about that.

As these women made their way to the tomb that morning, they were filled with sorrow, grief, fear, uncertainty, and a now what do we do behavior. They were not going there looking for a living Lord, they were looking for a cold, dead corpse. Do you know what their problem was? Their problem was they were still living as though it was still Saturday! When that awful Saturday dawned, all they could see was the shattered remains of their hopes and dreams. These ladies, along with the Lord's disciples and followers, had place all their faith and confidence in Jesus. They believe that He was the Messiah. The believed that He was the One Who was going to fulfill all the ancient prophecies. They believe that He was the One Who would be King of Israel. They believed that He would establish God's kingdom on the earth. All their hopes for life and eternity were bound up in what they believe about Jesus. Then, all their fondest hopes and dreams crumbled to the ground like so much dust as they stood there at the cross and watched Him die. Faith turned to grief and grief to utter hopelessness as they saw His broken body taken down from the cross, place in that tomb, and a stone rolled and sealed by the religious leaders and the Roman army. When that stone was rolled across the door of that grave, it was a ringing statement of finality. That stone said to them, "It's all over! It's all over! It's all over! Hope is gone! There is no future! There is no salvation! There is no kingdom! Jesus is dead! It's all over!"

If the life of Jesus ended with Him being buried in a tomb and with a stone being rolled across the door, there would be no hope. Paul says, "If in this life only we have hope in Christ, we are of all men the most pitiable" (1 Cor. 15:19 NKJV). And for that Sabbath day it was that way for the disciples, His followers, and for these women. Even today there are so many that are living as if it is still Saturday, and they do not realize that Sunday has come! People move through this world enslaved by their sins (Eph. 2:1-3 NKJV). They move through this world oblivious to the God who exist to save them (Rom. 1:18-21 NKJV). They move through this world and all it trials and tribulations especially during this Coronavirus Pandemic without joy, without peace, without hope, trapped in their sins and head for Hell. The problem with the majority of people is they are strapped in Saturday, they live in darkness of their sin and depravity, and are unaware that joy unspeakable and full of glory can be theirs if they only knew that the stone was rolled away by God for them, and that the tomb was empty for them, and that Jesus was alive for them. If they only knew that they could be delivered from the bondage and the darkness of sin by placing their trust in the risen resurrected Lord and Savior Jesus Christ that they could be save. Fishers of men, we must tell them what a difference a day makes!

A Message of Life

When these ladies arrived at the tomb, their fear is changed to amazement. Mark says, "But when they looked up, they saw that the stone had been rolled way; for it was very large" (Mark 16:4 NKJV). As they walked towards the tomb, they did so with their heads bowed and their eyes downcast because of their sorrow and their grief. As they neared the tomb, when they looked, they saw that the massive stone had been rolled away from the door and that the way into the tomb was wide open. They did not know that before they arrived that morning, there had been a great earthquake and that an angel had come to the tomb and removed the stone. All they see is the tomb opened and they fear the worst. Surely, they are afraid that the Lord's enemies have taken His body away. They were probably overcome with new fears that the body of the Lord might be subjected to greater indignities than it had already experienced. Seeing the stone rolled away must have chilled their hearts, so they ran the rest of the way to the tomb to investigate. When they go into the tomb, they find "a young man clothed in a long white robe sitting on the right side; and they were alarmed" (Mark 16:5 NKJV). Humanity was not the only one to send ambassadors to the tomb early that morning. Heaven sent an ambassador to deliver a message not only in word but also in deed. You see, the fact that God sent the angel early that morning was not to let Jesus out! Jesus already had been resurrected and alive before the angel arrived on the scene. That stone was rolled away so that men could look into the tomb and see that it was forever empty.

Another deed that the angel did before speaking to the women, was caused the Roman guards to "become like dead men" (Matt. 28:4 NKJV). Matthew 27:62-67 (NKJV) tells us that the chief priest and the Pharisees were concerned that the prophecies of Jesu might come true, and they wanted a guard to be posted at the tomb. You know it is sad when rank infidels know more about the Bible and believe it more than people who claim to know Jesus! That detachment of soldiers stood as an obstacle between the saints and their entrance into the tomb of Jesus. However, when the angel appeared, he made short work of the soldiers. These battle-hardened men fainted at his feet like a bunch of silly teenagers at a Harry Styles concert! When this angel does begin to speak to these women the message, his speech is designed to help them to stop living as though it was Saturday. It is message designed to help them experience the power of Sunday in their lives. Notice this angel's message.

A MESSAGE OF PEACE

"But he said to them, "Do not be alarmed"" (Mark 16:6a NKJV. The KJV uses the word "affrighted" (Mark 16a KJV). The word "affrighted" means "to be struck with terror" (*Dictionary* 1828). So, when the women see the angel, they were overcome with fear and terror. But he speaks to them and offers them a message of peace. He tells them that there is no need to fear. Things are not as they appear on the surface. But the way, they never are! Nothing is ever as bad as your mind, your heart, the world, the media, and the devil tell you they are. God is still in control; God is just fulfilling His plan.

Another part of this message that the angel delivered is a message of power. "You seek Jesus of Nazareth, who was crucified. He is risen! He is not here" (Mark 16:6b NKJV). The angel is letting them know that he knows why they are there. He knows they have come looking for the body of Jesus. He confirms what they already know that Jesus was "crucified" and then He died. They were not deceived by what they saw. They really did see Jesus nailed to a cross. They really did see His blood as it flowed from His body. They really did see Him yield up His Spirit. They really did see Him die. He wants them to know that His cry of "it is finished!" did not mean that He was finished! He died, but He did not stay died! This angel joyously cries out, "He is risen!" The angel wants them to know that the power of death has been swallowed up by a far greater power, life! The angel wants them to know that the empty tomb of the Lord Jesus is not a place of despair and defeat. That empty tomb is a place of glory, a place of power, and a place of hope. Jesus is alive! Just like the angel said! That was a message those women needed to hear that Sunday morning and it is the message you need to hear, and the sinner needs to hear today!

This message of power should have reminded them that His resurrection should not have taken them by surprise! After all, Jesus was making and teaching them how to behave as fishers of men and this was what He had been telling them would happen all along. Jesus compared His death, burial, and resurrection to the story of Jonah (Matt. 12:40 NKJV). He even "began to show to His disciples that He must suffer many things from the elders and chief priest and scribes, and be killed, and be raised the third day" (Matt. 16:21 NKJV). He repeats this same teaching over and over helping them to understand why He was going to the cross, why He was going to be buried, and why He was going to rise again (Matt. 17:23; 20:18-19; 26:31; John 2:19; 10:17 NKJV). Note: Mark and Luke tell us that Jesus taught this as well. The resurrection should not have caught them off guard. The crucifixion should not take them by surprise. They should have been holding worship service outside the tomb early that morning! They should have been there ready to meet Him when He came out of the tomb.

The last part of the angel's message was a message of proof. "See the place where they laid Him" (Mark 16:6c NKJV). After telling the women that Jesus has risen from the dead, the angel invites them to look at the place where the body had been. As they looked, we are told what they saw, later Peter and John arrived there and John records what he saw in John 20:6-7 (NKJV) which says, "Then Simon Peter came following him, and went into the tomb; and he saw the linen cloths lying there, and the handkerchief that had been around His head, not lying with the linen cloth, but folded together in a place aby itself." Just think, they saw the linen cloth that had been wrapped around the body, still lying there, undisturbed, as if the body had simply passed right though them. They also saw the napkin folded and laid to the side. They would have looked upon a scene of absolute calm and order. John states that when he saw these things in this empty tomb that is when he believed in the resurrection (John 20:8 NKJV). There is an old Jewish tradition concerning the folded napkin that was especially known to servants that serve the master's table. If the master were to get up and just throw his napkin on the table that meant that the master was not coming back. However, if the master were to get up and fold them napkin and put it in its place by itself it meant the master was not through and he would be right back. Jesus very powerfully without any words just simply folding this napkin letting followers know that He is not through, He will be right back!"

The empty tomb is still preaching today! That tomb still tells this world that Jesus is alive and the He can save all who come to Him by faith (Heb. 7:25 NKJV). To behave as fishers of men means that we need to tell those who are still trapped in the deadness and darkness of their sin and tell them that they don't have to remain in that condition. Tell them that the Lord Jesus Christ lives today, and He can deliver them from the Saturday of their sin and transport them to the Sunday of His new life. The message of the empty tomb can roll way the stone from the heart of those sad, sorrowful, grief-stricken women. That message brought them out of the gloom of defeat into the glory of life. It can do the same for you and for those who have not heard the message yet. What a difference a day makes!

A Mission of Liberation

After looking in on the empty tomb, the angel gave this little band of women a command. He said, "But go, tell His disciples and Peter that He is going before you into Galilee; there you will see Him, as He said to you." (Mark 16:7 NKJV). The angel sends them away from the tomb to carry a message to the disciples of the Lord. Those men were filled with fear and they were in hiding (John 20:19 NKJV), but God wants them to know that Jesus is alive. There is no need to fear because there is joy and hope! Peter, the disciple who had denied Jesus on the night of His trial, is singled out here in Mark's account by the angel. Now understand Mark is writing his gospel with the assistance of Peter, however, the point of the message sent by Jesus through the angel is that Jesus had not disowned Peter, but him to know that he is loved. Those three women came to that tomb that morning worried about rolling away one stone from a tomb. They didn't know it, but God was about to use them to roll countless stones away from the hearts of millions. They were the first to spread the good news as fishers of men that the tomb was empty!

Mark 16:8 (NKJV) says, "they went out quickly and fled from the tomb, for they trembled and were amazed. And they said nothing to anyone, for they were afraid." They came to that tomb with sorrow in their hearts and they leave the tomb in a different state of mind. This verse says that they "were amazed." That phrase refers to a "displacement of the mind". What they had seen and what they had heard at the empty tomb literally "blew their minds". It was almost more than they could comprehend. That phrase has the idea of "being overcome with awe of a religious nature". In other words, what they encountered at the tomb was not what they expected as they traveled there. But what they encountered changed their lives and replaced their sorrow with an overwhelming sense of the power of God. They knew that they were now a part of a great miracle and ran to tell others about their risen Lord!

Mark said as they went, they did not say anything about what they had seen and heard with anyone for they were afraid. That is just opposite of what the shepherds did the night Jesus was born. The shepherds as they went, they told everyone they met what they had heard, what they had seen, and what the Lord had done for them. They had an experience, and they shared it with everybody. These men had been saved just a short time, and they already had the courage to share the good news with everybody. These women who had spent time with Jesus, sat under His teaching that on the third day He would be resurrected; they were too afraid to tell the good news to everyone they met? As a fisher of men never let an opportunity pass you by to tell someone what you have seen and heard. Take great joy in telling everyone you meet the good news of what Jesus has done for you. Of course, we know from the other Gospel writers that these women did run to find the disciples and tell them (Matt. 28:8; John 20:1 NKJV). And the news did affect the disciples. As a matter of fact, many of them ran to the tomb and as previously stated, when John looked in and saw the evidence, he believed (John 20:8 NKJV). Later that day, Jesus would appear to more of the disciples. The message of these women caused more stones to be rolled away. Because of their testimony, many were brought out of the darkness and gloom of Saturday into the wonder and glory of Sunday!

Such is the power of the resurrection. When the resurrection is first encountered and believed, it fills the heart with amazement. When the Lord's resurrection is embraced by faith, it brings about change in the life of a person who receives its truth. When the death and resurrection of Jesus, which is the Gospel (1 Cor. 15:3-4; Rom. 4:25 NKJV), embraced by faith, a new birth takes place. A sinner becomes a saint; a child of the devil becomes a child of God; a new creature is born (John 3:3; 2 Cor. 5:17 NKJV). That new life draws its first breath, and it may not be perfect, but that new life is different. It is a life that Christ lives through (Gal. 2:20; John 7:37-38 NKJV). It is a life that strives to behave as a follower of Jesus Christ; it is a life that strives to behave as a fisher of men by learning and gaining more knowledge, wisdom, and understanding of God and the power of the resurrected Christ (Phil. 3:9-10 NKJV). It is a life that is no longer satisfied with Saturdays. It is a life that longs for the glories of Sunday to be real every day! It is a life that can't keep the good news to itself! It must go tell it on the mountain that Jesus Christ is Lord! That is the power of an empty tomb! It has the power to roll stones away from the stoniest of hearts. It has the power to deliver us from the Saturday of our death and revive us to live in His victory of Sunday! What a difference a day makes!

CHAPTER THIRTEEN

Our Great Salvation

This is a faithful saying, and these things I want you to affirm constantly, that those who have believed in God should be careful to maintain good works. These things are good and profitable to men. (Titus 3:8 NKJV)

HAVING LEARNED THE DETAILS OF THE DEATH, BURIAL, AND resurrection as a fisher of men you have now are equipped with the Gospel message. You see, the Gospel message is all about the death, burial, and resurrection and Paul sums up the gospel for us this way, "For I delivered to you first of all that which I also received: that Christ died for our sins according to the Scriptures, and that He was buried, and that He rose again the third day according to the Scriptures." (1 Cor. 15:3-4 NKJV). Therefore, having been equipped with this knowledge of the Gospel it is time for us behave as a fisher of men. The writer of Hebrews encourages believers to be more earnest in understanding this Gospel salvation that we have obtained, "Therefore, we must give the more earnest heed to the things we have heard, lest we drift away." (Heb. 2:1 NKJV). He goes on to encourage believers not to neglect our great salvation, "How shall we escape if we neglect so great a salvation, which at first began to be spoken by the Lord, and was confirmed to us by those who heard Him…" (Heb. 2:3 NKJV). If we are going to behave as a fisher of men then we must continue to grow in our walk with the

Lord, behaving as a follower of Christ, and by working on learning as much as possible about the Gospel of salvation and practice sharing the Gospel to improve your communication skills.

Since the death, burial, and resurrection is the main thrust of the Gospel plan of salvation, then what makes it so great. Well to understand that we go back to the Day of Pentecost. On the Day of Pentecost, Simon Peter stood up before a crowd of Jews from around the world and proclaimed a message that literally changed the lives of three thousand men that day (Acts 2:14-39 NKJV). It is also a message that has continued to reverberate down the halls of time and is as fresh today as it was two thousand years ago when it was first delivered. We are inundated with messages from the time we wake up in the morning until we go to bed at night. The television sends out messages about what we should drive, what we should eat, what we should wear, and who we are to vote for. Commercials use messages from a lizard who tries to get us to buy car insurance; messages from a chihuahua that tries to get us to buy tacos; and messages from a bear to get us to buy fabric softener. The government sends out messages to get us to accept their plans and goals for the country. The church sends out messages to try to reach people with the Word of God. The message Peter preached that day was God's precious plan of salvation. In just a few verses, Peter was able, by the help of the Holy Spirit, to declare the message that can change the life of everyone who hears it and receives it. It is a message that has not changed, nor lost its power. It is a message that still brings hope to the hopeless, life to those dead in sin, and forgiveness to those struggling under the burden of their sins. The message of the Gospel is the most important message the world has ever heard. It is far more important than anything the lizard or the government has to say. If you miss the message of the chihuahua or the bear your life won't change, but if you miss the message of the Gospel, your life will change forever!

That is why it is important that we the fishers of men take the message of the Gospel to a lost and dying world to change their lives. Because there are men, women, boys, and girls out in your community who have never heard God's precious Gospel plan of salvation. Maybe, they have heard the meandering of some socially motivated minister. Maybe, they have heard the drivel dispensed by many denominations. Maybe, they have heard some list of dos and don'ts, and they tried to keep them. But maybe they have never heard of God's precious Gospel plan of salvation and as fishers of men we cannot behave as if they have; we just cannot take that chance! So, let's look at the Gospel message as presented by Peter on the Day of Pentecost and from Paul as he writes Titus.

IT IS A MESSAGE OF LOVE

Let's start with Paul's encouragement to Titus. Paul writes, "For we ourselves were also once foolish, disobedient, deceived, serving various lusts, and pleasures, living in malice and envy, hateful and hating one another." (Titus 3:3 NKJV). In clear and vivid language, Paul reminds us of what we were before we met the Lord. He begins by telling us that we were foolish, meaning that we were ignorant of everything having to do with God, and unable to comprehend spiritual truths. He said that we were disobedient to God, authorities, and possibly even to our parents. We were deceived, continually being led astray deeper and deeper into sin by Satan. We were serving various lust and pleasures and have become slaves to our fleshly appetites and passions. We were living in malice having a live that is constantly bitter towards other people and/or given over to a lifestyle of evil. He said that we had envy which caused us to never be satisfied with what we have, but always grasping for more. We were hateful, this is a natural fruit of all the above. This kind of life makes us mean-spirited and hard to get along with, which leads to hating one another. That means we were walking without love for our fellow man. This is what we were, and what some still are today. The Bible reminds us repeatedly that mankind is fallen, ruined, spiritually bankrupt people (Eph. 2:1-3, 1 Cor. 6:9-10 NKJV). In our natural condition, we are worthy of nothing but judgement, wrath, and condemnation (Eph. 2:3; Ps. 9:7; 2 Thess. 1:8-9 NKJV). Even in our fallen condition, God still loves us (Jer. 31:3 NKJV). He could have left us in our sins and allowed us to go to Hell, but He loved us despite our condition!

Paul goes on to say, "But when the kindness and the love of God our Savior toward man appeared" (Titus 3:4 NKJV). In other words, despite our spiritual condition, God chose to display His love for us. How did God display His love for us? Paul answers this question in verse 6 "through Jesus Christ our Savior". God gave evidence of His love for fallen man by sending His Son into the world to die for us (Rom. 5:6-8; John 3:16; 1 John 4:9-10 NKJV). If you need evidence that God loves you, look no farther than Calvary! You don't need a feeling, just look to the cross! Look to Jesus and see Him as He dies for you on the cross (2 Cor. 5:21 NKJV) and know that you are special to the Lord. He loves you and that is the reason for the awful death of Jesus Christ. The cross says, "I love you!"

Paul explains this love in Titus 3:5 (NKJV), "not by works of righteousness which we have done, but according to His mercy He saved us, through the washing of regeneration and renewing of the Holy Spirit." From our perspective, there is no explanation for this kind of love. Why does God love lost sinners like He does? Why does He save us from our sins? Why would a Holy God set His love on sinners like us? Why would He give His only Begotten Son in our place? Why would He save us, cleanse us, and adopt us into His family? Why would He do something of this nature? He does not save because we deserve it. He does not save because He sees something good in lost sinners. He does not save because He knows what great servants we will become. The reason God saves sinners is because of His mercy. The word "mercy" speaks of kindness or good will toward the miserable and afflicted joined with a desire to relieve them. Justice gives us what we deserve. If we received justice, we would all spend an eternity in Hell. Praise God that He works in our lives according to "grace" and "mercy"! In His "mercy" God does not give us what we deserve. In His "grace" He gives us what we do not deserve. God's mercy is an extension of His grace (Eph. 2:8-9 NKJV).

IT IS A MESSAGE OF LIFE

The love of God is only part of the message of the Gospel. The message of the Gospel is also a message of life. When a lost sinner believes the

Gospel, the life of Christ is shared with them, (John 10:10 NKJV). Jesus said, "I am the resurrection, and the life: he that believes in Me, though he were dead, yet shall he live; and whoever lives and believes in Me shall never die…" (John 11:25-27 NKJV). Every person who comes to Jesus for salvation is given eternal life (John 10:28; John 3:16; John 6:47 NKJV). They are given eternal life that begins at the very moment of their salvation. If you are saved, you have eternal life right now!

Paul explains to Titus how salvation works in our lives. He begins by telling us how we are cleansed, "not by works of righteousness which we have done, but according to His mercy He saved us, through the washing of regeneration and renewing of the Holy Spirit." (Titus 3:5 NKJV). The phrase "washing of regeneration" refers to the cleansing that happens when we are saved. Some people view the "washing" as speaking of water baptism. They think that our sins are washed away when we are baptized in water. That is not what the Bible teaches! We are not cleansed by water baptism. Water baptism is merely an outward symbol of what the Lord Jesus did for us inwardly when He saved us by His grace. When God saved us, He washed us in the Blood of Jesus. He cleansed our sins away. The word "washing" refers to a "bath". When we come to Christ, we are given a spiritual "bath". Our sins are washed away forever (1 Cor. 6:9-11 NKJV). As far as God is concerned, the redeemed saints of God are clean, pure, and holy after being bathed in His blood (Isa. 1:18 NKJV). Revelation 1:5 (NKJV) says, "…unto Him that loved us, and washed us from our sins in His own blood." The word "washed" also carries the idea of being "released." (Strong's Concordance 1984). Jesus is the "Lamb of God that takes away the sin of the world" (John 1:29 NKJV). When the Lord saves us, He releases us from the power of our sin and put them away from us forever. When we are saved, we are forgiven, and our sins are gone (1 John 1:9 NKJV).

Next Paul explains how we are changed. In Titus 3:4 (NKJV) he uses the word "but" to transition from the description of what we were before we met Jesus into what He makes us by His grace. Then in Titus 3:5 (NKJV), there is the phrase "renewing of the Holy Spirit". The word "renewing" means renovating; to completely change for the better (*Dictionary* 1828). When God saves us by His grace, the Spirit of God comes to live in our hearts. When He comes in, He enters a ramshackle, ruined, rickety tent. He enters this tent (a life), that had formerly been condemned to destruction, and He remodels the place. He throws out the trash, cleans up the place, and renovates our lives completely. Literally, He starts over, rebuilding us from the inside out. He transforms us from the wretched creatures we are into redeemed saints of God. The evidence is striking, God's plan of salvation is a life changing plan! He makes us "new creatures" (2 Cor. 5:17 NKJV). He gives us a new heart (Ezek. 36:26 NKJV), and the new heart results in a new life! The message of Gospel has the power to change even the hardest of heart! It has the power that no other religion or movement has. Salvation is great because it takes the sinner and cleanses them and changes them into the children of the living God!

Not only does our great salvation cleanse and change a sinner but it also completes the sinner. Paul writes, "that having been justified by His grace we should become heirs according to the hope of eternal life" (Titus 3:7 NKJV). Our completion is revealed here in two important stages. First, we are completed because we have been "justified by His grace." The word "justified" means that our sins have been forgiven and we have been declared righteous by God the Father (*Dictionary* 1828). God accepts us because He has made us in His Son, the Lord Jesus Christ. He does not see us as we are; He sees us as Jesus, clothed in His righteousness. We are complete in Christ Jesus. And second, we are complete because we have been made "heirs according to the hope of eternal life." (Titus 3:7 NKJV) That simply means we have the hope of a better life after this life is over. The people of God have a home in Heaven to go to when they leave this world.

IT IS A MESSAGE OF AVAILABILITY

In Peter's message on the Day of Pentecost, he shows us more about the message of our great salvation. He said, quoting from the prophet Joel, "and it shall come to pass that whoever calls on the name of the Lord shall be saved" (Acts 2:21 NKJV). The first thing that we can notice from this verse is the availability of the Gospel message. Peter said that it is available to "whoever calls". You see, many things in life are exclusive. There are exclusive clubs, golf courses, restaurants, etc. Yet, when God, the Creator of the universe, designed a plan of salvation, He made it perfectly inclusive! When we think of this plan of salvation as fishers of men shouldn't ask "Who can this Gospel message work for?" Because the answer is simple and striking, because in God's economy, anyone can be saved! Fisher of men think about this: since God saved a dying thief (Luke 23:42-43 NKJV); a sin-stained woman (John 4:1-26 NKJV); a ruthless, ungodly tax collector (Luke 19:1-10 NKJV); some innocent little children (Matt. 18:1-9 NKJV), a brutal Roman Centurion (Luke 23:47 NKJV); a self-righteous Pharisee name Paul (Acts 9:1-9 NKJV); a demon possessed man (Mark 5:1-20 NKJV); a demon possessed slave girl (Acts 16:16-24 NKJV); a wealthy female merchant (Acts 16:11-15 NKJV); then He will save you and those who you think would not be a likely candidate to accept Jesus Christ as their personal Lord and Savior.

The truth of the matter is "whosoever" can be saved! The Bible expands on this theme in a myriad of places Some are especially noteworthy. "And the Spirit and the bride say, "Come!" And let him who hears say, "Come!" And let him who thirsts come. Whoever desires, let him take the water of life freely." (Rev. 22:17 NKJV). "For God so loved the world that He gave His only begotten Son, that whosoever believes in Him should not perish but have eternal life." (John 3:16 NKJV). "All that the Father gives Me will come to Me, and the one who comes to Me I will by no means cast out." (John 6:37 NKJV). "Ho! Everyone who thirst, come to the waters; and you who have no money, come, buy, and eat. Yes, come, buy wine and milk without money and without price." (Isa. 55:1 NKJV). These verses are sufficient to prove the case that God's plan of salvation is available to anyone who calls on the name of the Lord for their soul's salvation. The question that we as fishers of men need to be proposing to the lost sinner is, "Have you given you heart to Jesus and received this precious plan of salvation? It is available to you! Are you willing to receive this free gift of salvation?"

IT IS A MESSAGE OF SIMPLITY

As Peter continued to preach, he promised that those would simply "call on the name of the Lord" (Acts 2:21 NKJV) would be saved! It is one thing knowing that you are saved, and another altogether to understand how someone can be saved. Thankfully, the Bible tells us exactly how. When Peter delivered his message, he stated that it was as simple as "calling on the name of the Lord." Of course, Paul is quoting from the prophet Joel (Joel 2:32 NKJV) who has already made this statement of faith. Paul later quotes him again in Romans 10:13 (NKJV). But what does this phrase mean "to call upon the name of the Lord?" Is a person to just go around calling out the name the of the Lord? No! What this refers to is the call of faith. To be saved, a person must be aware of some important things. We as fisher of men are to present these important things to a lost sinner when we present the Gospel message to make them aware of the need of salvation. There are number of resources to present the Gospel message. Here are some examples: "The Roman Road"; "F.A.I.T.H."; "Gospel Tracks"; "ABC's of Becoming of Christian"; "The Cube"; "Personal Commitment Guide to Salvation" (from North American Mission Board); "Three Circles"; "One Verse Evangelism". What every resource you use, practice presenting the Gospel message, get familiar with that resource as much as possible, because you never know when the Lord will open a door of opportunity for you to behave as fisher of men.

Let's look at the "The Roman Road" as an example of the things a lost sinner needs to be aware of as you present the Gospel message. First, they need to know that there is a problem; that they are sinners. Romans 3:23 (NKJV) says, "For all have sinned and fall short of the glory of God." Romans 3:10 (NKJV) says, "There is none righteous, no, not one." Second, they need to know the consequences, that there is a price for their sin. "For the wages of sin is death, but the gift of God is eternal life in Christ Jesus our Lord" (Rom. 6:23 NKJV). "Therefore, just as through one man sin entered the world, and death through sin, and thus death spread to all men, because all sinned" (Rom. 5:12 NKJV). Third, they need to know that Jesus is the solution that paid that price for them. "For when we were still without strength, in due time Christ died for the ungodly. For scarcely for a righteous man will one die; yet perhaps for a good man someone would even dare to die. But God demonstrates His own love toward us, in that while we were still sinners, Christ died for us." (Rom. 5:6-8 NKJV). Fourth, they must understand the truth of the Gospel message that Jesus died, was buried, and rose from the dead, and then they must be willing to respond with a confession. "That if you confess with your mouth the Lord Jesus and believe in your heart that God has raised Him from the dead, you will be saved. For with the heart one believes unto righteousness, and with the mouth confession is made unto salvation." (Rom. 10:9-10 NKJV). Then lastly, they must be willing to ask the Lord Jesus to save their soul. "For whosoever calls on the name of the Lord shall be saved." (Rom. 10:13 NKJV). Then you need to follow that up by giving them the assurance of them calling on the Lord. "Therefore, have been justified by faith, we have peace with God through our Lord Jesus Christ." (Rom. 5:1 NKJV). "There is therefore now no condemnation to those who are in Christ Jesus who do not walk according to the flesh, but according to the Spirit." (Rom. 8:1 NKJV). "For I am persuaded that neither death nor life, nor angels nor principalities nor powers, nor things present nor things to come, nor height nor depth, nor any other created thing shall be able to separate us from the love of God which is in Christ Jesus our Lord." (Rom. 8:38-39 NKJV).

This may sound difficult to follow, again this is one of many resources that are available to the fisher of men. Find one that you are most comfortable with and practice makes perfect. Remember Jesus Christ was able to sum up the Gospel for us in one easy to understand passage in John 3:1-18 (NKJV). In those verses, Jesus tells us that salvation is obtained by simply believing. That is, all a sinner must do is come to the place where he/she is willing to trust Jesus and Jesus alone for salvation of their soul. We are to turn from good works, from religion, from church membership, and we are to realize that salvation is by grace and faith alone in Christ alone (Eph. 2:8-9 NKJV). In my mind, nothing could be easier! Salvation is simple!

THE SUBSTANCE OF THE MESSAGE

God's plan of salvation is 100% reliable! In other words, you can count on it doing that which the Lord has promised it will do! This is the only plan known to man that will never fail, never be revoked, and is absolutely worthy of your faith! Peter sums up the benefits of salvation in three words, "shall be saved" (Acts 2:21 NKJV). But what does it mean to be saved? Those who don't know the lingo would ask, "Saved from what?" So, what does the word "saved" mean anyway? Saved is one of those words that Christians use to describe that which they have received from the Lord. If you are lost, this word might sound a bit "churchy" or strange to you. But the word "saved" literally means to "rescue from all harm and danger; to keep safe and sound: to deliver; to save". It is a word that is special to every child of God who has experienced salvation. When we say that we are saved, we are saying a mouthful. It may be helpful for us to consider what some of the benefits of salvation are for the saints of God.

Here is what being saved does for you. Salvation brings deliverance from the wrath of God. "Much more then, having now been justified by His blood, we shall be saved from wrath through Him." (Rom. 5:9 NKJV). This also mean that we are delivered from Hell! Salvation brings forgiveness of sins. "And you, being dead in your trespasses and the uncircumcision of your flesh, He has made alive together with Him, having forgiven you all trespasses" (Col. 2:13 NKJV). It produces a perfectly clean life! However, don't get that idea that Christians never sin, it just means that the saved child of God sins are no longer imputed to him. When we come to Jesus, we are cleansed and declared righteous by the Heavenly Father. Our sins were assigned (imputed) to Him on the cross (2 Cor. 5:21 NKJV) and His righteousness is imputed to us at salvation (1 Cor. 6:9-11 NKJV). Salvation brings absolute security (John 10:28; Heb. 7:25 NKJV). Salvation brings the promise of Heaven (John 14:1-3 NKJV). Salvation brings about a changed life (2 Cor. 5:17 NKJV). There are dozens of other things that come our way when we are saved! Such as, we become the children of God (1 John 3:2 NKJV). We become heir of God (Rom. 8:17 NKJV). We become the servants of God (1 Cor. 6:19-20 NKJV). We become salt and light in the world (Matt. 5:13-16 NKJV). And the benefit list goes on forever! It is plain to me that being saved is the greatest blessing that any dirty, lowdown, wretched sinner can ever receive as a gift from the very hand of God. What about you? Are you a follower of Jesus Christ? Are you willing to behave as a fisher of men and share the world's great gift given to mankind?

THE SITMULUS OF THE MESSAGE

God's plan of salvation is to be desired because it offers something to mankind that no other plan can. It offers the assurance of Heaven! Every other plan devised by man offers the promise of some otherworldly type of adventure. Hindus look for Utopia. Muslims look for Nirvana. Jehovah's Witness long for heaven on this earth. All these hopes and dreams will ultimately fail! Only God's plan of salvation offers a home in Heaven that is guaranteed and not a pipe dream!

But what brought about this wonderful Gospel message? What was the event that enables God to offer this precious plan to fallen men? The answer is found in the next part of Peter's message. Peter said, "Men of Israel, hear these words: Jesus of Nazareth, a Man attested by God to you by miracles, wonders, and signs which God did through Him in your midst, as you yourselves also know; Him, being delivered by the determined purpose and foreknowledge of God, you have taken by lawless hands, have crucified, and put to death; whom God raised up, having loosed the pains of death, because it was not possible that He should be held by it." (Acts 2:22-24 NKJV). In the words of Peter, this plan of salvation came about because a man named Jesus Christ went to an old rugged cross and died between Heaven and earth to pay the sin dept of the entire world. He died for you on the cross and according to the Bible, He got up the third day and He still lives to save the lost. This is the heart of the Gospel. Its power lies in the fact that Jesus Christ shed His innocent blood to pay for sin and then He arose from the dead to offer eternal life to all who will receive Him by faith. That is the Gospel and that is what will save the human souls. There is nothing else, "Jesus said unto him, "I am the way, the truth, and the life, No one comes to the Father except through Me."" (John 14:6 NKJV). The preaching of the cross may be foolishness to a pagan world, but it is the power of God to those who have experienced it (1 Cor. 1:18 NKJV). Two thousand years ago, Peter preached this same Gospel to a crowd and three thousand souls were saved. We must behave as fishers of men and share our great salvation!

CHAPTER FOURTEEN

If a Fisher of Men Could Spend Five Minutes in Hell

And being in torments in Hades, he lifted up his eyes and saw Abraham afar off, and Lazarus in his bosom. (Luke 16:23 NKJV)

SUPPOSE IT WERE POSSIBLE FOR EVERY FISHER OF MEN TO SPEND FIVE minutes in Hell. I am not saying you want to, but suppose it was possible that we could experience what Hell is like for a short amount of time. Just think about that would affect our behavior as fishers of men! It is not the will of God for anyone to go to Hell (2 Pet. 3:9 NKJV). In the original plan for creating Hell, God created Hell for the Devil and His angels (Matt. 25:41 NKJV), however, when man sinned and became eternally separated from God, the wages of sin was death (Rom. 6:23 NKJV). That means sending an individual, who has never accepted Jesus Christ as their personal Lord and Savior, to a place of darkness, torment, and never-ending death in the flames of Hell.

With the mention of Hell, it brings with it many different reactions. Some people react with concern and are moved to share Jesus with the lost. Others react with fear and come to Jesus seeking salvation for their souls. Still others react with hate and revulsion and say that it is not a proper topic to talk about. Yet, there are those who seek to deny or prove that Hell never exists. In the Bible you will find that God and

Jesus declare that Hell is a very real place. "The wicked shall be turned into hell, and all the nation that forget God" (Ps. 9:17 NKJV). Jesus in His earthly ministry spoke more about Hell than He did any other subject, including Heaven. Jesus describes Hell more vividly than He does Heaven. Of 162 references to Hell in the New Testament, 70 are spoken from Jesus Himself. There is no denying that Jesus believed in the reality of a place called Hell, and therefore He went about, (setting the example for us a fishers of men), warning people about the horrible place.

When people try to deny the doctrine of Hell, there are three basic approaches. First, there is the Rationalism approach which says, "There is no God, therefore there can be no Hell." But the Bible says, "let God be true and every man a liar." (Rom. 3:4 NKJV). Second, there is the Ridicule approach which says, "There may be a God, but it is silly to speculate about millions of disembodied spirits frying in lake of fire somewhere." Or "This is the twenty-first century, wake up!" Third, there is the Religion approach which says, "There is a God, but He is a God of love and therefore He would not and could not send anyone to Hell." Man may try to use religion as a soapbox to preach that Hell is a myth, but let me quote Romans 3:4 (NKJV) again, "Let God be true and every man a liar!"

We may not all like to think about Hell, however, Hell is a literal place and a reality. And for this reason, God sent His Son to redeem back the people He so dearly loved. This redemptive program of God was motivated by the desire to save people from a destiny in Hell and to save them to an eternal relationship, an eternal fellowship, and an eternal life with God in Heaven. So, if the teaching of the Bible concerning Hell are a myth, then we have no real need for churches, for Holy Bibles, for preachers, worship, prayer, giving, tithes, discipleship, evangelism, deacons, elders, etc. If there is no Hell, then there is no Heaven, there is no Savior, because there is no Hell. Therefore, that would mean that Jesus lied to us and He has disqualified Himself. The truth of the matter is God the Father, Jesus the Son, and the Holy Spirit is real; Heaven is real; Hell is real; and the Satan and his angels are real.

In Luke 16:19-31 (NKJV), Jesus shares a story, this is not a parable this story that actually happened! The rich man spoken of in this passage is still in Hell and there will be others that will join him there. But have you ever speculated what you could learn and be motivated by if for five minutes you got to experience Hell? Have you ever examined your heart and been convicted of the calloused, cold-hearted indifference of your heart toward the spiritual warfare of those for whom Christ died? Have you ever examined your heart to see if you have compassion for the lost of this world? I must confess that there have been times in my life that I have been cold, non-caring, times of no compassion towards anyone lost and headed for a place called Hell. I must say that if it were possible for me to experience Hell for only five minutes as a fisher of men it would help me to behave better as a fisher of men, it would help me as a pastor to minister with a compassion like that of Jesus, and it would help me to behave like a follower of Christ. If parents could just have a five-minute experience of Hell, they would be able to see the awful danger to which they were exposing their children by an attitude of total indifference concerning their spiritual and moral well-being. If every church congregation could just have a five-minute experience of Hell, it would motivate each church to go out and proclaim the Gospel message to a lost and dying world. It would motivate each mature fisher of men to disciple the babes in Christ to behave as fishers of men. So, let's look at what we could learn about Hell.

Hell is a Real Place

The translators of the King James Version translated two different Greek words (*hades* and *Gehenna*) with one English word, "hell". *Hades* usually refers to the "grave" or the "place of the dead." (Strong's Concordance 1984). There is only one place in the New Testament that "*hades*" is translated as referring to a place of torment for the wicked found in Jesus' story of the Rich man and Lazarus (Luke. 16:23 NKJV). The Greek word *Gehenna* refers to "eternal flames", therefore "hell" as most people think about it is *Gehenna* not *hades* (Strong's Concordance 1984). The Greek word *Gehenna* is used in number of New Testament text to designate the fiery place for punishment of sinners and is often translated "hell" or "the fires of hell (Matt. 5:22, 29-30; 10:28; 18:9; 23:15; Mark 9:43, 45,47; James 3:6 NKJV). It is also connected with the final judgment and suggest that the punishment is eternal. Hell is not a myth or a bad dream or the creation of fantastic fiction writer. It is a real place, where real people will go to spend eternity experiencing real torture.

Many see this Luke 16:19-31 (NKJV) as merely another "parable" from Jesus. Remember that a parable is an earthly story that has a heavenly meaning. The word parable means "to lay alongside of"; in other words what Jesus would do when He told a parable He would share a lesson in story form using something in physical or material world and then He would lay it alongside of a spiritual truth. This is not what Jesus is doing when He shares this true story. Because Jesus never called anyone by name in a parable. Here, He calls "Lazarus" by name. Hell is real and there are no philosophical debates raging within the heart of the rich man concerning the existence of Hell. He is thoroughly convinced that Hell is an absolutely reality.

Furthermore, the rich man now understands that Hell is not an annihilation. You see, Hell does not spell the end of man's existence as many groups teach neither does man burn up like a broom sage field. Hell is a real place where the soul of a lost person goes on living in torment forever when they die in unbelief. Don't let the world try to tell you that a loving God won't send people to Hell. Because a loving God will allow men to send themselves to Hell. The rich man has no doubts that God will allow man to follow his unbelief all the way into Hell. The world will try and quote to you John 3:16 (NKJV) to prove that a loving God will not send people to Hell, and what they fail to read, quote, and memorize is John 3:18 (NKJV) which says, "He who believes in Him is not condemned; but he who does not believe is condemned already, because he has not believed in the name of the only begotten Son of God." God does not make the choice for a person to go to Hell; a lost person does when they reject God's amazing grace. When a person chooses to live their life without Jesus in their hearts, then they are headed to a place called Hell, and a loving God will send a lost sinner there because of their choice not to receive the free gift.

Hell is a Place of Uninterrupted Consciousness

According to Luke 16:23 (NKJV), in Hell sinners can see. Luke speaking about the rich man said, "And being in torments in Hades, he lifted up his eyes and saw…" The rich man looks at his surrounding through the scalding tears in his eyes and see "Abraham afar off, and Lazarus in his bosom." This passage is clear, this is a real man in a real place, experiencing real torment. As fishers of men, we need to make this clear, that if a person dies with their faith in Jesus or if they die lost, they will not spend one second in the grave. But you will at the very instant of death go to either Heaven to be with the Lord Jesus (2 Cor. 5:8 NKJV) or will go immediately into Hell if they die lost (Luke 16:22-23 NKJV). Never believe for an instant that death is the end, or that man is no different than a dog, which dies and is no more. Man was given an immortal soul and that soul will live on forever whether in Heaven or in Hell.

Luke then tells us that in Hell sinners can feel pain and get thirsty, "Then he cried and said, "Father Abraham, have mercy on me, and send Lazarus that he may dip the tip of his finger in water and cool my tongue; for I am tormented in this flame."" (Luke16:24 NKJV). This verse illustrates for us the pain and suffering that exist in Hell. John says, "He himself shall also drink of the wine of the wrath of God, which is poured out full strength into the cup of His indignation. He shall be tormented with fire and brimstone in the presence of the holy angels and in the presence of the Lamb. And the smoke of their torment ascends forever and ever; and they have no rest day or night, who worship the beast and his image, and whoever receives the mark of his name." (Rev. 14:10-11 NKJV). You see, Hell is not a state of mind. It is a real place, where real souls suffer real torment.

Of all the agonies of Hell, perhaps the worst one of all is depicted by the word "remember" (Luke 16:25 NKJV). This word tells us that men in Hell have the capacity to remember the events of this life and that they are forced to deal with those memories eternally. They will remember every sermon they heard and rejected. They will remember when the Lord convicted their hearts, and they turned a deaf ear to the pleas of the Holy Spirit. They will remember how God manifested Himself in thousands of ways to draw them unto Himself. They will remember and they will know that they have no one to blame for their situation but themselves! This rich man remembers every witness who ever came to his gate. He remembers Lazarus lying there. He remembers turning a deaf ear to the plain needs of Lazarus. He remembers the opportunities he wasted in life. He remembers that he could have been saved. He remembers that he could have lived for the Lord. He remembers in glaring detail the chances he had, and he realizes that they are now gone forever.

Sinners in Hell can also hear, get frustrated and angry. Matthew writes, "and will cast them into the furnace of fire. There will be wailing and gnashing of teeth." (Matt. 13:42 NKJV). The rich man hears Abraham say to Him that no one can cross the great gulf fixed between Heaven and Hell, so he responds to Abraham by ask him to send someone to his father's house (Luke 16:25-27 NKJV). This means that the rich man was hearing all that wailing and the seeing the gnashing of teeth. Hearing the screams of millions of parched throats; hearing his fellow sufferers moan, curse, and scream and he becomes frustrated and angry. This means that this real place called Hell is a place of punishment. "Then He will also say to those on the left hand, "Depart from Me, you cursed, into the everlasting fire prepared for the devil and his angels."" (Matt. 25:41 NKJV).

In Hell there is a fire that never goes out, "If your hand causes you to sin, cut it off. It is better for you to enter into life maimed, rather than having two hands, to go to hell, into the fire that shall never be quenched; where 'their worms does not die, and the fire is not quenched.'" (Mark 9:43-44 NKJV). Hell is a place of wrath. In the Old Testament, the prophet Habakkuk cried out for the Lord to remember mercy during a time when His wrath was being poured out (Hab. 3:2 NKJV). This has always been God's way! When He destroyed the earth with water in Genesis 6-8 (NKJV), He extended grace to Noah and his family. He remembered mercy and even placed a rainbow in the clouds to declare His mercy. Even after the world rejected Him, He sent His

Son Jesus to die for the sinners any way! That's grace! That's mercy! The Lamb of God died in your place and my place and for every lost soul that would ever live on the cross at Calvary! And as He died, He demonstrated in perfection the love of God for sinners (Rom. 5:6-8 NKJV).

Hell is a place of eternal separation from God. Luke says, "And besides all this, between us and you there is a great gulf fixed, so that those who want to pass for here to you cannot, nor can those from there pass to us" (Luke 16:26 NKJV). Notice that the rich man found himself separated from Lazarus and Abraham by a great gulf, The Bible says that this gulf is "fixed". That is, it will never be taken away. This separation is eternal! This rich man found himself separated from everything that Lazarus enjoyed. No doubt, one of the greatest torments of Hell will be the eternal separation from all the joys and wonderful thing that life itself has to offer. For instance, there will never be a sunrise or sunset in Hell. The laughter of a child will not be heard in Hell. There won't be a blowing of a gentle summer breeze, nor the fragrance or beauty of flowers. There will be no one to tell you they love you. Hell will be devoid of the good things of life. No family, no friends, no fellowship, nothing but endless isolation and eternal separation.

In Hell, the Lost sinners will never hear another Gospel message, another Gospel song, nor will anyone ever witness to them again. They will never be handed a Gospel tract. There will be no churches in Hell. None of the things that point the lost to Jesus will make their appearance in that place called Hell. But, of all the things the sinner will not see in Hell, the worst will be eternal separation from the presence of God. "In flaming fire taking vengeance on those who do not know God, and on those who do not obey the Gospel of our Lord Jesus Christ. These shall be punished with everlasting destruction from the presence of the Lord and from the glory of His power." (2 Thess. 1:8-9 NKJV). Imagine being in a place where there was no mercy, no grace, no love, or presence of God. Nothing but an endless Hell and an endless separation from the One who loved you more than any other.

Hell is a Place of Unanswered Concerns

Now that the rich man is in this place called Hell, NOW he is concerned about life after death. He may not have ever given eternity a single thought while he was alive, after all he was living in a mansion and enjoying his wealth. But now, his is very conscious and concerned about the fact of life after death. And what every fisher of men and lost person needs to understand is the fact that you may be alive today but one day you will die. After you die, your soul continues to live forever in either Heaven or Hell. Hebrews 9:28 (NKJV) says, "and as it is appointed for men to die once, but after this the judgement." Therefore, it is important for us to behave as fishers of men, because today is the day of salvation for those who live in darkness and are headed for a place called Hell.

Here is this rich man and now he is concerned about life after death and NOW he is concerned about repentance. This man lived like he wanted to live, done what he wanted to; now that he is dead, now he has a change of attitude. Listen, after a person dies it is too late for one to repent of their sins. People today may not even think about repenting of their sin little lone deal with their sin at all, but there is coming a day when it will be too late to get right with God. It will also be too late for a person to accept Jesus as their personal Lord and Savior.

So now, that the rich man has seen what Hell is like, NOW he is concerned about others. He says, "I beg you therefore, father, that you would send him to my father's house, for I have five brothers, that he may testify to them, lest they also come to this place of torment" (Luke 16:27-28 NKJV). While he was alive, we don't know what kind of relationship this man had with his five brothers. He might have loved them, and he might have shared his wealth with them. But you can be certain that he never gave a moment's thought to where they would spend eternity. Now, he is in Hell and knows that they are just like him. He knows that where he is, his brothers will soon be. Now, he is concerned for his brothers and wants God to send Lazarus, from the grave, to them and tell them about happens after a person dies. "Abraham said to him, 'They have Moses and the prophets; let them hear from them'" (Luke 16:29 NKJV). My dear brothers and sisters in Christ, we must behave as fishers of men and reach the lost and dying sinner while there is still time! Let us open our mouths and share Jesus with every opportunity that God places in front of us. Let's go and make followers of Jesus Christ by sharing the Gospel Message telling them about a Savior who loves them, died for them, rose from the grave to save them, and gives them eternal life if they will trust Him by faith.

Hell should awaken the Church

Let me just say to us as fishers of men, "The church, the bride of Christ, is not a social club!" The church is not just some place you can say that you belong to, it is not something you add to your resume as an organization that you belong to. As a pastor I do not just get up and preach Sunday morning, Sunday night, Wednesday night, or anytime I have the opportunity to preach because I enjoy it, nor do I desire to be an entertaining preacher. I preach because I was called by God to preach the Gospel of our Lord Jesus Christ to those who will listen. I am to be concerned about the welfare of the congregation as well as the destination of those who do not know Jesus Christ as their personal Lord and Savior. I am to help open the eyes of the church who sometimes turns a blind eye to the lost sinner. These days in which we live in has been called perilous times and it is high time the church awakens to the sin that has engulf our church, city, county, state, nation, and earth. If we could spend five minutes in Hell, I believe it would awake the church!

The church is not just a service organization. We don't come to church just so we can develop programs like feed the homeless, food pantries, women on missions, men's prayer breakfast, youth gathering, or children's movie night. We are not just to plan one event after another or host potluck dinners. The church today has become so comfortable with just going through the motions of these programs, these events, and these dinners that we have lost the focus as to why we do programs, events, and dinners. If Jesus Christ is not at the center of these things, and the goal being to bring in lost souls with these programs, events, and dinners then the church has fallen asleep, or become complacent to the needs of lost sinners. The church is comfortable with and satisfied with those who come to church that they are not willing to go out and bring anyone else in. The church is God's fisherman harbor charged with making disciples (fishers of men) and sending out the fishers of men to persuade people to forsake their lives of unbelief and rebellion against God and trust Him for their soul's salvation (Matt. 22:9; 28:18-20 NKJV).

Hell would cause Personal Spiritual Growth

Our prayer life as fishers of men would take on a new meaning if we were able to spend five minutes in Hell. It would cause us to realize that prayer brought us into vital contact with the eternal God. Plus, through prayer God would be able to work His work within us to make us more effective in our witnessing as we go out and share the Gospel message. James 5:16 (NKJV) says, "The effective, fervent prayer of a righteous man avails much." It helps to pray and talk to God daily. If we would use this secret weapon before we go out to fish for men just think how much more, we would be affective. If after spending those five minutes in Hell, just think how much earnest we would be weeping at the altar for God to save souls. Prayer is the avenue that God uses to open doors of opportunity for us to share the Gospel message.

Not only would our prayer life affected by the sights of that brief experience, but we would also become more diligent students of the divine Word of God. "Study to shew thyself approved unto God, a workman that needeth not to be ashamed, rightly dividing the word of truth." (2 Tim. 2:15 KJV). The more we study God's Word the more effective we can be at meeting the needs of those we seek to share the Gospel message with. James writes this principle this way, "and one of you say to them, "Depart in peace, be warmed, and filled," but you do not give them the things which are needed for the body what does it profit?" (Jam. 2:16 NKJV). You see, in the same way if you don't provide those items of clothing or food to help someone who needs it for their body it profits them nothing. How much more do we need to strengthen our lives in wisdom and knowledge of God's Word so that we can go to work fulfilling the great commission. James continued saying, "Thus also faith by itself, if it does not have works, is dead." (Jam. 2:17 NKJV). Since we are living in a day and age where not many people know that much about the Bible, how are you going to use God's word to point someone to Christ if you, yourself does not know anything about the Bible?

Hell would Enable us to Learn Why People go to Hell

If we could spend those five minutes in Hell, we would indeed see some valuable truths and be motivated to share the Gospel. We would even understand or at least know why people go to Hell. Think about this: the question is not "Why would a loving God send anyone to hell?" The question is "Why would anyone choose Hell over a loving God?" In all honesty God does not desire for people to go to Hell. "The Lord is not slack concerning His promises, as some count slackness, but is longsuffering toward us, not willing that any should perish but that all should come to repentance." (2 Pet. 3:9 NKJV). The reason God waits is to allow lost men and women ample time to repent and turn to Him. It is not God's design or desire that anyone should die lost and go to Hell. He desires to see all men saved, so that they can spend eternity with Him in Heaven. Therefore, He waits, and He loves, and He calls, and He gives mankind opportunity after opportunity to get right with Him. However, one day, God's patience will be exhausted, and He will return to this earth. Then, it will be too late to repent, but there will be nothing more to look forward to but an eternity in Hell. Please understand that people do not go to hell because of the desire of God.

Another reason, people do not God to hell because they have sinned so greatly that God is unable to save them. Remember, salvation is simple "Believe on the Lord Jesus Christ, and you will be saved" (Acts

16:30 NKJV). "For I am not ashamed of the gospel of Christ, for it is the power of God to salvation for everyone who believes." (Rom. 1:16 NKJV). People will tell you that there is something in their life that they have done, and they don't think God will save them. Others will tell you they have to get some things straighten out before they can be saved. No! No! Just remind them that all they need to do is believe. God will forgive their past and He will help them straighten out their life. But unless they ask Jesus into their hearts and get saved, they will go to Hell for their sin.

People go to Hell because they refuse to repent. Notice how Jesus closes His story. "And he said, 'No, Father Abraham; but if one goes to them from the dead, they will repent.' But he said to him, 'If they do not hear Moses and the prophets, neither will they be persuaded though one rise from the dead.'" (Luke 16:30-31 NKJV). Jesus had already said, "but unless you repent you will all likewise perish." (Luke 13:3 NKJV) No more chances! While the rich man lived, he had the same opportunities that Lazarus had. They both had the testimony of the Law of God (John 5:39; Gal. 3:24 NKJV). They both had the revelation of God in creation (Ps. 19:1-4 NKJV). They both had light (John 1:9 NKJV) and they both had a choice to make. Lazarus chose to repent and put his faith in God, while the rich man refused to repent, embrace his unbelief, and place his trust in riches, power, and self. Because the rich man chose sin over the Savior, he is in Hell and he is in a place where God will never call him again.

People go to Hell because they live a selfish life of sin. Three times the writer of the Book of Judges makes the statement "there was no king in Israel," (Judg. 17:6; 18:1; 19:1 NKJV), and for a second time the writer shares that "everyone did what was right in his own eyes." (Judg. 17:6; 21:25 NKJV). The reason that Israel does not have a king today is because they chose Barabbas over Jesus (Luke 23:13-25 NKJV). And because there is no king in Israel people are living a selfish life of sin in rebellion against God and doing whatever pleases them. Regardless of the consequences, "for the wages of sin is death" (Rom. 6:23 NKJV), these rebellious selfish people will continue in their sin until the King comes back and sets up His kingdom.

Praise God that His children, we the fishers of men, do not live in the Book of Judges like the world today is living. We live in the Book of Ruth! The story of Ruth took place during the time of the judges (Ruth 1:1 NKJV). It is more than just a love story about a man seeking a bride, it is also redemptive and harvest story about a wealthy man willing to pay the debt to purchase his beloved bride and make her his own, which represent Jesus bringing in the sheaves. Through faith in Jesus Christ, all of God's people share in His love. We belong wholly to Him because He redeemed us by His precious blood that He shed for us on the cross of Calvary. As fishers of men, we labor together to bring in the harvest, because we have a wonderful life in a world that is torn apart by sin and selfishness! As fishers of men, we should take great joy in the privilege to share the greatest gift given to men! The question is which book are you living in: The Book of Judges or the Book of Ruth?

People go to Hell because often as fishers of men we neglect to "go", "share", and "make". We need to tell others of God's great love for the world (John 3:16 NKJV). You see, as we behave as fishers of men by being obedient to the Lord's commands (Matt. 28:18-20 NKJV), we become the means whereby people hear the Word, come under conviction, and seek forgiveness for their sin. For a fisher of men to neglect to share the Gospel, means that we are misbehaving and acting as the world around us in a selfish life of sin. If you are okay, as a fisher of men, letting people go to hell, then your relationship with God is out of whack. When you are at odds with God then you will be at odds with people. If you are neglecting people, then you are neglecting God. But just how hard hearted does your heart have to be for you to be okay with people going to Hell? To me it is too terrible to even fathom the idea of people going to Hell and spending an eternity in such a wretched place. That why I say if every Christian could go to Hell for five minutes and just see what Hell is like. God does not want anyone to go to Hell. He has given His Son Jesus Christ to prevent people from going to Hell. God has done all withing His power to save people. Every fisher of men should behave and cooperate with the Holy Spirit in Jesus' completed work of salvation by share the grace of God and keeping people from a hopeless eternity.

CHAPTER FIFTEEN

Fishermen and Hunters

"Behold, I will send for many fishermen," says the Lord, "and
they shall fish them; and afterward, I will send for many hunters,
and they shall hunt them from every mountain and every hill,
and out of the holes of the rocks." (Jeremiah 16:16 NKJV).

As a fisher of men, you would do well if you would learn
what the Bible teaches about prophecy. Just as a pastor, preacher, or
teacher would benefit in their ministry to proclaim prophecy; a fisher
of men would reap the benefit of motivation to share the Gospel of
our Lord and Savior Jesus Christ to a people who has no ruler. "Why
do You make men like fish of the sea, like creeping thing that have no
ruler over them?" (Hab. 1:14 NKJV). Jeremiah's message of prophecy
is written to the people of Israel (Jer. 16:1-21 NKJV). It was delivered
in a time when the people knew the terms of His covenant and the
extent of their own sins, however, they had been led astray by false
prophets and they had become comfortable in their own sins. It was
as if their conscience was seared with a hot iron and the thought of
the consequences did not bother them. You see, Israel had a false
hope of assurance that God would never leave them or even allow
the Gentiles to desecrate the Holy City and the temple. How wrong
were they!

Jeremiah's explanation of his message of prophecy was quite simple: they failed to learn from the mistakes of the past and breaking the law of God. Plus, they did not heed the lessons taught by past judgments that God sent. Which made them even more guilty than their forefathers. At this point God had already allowed the Assyrians to come in and take the northern kingdom captive because of the sin of idolatry. Not to mention God had sent in prophet after prophet to warn them of their sins and they did not listen. So, Jeremiah uses several images to describe the captivity that was going to take place. One of those images is that of the fisherman and the hunter (Jer. 16:16 NKJV). What would eventually fulfill the prophecy is that the Babylonians would cast their nets and catch the Jews (Ezek. 12:13 NKJV), and not one "fish" would escape. If anybody tried to run and hide in the hills, the fishermen would become hunters and track them down. The reason for this prophecy of judgment is because the people of Israel had owed a great debt to the Lord for the way they treated His law and His land. Now it was time to pay the debt. "I will repay double for their iniquity and their sin, because they have defiled My land; they have filled My inheritance with the carcasses of their detestable and abominable idols." (Jer. 16:18 NKJV).

However, God is a God of mercy and He gives Jeremiah a message of hope to give to the people of Israel. He tells the people that one day they will return to their land, and so great will be this restoration that it will be looked upon as the "second exodus". Plus, they would be an established nation with a rebuilt temple that would never again turn to the idols of the Gentile nations. Then at the end of Jeremiah's message of prophecy, he has a great moment of faith and prophetic joy, for Jeremiah not only saw the gathering of the Jewish nation but the gathering of Gentile nations from all over the world. They would come to the Holy City just to worship the true and living God of Israel. Isaiah had this same vision (Isa. 2:1-5; 11:10-16; 45:14 NKJV), and so did Zechariah (Zech. 8:20-23 NKJV). In that day, the Gentile nation will confess their sin of idolatry and admit that the idols were worthless. Then they will be taught to know the Lord. Meanwhile it is the task of the church and every fisher of men to spread the Gospel Message to the ends of the earth.

Even though Jeremiah's prophecy has been partially fulfilled. There is one verse that is interesting to look at, seeing how it fits the theme of this book, that is Jeremiah 16:16 (NKJV). I can see and support that this prophecy was literally fulfilled as the Babylonians put the people of Israel in captivity. However, let me point out that there are three symbolism interpretations that we can draw from this one verse. Especially, when you look at it from the divine purpose for Israel that God has revealed to us in Genesis 18:18; 22:18; 26:4 (NKJV). Israel is to be light unto the world, they are to be fishers of men bring people to Jehovah God. And through them God would bless the nations by sending His Son, Jesus (John 3:16 NKJV).

Before we look at the symbolism let me give you the difference between fishermen and hunters. Let me be clear, I am talking about the spiritual lessons using the physical characteristics of the sports to show the message. Plus, I am not promoting fishermen over hunters, because I am a fisherman, and my wife is a deer hunter. Here are some of the differences that I want you to see: first fishermen they cast their nets while hunters drag their nets. Casting is the art of throwing your bait or net forcefully in one specific direction. It also means to cast light (or shadow) on something. Therefore, fishers of men are to cast light upon the darkness in the hearts of men in one direction, pointing them to the Lord Jesus Christ. To drag a net like a hunter means to pull away, haul way. It gives us the idea that the hunter comes to pull the scales away from the blind eyes of the sinner and expose them to the truth. In the Parable of the Dragnet (Matt. 13:47-52 NKJV), Jesus gives us the illustration what the kingdom of Heaven is like. The dragnet is a net that is drawn through the water or on the ground to trap the prey, with nowhere to hide. The second difference is fishermen go to one location the water, while hunters will go everywhere using whatever method, they can use to find their prey. They are, in a since, to "go out into the highways and hedges and compel them to come in, that my house may be filled" (Luke 14:23 NKJV).

Looking at Jeremiah 16:16 (NKJV), the first thing I see is that the fishermen are symbolic of the prophets that God sent to warn the people of the impending judgment. The hunters are the Babylonians who spread their nets out like snares or drag nets to gather the people of Israel. The second symbolism, I see the fishermen as Jesus calling the disciples and promising to make them fishers of men, who cast their nets out and begin building up the church, who are to go out to share the Gospel of Jesus Christ, telling them about sin, death, the need for a Savior, and about the Second Coming of Christ. The hunters I see as the death for the wages of sin is death (Rom. 6:23 NKJV) and no one can hide from death (Heb. 9:27 NKJV). The third symbolism, I see the fishermen as the 144,000 Jewish preachers who go during the tribulation proclaiming (casting) the Gospel message. The hunters I see as terrible judgment that will be poured out during the Tribulation, with all the plagues, death insects, viruses, poison water, fervent heat, and fallings stars. This will be a time when no one can run and hide from so like hunters these judgments fall on those who do not know Jesus Christ as their personal Lord and Savior in the tribulation. I show you all this to encourage you to learn about the prophecy of the Second Coming of Jesus and see the importance and urgency of sharing the Gospel in the days that we live.

There are some people who think that we should not study prophecy. They believe that prophecy is unrelated to reality and everyday life. They think that studying about the Second Coming of Jesus Christ, Heaven, the Antichrist, and the mark of the beast is just unnecessary. Let me remind you that 25% of the Bible is given to prophecy and if 25% of the Bible is prophecy then did the Holy Spirit make a mistake when we have the prophecy of God's word? Of course not! There is incredible, wonderful blessings in the study of prophecy. So, what is the benefit that we gain from prophecy and why should we learn it? Revelation 1:3 (NKJV) says, "Blessed is he who reads and those who hear the words of this prophecy and keep those things which are written in it; for the time is near." As fishers of men, we are to read prophecy, we are to heed prophecy, and then we are to proclaim prophecy to a lost and dying world. Just think you can turn prophecy into praise. You can praise God in an incredible way when you learn about prophecy because without prophecy, nothing makes sense. You can turn prophecy in to prayer. Prophecy, once you learn it, leads to intercede on behalf of those who are lost in sin. You can turn prophecy into proclamation. Why? Because it is our duty.

Let me tell you what prophecy is about and then we will discuss our duty to proclaim prophecy. Real prophecy is the testimony of Jesus. Prophecy is not looking for something to happen; it is looking for someone to come. The testimony of Jesus is the Spirit of prophecy. Let me ask you: Do you believe Bible prophecy? If you do believe in Bible prophecy, then the fruit of believing is that everywhere you go you are behaving as fishers of men sharing the Gospel of our Lord and Savior Jesus Christ. If you aren't studying prophecy, then what are you doing to warn sinners about the wrath to come? The apostles knew, thru prophecy that Great Tribulation was coming. If they knew that the Rapture of the church is coming, then after that the Great Tribulation would occur, the Antichrist would come on the scene, there would be a mark of the beast, and there would Hell on earth; then how much more should we learn about prophecy.

Before Jesus went to the cross to die for our sins; He painted a clear picture of what the world would look like as the end of time approached (Matt. 24-25 NKJV). He laid out a clear blueprint for the end of the age and told us that we could know that the end was near when certain characteristics began to be seen in the world (Matt. 24:1-8 NKJV). While these verses have a primary interpretation to events that will take place in the Tribulation Period; we will see these things beginning to take place, even before Jesus comes for His people in the Rapture. That's why it is important that we behave as fishers of men and proclaim the prophecy of the Second Coming of Jesus Christ. In Romans 13:11-14 (NKJV), Paul tells everyone who claims to have a personal relationship with Jesus Christ that you have a duty before God to proclaim this prophecy. Paul gives us another perspective to our marching orders called the Great Commission as we learn about our Christian duty.

You Have a Duty to Wake Up

Paul writes, "And do this, knowing the time, that now it is high time to awake out of sleep; for now, our salvation is nearer than when we first believed." (Rom. 13:11 NKJV). When you first wake up in the morning, possibly the first thing you do is open your eyes and then look at the clock to see the time. What Paul is saying in this this verse is that we need to first open our eyes and look at the signs of the time around us. This whole verse has to do with the return of the Lord Jesus Christ for His people. The idea here is that the believer is to keep his eye on the changing world around him and understand that the coming of the Lord is near. Sadly, many believers cruise lazily through life no even considering that fact that Jesus might return at any moment. Yet, all one must do is cross-reference the daily news with the Word of God to see that the His coming is at hand. Therefore, the advice Jesus gave concerning the Second Coming is still good advice today. Jesus said, "Watch therefore, for you do not know what hour your Lord is coming." (Matt. 24:42 NKJV). That is what Paul is implying as he tells us that our salvation is nearer than when we first believed. Every day we are one step closer to glory and we need to wake up and recognize the time by behaving as fishers of men in anticipation of His return.

Paul as tells us that we are redeemed because the time for slumber has long since passed. Therefore, Paul uses strong words, such as: "high time", meaning that it is time to wake up! Too many children of God are sleeping on the job. Living their lives as they please without any thought for the will of God, the plight of the lost or the return of the Lord Jesus Christ! We need to wake up and be sensitive to the needs of lost sinners around us as well as our fellow fishers of men! Now is not the time to be drowsy and unaware of what is going on. Now is a time for the church to be alert and active. Paul tells this same thing to the Ephesians, Paul says, "Redeeming the time, because the days are evil." (Eph. 5:16 NKJV). He encouraged the Colossian church this way, "Walk in wisdom toward those who are outside, redeeming the time" (Col. 4:5 NKJV). Now it is time to become active in the business of the Lord. His Holy Word reminds us that there should be a sense of urgency to the work of a fisher men in serving God. Every day people are dying without the Lord and going to Hell. Every day the forces of evil are growing stronger and working harder in the world. There is a tremendous need for fishers of men everywhere to wake up from there slumber to recognize the seriousness and the lateness of the hour and get busy serving the Lord with all their might! If you are planning to tell your neighbors about Jesus, the time is now! If you are going to tell your family about Jesus the time is now. If you are going to go to work for the Lord, the time is now! We have a duty to wake up!

You Have a Duty to Dress Up

Paul says, "The night is far spent, the day is at hand. Therefore, let us cast off the works of darkness, and let us put on the armor of light." (Rom. 13:12 NKJV). Paul's vivid imagery is that of a man waking up in the morning and throwing off all the garments associated with the night. He throws off the bedclothes. He removes his night wear and gets dressed for the day. Far too many believers are still walking around dressed in the clothing of darkness! What I mean by that is that their behavior and attitude resemble that of the lost person around them. When we were saved, we become "new creatures" (2 Cor. 5:17 NKJV), and at that time we are forever changed by the power of God, and therefore we are to be different from what we used to be; different from the world around us. When Lazarus came out of that tomb, having been raised from the dead, what was it that Jesus said? He said, "Loose him, and let him go!" (John 11:44 NKJV). Why? Because he was a living man, and a living man had no use for grave clothes! As redeemed children of the Lord, why would we want to wear the grave clothes of sin? Why resemble or still look like the world today? Why would you want to resemble the dead? Why would you want to still talk like the dead? Why would you want to participate in the activities of the dead men around you? The answer is simple, as a fisher of men you shouldn't, but we do! May God help us to throw off the garments of the night, because we don't want to be wearing dirty garments when Jesus comes back. Therefore, that is why Paul reminds us again that the "night is far spent", meaning that the time for slumber has passed! A new day has dawned in our hearts and we are called to walk in the day!

Just as we are commanded to "cast off" the garments of darkness, we are also commanded to "put on the armor of light" (Rom. 13:12

NKJV). This also speaks of a once for all putting on! Just as a person does not get dressed in the morning only to immediately get ready for bed again, the believer is to make a permanent break with the works of darkness and to dress up in the things of the Lord to behave as a follower of Christ and a fishing for men! Paul uses the word "armor" which it is possible that he is speaking to a new babe in Christ. This imagery gives us the idea of a believer forever laying aside the ways of the old life and dressing up once for all in the ways of the new life by putting on the whole of armor of God. God's idea for the Christian life is to be one of total commitment and dedication. While most Christians see the Christian life as one of compromises. They honor God over here while doing as they please over there. This is poor behavior for the follower of Christ, little lone it's not a very good witnessing behaver of a fisher of men.

So, what does this have to do with knowing prophecy. Well, if you continue to dress up in the garments of darkness your witness speaks as if you really don't believe that Jesus is coming back. And all you are doing is wasting time (the night is far spent), and you are accomplishing nothing for the kingdom of God. If you are not dressed up in the armor of light it means that you are prepared and you are looking for the return of Christ. It means that you genuinely believe by faith in Jesus. It means that you are motivated, compassionate, prayerful, and desiring that all men come to repentance. It means that you are sold out to Jesus, totally and absolutely committed to Him.

You Have a Duty to Line Up

Paul continues to say, "Let us walk properly, as in the day, not in revelry and drunkenness, not in lewdness and lust, not in strife and envy" (Rom. 13:13 NKJV). The phrase "walk honestly" which means to "behave properly" (*Dictionary* 1828) reminds us that as fishers of men we are to live an outward life that is consistent with who we say we are on the inside. There should be no pretense in our lives. If we say we are saved, we should live as though we are saved. We are to be sure that our practice matches our profession of faith. With the new birth comes the desire to live a life that is pleasing to the Lord. A life that is honest. A life that is a living sacrifice to His glory in the world (Rom. 12:1-2 NKJV).

Then after telling how we should live; Paul turns his attention to how we should not live by mentioning six sins of the flesh that were no doubt prevalent in Paul's day. These same sins can be seen in Paul's letter to Timothy when Paul warns him about perilous times. He writes, "But know this, that in the last days perilous times will come" (2 Tim. 3:1 NKJV). Then he lists the sins that will be even more prevalent as we get closer to the time of Christ's return. And if you know prophecy you can see in our world today that these sins are increasing at an alarming rate. Therefore, we as children of God should not be walking in these sins but should be behaving like a fisher of men.

Let's look at these six sins that Paul lists for us in Romans. Rioting refers to wild parties, sexual orgies, brawling, etc. Drunkenness refers to habitual and intentional intoxication, which can speak of alcohol or drug abuse. Note: The New Testament usually speaks of drunkenness and rioting together as one intensifies the other (Rom. 13:13; Gal. 5:21; 1 Pet. 4:3). Lewdness (NKJV) or chambering (KJV) refers to sexual activities that are engaged in outside of the marriage relationship of one man and one woman. The word "lust" is tied to "lewdness" and it refers to unbridled, uninhibited sexual desire and activity. It speaks against the casual attitude society hold concerning sex, where every form of sexual expression is indulged in and encouraged. Strife refers to a mindset that seeks its own way first and foremost without regard for the cost to others. It speaks of those people who are constantly bickering; engaged in competitive antagonism, and petty disagreements. It speaks of people who are plain mean. Always looking for a fight, walking around with a chip on their shoulder. Envy refers to a spirit of jealousy and an attitude of me first and everyone second. Listen if any of these sins are in the life of a fisher of men then there is only one remedy; it's called confession and repentance (1 John 1:9 NKJV).

The Days of Noah

If we are going to know about prophecy, then let's ask the question: "Is the days of Noah here again?" If we take the time to look seriously at the way the world was during the days of Noah before the flood, and the way it is now before the return of Christ, we will see some clear parallels between our world and theirs (Gen. 4-6 NKJV). By observing the characteristics that prevailed in Noah's day, we can determine whether the days of Noah are here again. If they are, then we need to be ready, for our "redemption draws near" (Luke 21:28 NKJV). Let's look at the evidence and observe the characteristics that prevail in those days so that we can know about prophecy in our day.

The first characteristic that we can see is that those days were characterized by perversion. In Genesis 4:1-15 (NKJV) there was a religion without a blood sacrifice. Cain's offering to God was that of fruit of the ground. His offering was not respected by God. Why? Because Cain ignored the plain mandate ordained by God Himself. In Genesis 3:21 (NKJV) it is plain to see that an animal was sacrificed to atone for the sin of Adam and Eve to make the tunic of skin which God used to cloth them. This same mentality abounds in our world today, people have "a form of godliness but deny its power" (2 Tim. 3:5 NKJV). Therefore, because people today want to be godly without having to accept Jesus, we are living in days of widespread apostasy. Listen to what Paul tells Timothy in both letters. "Now the Spirit expressly says that in latter times some will depart from the faith, giving heed to deceiving spirits and doctrines of demons, speaking lies in hypocrisy, having their own conscience seared with a hot iron, forbidding to marry and commanding to abstain from foods which God create to be received with thanksgiving by those who believe and know the truth." (1 Tim. 4:1-3 NKJV). In 2 Timothy 4:3-4 (NKJV) he says, "For the time will come when they will not endure sound doctrine, but according to their own desires, because they have itching ears, they will heap up for themselves teachers; and they will turn their ears away from the truth and be turned aside to fables." Sadly, this is the idea that is prevailing in churches today and people swallow up this social, psychological so-called gospel hook, line, and sinker.

Those days were characterized by prosperity. In Genesis 4:20 (NKJV) we see a man by the name of Jabal. He was the first person to practice the domestication of animals. What that means is that men no longer had to hunt and scrounge for their food, they merely raised it. This allowed people to have more than they needed. It was a time of material prosperity and Jabal cornered the market. Now despite the economic trouble that we have seen in 2020-2021, the U.S. is still enjoying prosperity. Everyone is still spending money and these days are marked by people having more than enough.

Those days were characterized by pleasure. Genesis 4:21 (NKJV) tells us about the brother to Jabal whose name was Jubal. He invented musical instruments and was the father of the entertainment industry. There is no denying the fact that we are living in a pleasure mad world. Americans spent billions on movies, sports, music, and hobbies. Now days you can have all that on your phones. There are all kinds of apps for almost any kind of entertainment you want because we love to be entertained. When I was growing up our entertainment consisted of matchbox cars that you could get for a quarter. We did not spend time inside on a beautiful day. We went out with a ball and a glove, played soccer, or just going outside in the evening and catching the lightening bugs. Today, kids have the Xbox 360, PlayStation 4, along with social media platforms: tiktok, snapchat, Facebook, and Twitter. We are a pleasure mad society!

Those days were characterized by progress. A man named Tubal-Cain discovered and learned how to extract metal from ore and invented the smelting business (Gen. 4:22 NKJV). This allowed men to produce stronger farm implements and stronger weapons. Genesis 4:17 (NKJV) talks about the rise of cites. The days preceding the flood were marked by scientific and engineering advancements. The ark for example in Genesis 6:14-16 (NKJV), even though the plans were handed down by God, the boat was built by man. That kind of achievement required a tremendous amount of technological knowhow. Some people believe that the people who existed before the flood were ever more advanced than we are today. There are many inventions and advancements that could be mentioned that clearly reveal how we are progressing in the scientific and engineering fields, as well as in every arena of human life. Advancements in the medical field, alone, are almost beyond belief. If you look at those days, you might be led to believe that humanity was doing quite well. They were prosperous. They were developing a complex culture, complete with great cities, art, and the ability to sustain life. They were advancing in the fields of agriculture, metal, music, and science. Yet, for all their achievements, they did not know God. Sound familiar? Our society is advancing at an amazing rate; but mankind has chosen a path that leads him ever further away from God.

Those days were characterized by polygamy. Lamech is the first man to marry two wives (Gen. 4:23 NKJV). He is the first man who took clear steps to undermine the home and the family. God had set the standard for the home and family in Genesis 2:18-25 (NKJV). Lamech perverted this commandment because in those days it was a time marked by lust and lewdness with blatant disregard for God's will. Sadly, Lamech would not be the last! In Genesis 6:1-4 (NKJV), we are told that there was an intermingling of the godly line of Seth with the cursed, reprobate line of Cain. This produced a generation of men called "giants" and "men of renown." Basically, what you have here is a generation of demon-possessed men who dominated that society for their own pleasure and profit. In our day we know that marriage as it is defined today in the Bible as one man and one woman is under attack. The traditional family is being challenged by homosexuality and lesbianism, and the acceptance of these lifestyles is becoming the order of the day.

Those days were characterized by pride. According to Genesis 4:24 (NKJV), Lamech declares his value to be far greater than that of his ancestor Cain. He sets himself up as the be all and the end all of life. He is the first real humanist. He sees himself as number one and believes that all his actions are right. His name even means "powerful", and he lived as if all power resided within him. If you look at the names of Cain's offspring in Genesis 4:17-18 (NKJV), you will notice that some of the names include the suffix *"El."* This is a name for God, basically referring to Him as the God of creation, or to God in a general sense. Then you come to the name "Mehujel." This name literally means "blot out that Jah is God." In other words, they paid God lip service for a while; but the day came when they want God out of their lives. They wanted to live as though He did not exist. We are living in days just like that now. When I hear liberal politicians, homosexuals, and other people using the name of God in vain, I realize that the days of Noah are here. They want to pay Him lip service; but they do not want Him involved in their affairs, or affairs of the world at all. If there was ever a day when men "did what was right in his own eyes" (Judg. 21:25 NKJV), it is the day in which we live. Men have no regard for the Word of God. They do not fear the Lord, but live as they want to live without a thought of a Heaven to gain or a Hell to shun. That is why it is important that we know prophecy and about the return of Jesus Christ.

Finally, those days were characterized by pollution. There are three types of pollutions that characterized those days. The first pollution is that of social pollution, this is clearly seen in Genesis 6:5-6, 11-12 (NKJV). In those verse we see the exposed moral and social climate of that day. It was a time when men did as they pleased without thought for the welfare or property of others. Murder and crime were rampant in that society. Of course, when men throw off God and His restraining influence; they will degenerate into the depths of depravity and wickedness. That is where we are in our world today and things will continue to get worse the closer, we get to the end of time! We raised a generation to believe that there is no God, no Heaven, and no Hell. Therefore, we are seeing them live without any standards of right or wrong, believing that man is the product of random chance and evolution and he can do as he pleases.

The second pollution is sexual pollution. In the days of Noah, it was a time of unequal yokes in marriage (Gen. 6:1-4 NKJV), and tolerance of evil and wicked lifestyles (Gen. 4:19-24 NKJV). In fact, the bloodline of humanity had become so tainted and polluted, that only Noah was considered pure in his generation (Gen. 6:9 NKJV). Chastity and morality have gone out the window. Sex is no longer reserved for the marriage relationship as God intended. Now, sex is for the classroom and the locker room. Virginity is no longer seen as a precious gift to be cherished and preserved for one's life mate; it is seen as a commodity to be traded for affection, acceptance, and pleasure. Just looking at our society it is easy to see that we are a people obsessed with sex! Consider the rise of teachers having sex with students, the rise of child molesters, and the rise of pornography available on the internet and in our society. Things that are done in back rooms and talked about in whispers are now displayed openly for all to see. Traditional values and morality are under increasing attacks in these days. Homosexuality and Lesbianism are not merely tolerated; they are promoted as "alternative lifestyles" and woe to the person who dares to speak out against it! There is no doubt that we are living in perilous times and they are getting worse by the hour!

The third pollution is spiritual pollution. Genesis 6:12 (NKJV) tells us that "God looked upon the earth, and indeed it was corrupt; for all flesh had corrupted their way on the earth." Men had turned from the worship of the true and living God to embrace the world. They worshiped Satan and his lies while they shunned the truth of the Lord. The same is true in our day. People are caught up in the supernatural, psychics, and angels. If you were to look at bookstores online or in person you will find an increase number of books on witchcraft, astrology, spiritism, psychic phenomenon, demonic religion, and Satanism. Man is a religious being and he will worship something. When God is removed from a culture, He will be replaced with satanic counterfeits. It has always been that way and it always will be (Rom. 1:18-28 NKJV). The Cainites set the moral and spiritual temperature at that age. They controlled public opinion and they decided what was in and what was out. The Sethites, on the other hand, seemed to have very little voice in that society. It is much the same way today. The world, for the most part has turned its back on God, set the moral and spiritual tone for our society. They pay lip service to the Lord and deny Him the love, devotion, and worship He deserves.

Have the days of Noah arrived again? Can you see the signs of the times? I get the feeling that if we were to get into a time machine and travel back to Noah's day, we might just see the similarities between that day and our day. Now don't think that prophecy is a negative tool that a fishers of men have. Oh no! Even in the dark days of Noah, God still had His man and God was still working in a big way. He was still moving in grace to redeem the lost in that day just as He is in these perilous times. God was still working to bring things to a conclusion that would honor Him, just as He is in this day. Jesus said, "And when these things begin to come to pass, then look up, and lift up your heads; for your redemption draws near." (Luke 21:28 NKJV). This is referring to those who would be living during the Tribulation. He is telling those people that He is coming again, and when He does, He will make things as they ought to be. He will straighten out the messes in this world and make it right again. Let me just remind you that before He comes in power and glory to establish His kingdom here on earth; He will first come in the clouds and call His bride to meet Him there. If the world is ripe for judgment, then it is just about time for the Rapture. Since that is true then "the night is far spent, the day is at hand. Therefore, cast off the works of darkness, and let us put on the armor of light" (Rom. 13:12 NKJV).

While we are waiting in this world for the Lord to return, we should be careful that we behave as fishers of men. We are to adopt His character as our character. We are to adopt His lifestyle as our lifestyle. He is Truth, we are to walk in truth. He is Light, we are to walk in the light. He is faithful, we are to be faithful. He is holy, we are to be holy. He loves the Father; we are to love the Father. He walked in total obedience to God, we are to walk in total obedience to God (1 John 2:6 NKJV). Therefore, until He comes, let us determine that will live Christ-like in front of a hell-bound world and behave as fisher of men in light of knowing the prophecy of His coming.

CHAPTER SIXTEEN

When Jesus Comes Again

Let not your heart be troubled; you believe in God, believe also in Me. In My Father's house are many mansions; if it were not so, I would have told you. I go to prepare a place for you. And if I go to prepare a place for you, I will come again and receive you to Myself; that where I am, there you may be also. (John 14:1-3 NKJV)

NO AMOUNT OF EFFORT CAN STOP THE CLOCK OF HISTORY. NO MORTAL, no matter how influential, wealthy, or well-known can break the tyranny of time. Every day that passes, every flash of a digital crystal, brings us closer to the dramatic events predicted in the Bible. As stated in the previous chapter knowing prophecy can prove vital to sharing the Gospel of Jesus Christ. It can motivate you to reach out the lost and dying world, and/or it can humble you to know what you have been saved from: "the wrath to come." (1 Thess. 1:10 NKJV). We can prepare for the unavoidable, we can behave as fishers of men by seeing the urgency of the coming of Christ, however, we cannot stop Him from coming. Not for a moment and that is an unsettling thought. The prophetic passages of the Bible are filled with frightening scenes and complicated symbols; however, we can still know and understand the basics when it comes to the return of Christ.

Here are some indications that Rapture may be near than we think. First, there is the formation of the State of Israel in 1948 (Luke 21:29 NKJV). The fig tree (Israel) is shooting forth and is beginning to put forth its leaves (Luke 21:29-31 NKJV). For the first time in centuries, the Jews have a national existence in their own homeland. This means that the kingdom of God is near. Next, we can see the rise of many other nations (Luke 21:29 NKJV). Jesus predicted that not only the fig tree would shoot forth but all the trees as well. Since 1948, we have seen the rise and fall of many nations. Another indication is that Israel would return to the land in unbelief (Ezek. 36:24-25 NKJV). Ezekiel prophesied that it would only be after their return that they would be cleansed from their sins. Israel today is largely an agnostic nation meaning that there are many Jewish people who is still looking for a Messiah. Then we can see in later days that there will be a drastic decline of moral standards (2 Tim. 3:1-5 NKJV). The news media and social media offer plenty of evidence of this. Not to mention that there has been an increase in violence and civil disobedience (2 Thess. 2:7-8 NKJV). A spirit of lawlessness is abounding in homes, cities, states, nations, in politics and even in some cases the church. There is this sense of that people have a form of godliness but deny its power (2 Tim. 3:5 NKJV). Here in these perilous times, there is a rise of the anti-Christian spirit (1 John 2:18 NKJV), manifested in the multiplication s of false cults which profess to be Christian but deny every fundamental doctrine of the faith. They deceive others by imitation (2 Tim. 3:8 NKJV).

To these could be added other indications such as earthquakes in many countries, the treat of worldwide famine, the treat of out breaks of life threating pandemics, and the increase of hostility among nations (Matt. 24:6-7 NKJV). The failure of governments to maintain law and order and to suppress terrorism creates a climate for a one-world dictator. The building of nuclear arsenals gives added meaning to such questions as, "Who is able to make war with him [the beast]?" (Rev. 13:4 NKJV). Worldwide television facilities may be the means for fulfilling Scripture describing events that will be seen simultaneously all over the planet (Rev. 1:7 NKJV).

Return of the King

Most of these events are foreseen as occurring before Christ returns to the earth to reign. The Bible does not say they will take place before the Rapture but before His appearing in glory. How much can we know about the end times? Well, not everything, certainly; however, the Bible does give us enough information that we can be ready. Take the promise found in John 14:2-3 (NKJV), because Jesus can be trusted, we know that He will keep His promise to return for His own. He promised His fishers of men: "I go to prepare a place for you. And if I go and prepare a place for you, I will come again and receive you to Myself; that where I am, there you may be also" (John 14:2-3 NKJV). So, have you ever wondered what all the return of Christ involves? Let take a moment and discuss three general overviews as to what will take place.

What will Happen?

In 1 Thessalonians 4:16 (NKJV) it says, "For the Lord Himself will descend from heaven with a shout, with the voice of an archangel, and with the trumpet of God." At a predetermined time, the Son of God will leave the Father's side and descend toward earth. As He does, three mighty sounds will echo across the halls of heaven and sweep over the earth: a shout, the voice of an archangel, and a blast from the trumpet of God.

When these sounds are heard, all believers since the time of Christ will be resurrected. Their bodies will be transformed and reunited with their soul as they meet Jesus Christ in the air. Then every living Christian will be removed from earth, given new bodies, and caught up to join Jesus and the resurrected believers for a great and glorious meeting in the air. Christ will take then to be with Himself, and they will always be with the Lord.

Paul had this same idea as he wrote to the Corinthians. In 1 Corinthians 15:51-52 (NKJV), he wrote, "Behold, I tell you a mystery: We shall not all sleep, but we shall all be changed; in a moment, in the twinkling of an eye, at the last trumpet. For the trumpet will sound and the dead will be raised incorruptible, and we shall be changed." Let's think about these verses briefly.

First, this event will be sudden. The word "moment" comes from the same word that gives us the word "atom" (*Dictionary* 1828). It refers to "something that is indivisible". It speaks of the smallest amount of time imaginable. The word "twinkling" was used to refer to "the flap of a wing; the buzz of a gnat; or the twinkling of a star" (*Dictionary* 1828). Scientist have estimated that a blink of the eyes takes place in $1/30^{th}$ of a second. A twinkle on the eye takes place in $1/10,000^{th}$ of a second. In other words, when Jesus comes, He is coming suddenly! He will come for His people and He will come unannounced. His people will be here one moment and the next they will be gone! It makes no difference whether they are dead in the grave or alive on the earth; all of God's saved people, will be taken away suddenly! That is why Jesus said, "Therefore, you also be ready, for the Son of Man is coming at an hour you do not expect" (Matt. 24:44 NKJV).

Second, the event will be selective. Notice the words "we" and "all" in 1 Corinthians 15:51-52 (NKJV). To whom do they refer? The answer is back in verse 50. Paul is speaking to the "brethren". When Jesus comes, He is not coming for everyone. He is only coming for those who have placed their faith in Jesus Christ for their soul's salvation. Only those who are saved will go. Not those who have been baptized; not those who have joined the church; not those who have prayed a prayer; not those who have been good neighbors; Jesus is coming for those who have been "born again" (John 3:3, 7 NKJV). He is coming for those who have "called upon the name of the Lord will be saved" (Rom. 10:13 NKJV).

Third, the event will be a sad event. Those who are left behind in the Rapture will not even realize what has happened. They will remain in their lost condition and eventually go to Hell without Jesus. If you are left, you will enter what is called the Great Tribulation. You will experience Hell on earth and then you will die and go to Hell for all eternity. What is sad about this event is the fact that it did not have to end that way. We need to behave as fishers of men and tell them Jesus is the only way to go to heaven and escape the wrath to come.

When will it take Place?

Let me clear as I can: "I don't know!" To be truthful neither does anyone else know when this event will take place. Even Jesus did not know when that day will come. In Mark 13:32 (NKJV) Jesus said, "But of that day and hour no one knows, not even the angels in heaven, nor the Son, but only the Father." Let me explain that Jesus is both God and Man. He had all the attributes of God and all the characteristics of a perfect man. There was never a time when He was not fully God. So, how then can it be said of Him that He does not know the time of His Second Advent? Go and compare this verse with John 15:15 (NKJV) where Jesus said, "...for a servant does not know what his master is doing..." As a Perfect Servant, Jesus wasn't given the privilege of knowing the time of His Coming (John 12:50; 17:8 NKJV). However, Jesus as God the Father, He does know it. But as a Servant, it was not given to Him to know it for the purpose of revealing to others.

That is why Jesus instead taught His disciples that as fishers of men maintain an attitude and condition of readiness (Matt. 24:44 NKJV). Jesus encourages them to behave as a watchman by teaching them two similar parables recorded in Luke 12. In the first parable (Luke 12:35-40 NKJV), He compared His coming to the return of the master of the house from a wedding. In the second (Luke 12:42-48 NKJV), He compared His coming as a man has left his household affairs in the hands of a servant. The key element in both parables is that the day of the master's return could not be known by the servant. But those servants were to maintain constant readiness. The same is true for a fisher of men we are to behave with an attitude of constant readiness as we wait Christ's return. It could occur at any moment.

What will Heaven be Like?

As a fisher of men how often do you think about your eternal future? What kind of effect does Heaven have on the way you behave as a fisher of men, right here and right now? You see, the thought of a better place for the saints of God to live after their time on earth has cheered and motivated the hearts of God's people for thousands of years. Abraham who lived some 3,500 years ago longed to go to Heaven when he died (Heb. 11:8-10 NKJV). To him it was worth leaving his home and family; it was worth becoming a stranger and a pilgrim; it was worth all the hardships and pain of following God. Simon Peter caught a little insight into the inheritance that awaits every child of God in Heaven (1 Pet. 1:3-5 NKJV). For Peter it totally changed his life. To him it was worth the hardship that he endured, and Heaven was worth more to him than his own life.

On the Isle of Patmos, John received a clear revelation of what that city looked like, and all the glories it contains. He wrote extensively about Heaven in Revelation 7; and Revelation 21-22 (NKJV). John saw Heaven while being exiled from his home, family, and friends. He endured loneliness, pain, suffering, and the cost of being a fisher of men. To John Heaven surely was worth it all! Paul describes an amazing experience that he had in which he was caught up into "the third heaven" or the very realm of God. Paul was carried away in the celestial city of God and saw things that he was not allowed to repeat (2 Cor. 12:1-10 NKJV). That one vision of Heaven was enough to strengthen Paul as he faced the many trials that came his way (2 Cor. 11:22-32 NKJV). Paul saw that city and lets us know that Heaven is worth all the pain that comes our way. It's worth the hatred and the persecution. It's worth the sorrow and the attacks. Heaven is surely worth it all!

But how do we know what heaven will be like? Paul quotes Isaiah and writes, "Eyes has not seen, nor ear heard, nor have entered into the heart of man the things which God has prepared for those who love Him." (1 Cor. 2:9 NKJV). The thought of Heaven should create excitement in the hearts of fishers of men. With that great and blessed hope fishers of men should behave and go out and tell lost sinners about the Gospel of Jesus Christ! However, as points out, we don't have a whole lot of information about Heaven. Paul does go on to say, "But God has revealed them to us through His Spirit. For the Spirit searches all things, yes the deep things of God." (1 Cor. 2:10 NKJV). The "them" in that verse is talking about the "the deep things of God", which I believe includes Heaven. Therefore, the Bible gives us just enough information to whet our appetites for that wonderful, beautiful, Holy city that Jesus has prepared with His own hands (John 14:2 NKJV).

So, what will heaven be like? Let's consider Jesus' own words found in John 14:1-3 (NKJV) to help us understand more about Heaven because for this along with prophecy of Jesus coming will help us behave as fishers of men.

THE PLACE CALLED HEAVEN

The first thing I want you to notice is that it is a special place. Jesus said, "Let not your heart be troubled; you believe in g God, believe also in Me. In My Father's house are many mansions; if it were not so, I would have told you. I go to prepare a place for you." (John 14:1-2 NKJV). Did you catch that Jesus calls Heaven "My Father's house"? Heaven is special because it is the place where God dwells. A place like that would have to be Holy! It would have to be a place that is filled with the glory of God! A place that is full of peace, blessings, and abundant joy! Heaven would have to be a place that is made out of love. Listen all those qualities about Heaven I just described are all the characteristics of our Heaven Father! And any place that is called the "Father's house", would have to be a place just like Him! Can you imagine, a place like Heaven is enough to make one just want to go there. Paul writes, "For to me, to live is Christ, and to die is gain." (Phil. 1:21 NKJV). To Paul Heaven is a place that gave him great hope of receiving all the promises of God, "the deep things of God" (1 Cor. 2:10 NKJV). But Paul used that hope of a special place "to live" for Christ by telling people about the Gospel of Jesus Christ. He goes on to tell the Philippian church, "But if I live on in the flesh, this will mean fruit from my labor; yet what I shall choose I cannot tell." (Phil. 1:22 NKJV). Yet, he was torn between the two; he writes "For I am hard-pressed between the two, having a desire to depart and be with Christ, which is far better." (Phil. 1:23 NKJV). To Paul it would be much easier to depart from this world and go to Heaven and be with Christ, "nevertheless to remain in the flesh is more needful for you." (Phil. 1:24 NKJV). Christians should behave as fishers of men because we are needed here on earth to make disciples and tell a lost and dying world about Jesus; all the while having Heaven on our mind.

The next thing we notice about Heaven is that it is a splendid place. Jesus said that "in His Father's house are many mansions." (John 14:1 NKJV). The word "mansions" refer to "a dwelling place, an abode, a staying place." (*Dictionary* 1828). In other words, Heaven will be a place of variety and there will be room enough for everyone. It will be huge! That is why we sing "Yes! There is room at the cross for you!" (Stanphill 1991). In the Book of Revelation, John describes Heaven, that future city of the New Jerusalem, as cubical in shape (Rev. 21:15-16 NKJV), however, you must realize that it is a cube of 1,400 miles. Roughly the distance between Maine and Florida on all sides. Now that's a big city is it not?

Take the diameter of the moon it is approximately 2,160 miles and the New Jerusalem will be 2,600 miles in diameter. Think of it; a city shaped like a cubed skyscraper, whose dimensions are as high and as wide as they are long, with a diameter larger than the moon. To put it another way, the New Jerusalem will be around 2,250,000 square miles, or 15,000 times the size of London, England! Now imagine there is a city where there is room for all; where there are no ghettos, no mean streets; no wrong side of town; no poverty, pollution, or political agenda. Imagine a city of absolute beauty and sinless perfection. If you can imagine that, then you can imagine home!

John describes for us the materials that Jesus used to construct that glorious city (Rev. 21:18-21 NKJV). He tells us that the walls are made of diamond and the city is made of pure, transparent gold (Rev. 21:18 NKJV). He says that the city rests on a foundation of precious gemstones. Imagine a city that gleams with the brilliance of God's glory. Imagine that pure light as it shines through the diamond walls, the gold, and all the multi-colored precious stones of that Heavenly city. It will be a glorious sight to behold! What is interesting to me is the fact that the gates of that city are made from pearls (Rev. 21:21 NKJV). If you know anything about pearls, you know that they are made out of suffering and pain. In an oyster, sometimes a grain of sand is trapped inside. Then that grain of sand begins to irritate the oyster, causing the oyster to build up layer upon layer of calcium around that grain of sand. After a long period of time a pearl is formed. Meaning that the pearl is the only gemstone that is made by a living organism. The pearl is the oyster's answer to pain. Those gates will remind us that while salvation and the Heaven salvation provides are free; salvation was not cheap! Everything we have was born out of the pain of our Savior on the cross of Calvary. Every time we enter that city, we will be reminded of the price He paid to redeem our souls. Plus, the pearly gates remind us, that there is but one way to go into Heaven, and that is through the suffering and pain, the shed blood, the death, and resurrection of Jesus Christ on the cross of Calvary. Jesus said, "I am the way the truth, and the life. No one comes to the Father except through Me." (John 14:6 NKJV). Where is the Father? In that splendid place called Heaven.

The last thing we notice that Jesus about Heaven is this, "Let not your heart be troubled" (John 14:1 NKJV). This is just a reminder that Heaven will be a place of peace for the people of God. None of the many afflictions of earth can touch us there. "And God shall wipe away every tear from their eyes; there shall be no more death, nor sorrow, nor crying. There shall be no more pain, for the former things have passed away" (Rev. 21:4 NKJV). No one will die in Heaven. There will not be any heart breaks, no weeping, no pain, and no hurt. No one will have to do any work just to survive in Heaven, because God is our Great Provider. Every saint of God will enjoy the perfection of that city, along with the awesome presence of our Lord and Savior Jesus Christ and our Heavenly Father! All this is enough to make us want to go there and should cause us to behave as fishers of men to want everyone to go as well. But wait there's more!

THE POPULATION OF HEAVEN

Just think that Heaven is going to be personal. Jesus said, "I go to prepare a place for you." (John 14:2 NKJV). Heaven is a place that has us in mind! It is a place prepared by Jesus for us to be with Him forever! We will be changed to suit our new environment, because "that flesh and blood cannot inherit the kingdom of God; nor does corruption inherit incorruption. Behold, I tell you a mystery: We shall not all sleep, but we shall all be changed; in a moment, in the twinkling of an eye, at the last trumpet. For the trumpet will sound, and the dead will be raised incorruptible, and we shall be changed. For this corruptible must put on incorruption, and this mortal must put on immortality." (1 Cor. 15:50-53 NKJV). We will have a new body just like that of Jesus and Heaven will be a place decorated by Jesus for us personally to enjoy.

God created the earth in six day. He fashioned the earth's biosphere with its variety of plants and animals. He balanced our atmosphere with the perfect blend of oxygen, nitrogen, and other gases. He did it all in six days and could have done more in a microsecond if He had chosen to. Therefore, think of what Heaven will be like; a place prepared for us since Jesus made His promise two thousand years ago.

In Heaven we will be with our Savior. Jesus said, "I will come again, and receive you unto Myself; that where I Am there you may be also." (John 14:3 NKJV). The redeemed saints of God will spend eternity with the very Lord Who paid the ultimate price for their redemption when He died on the cross. We will see Him, and we will worship Him in perfect bodies, sing His glories with perfect voices, and shout His praises in perfect holiness in Heaven (Rev. 4-5 NKJV). Not to mention we will be with other saints. Jesus said, "that where I Am there you may be also" (John 14:3 NKJV). The pronoun "you" in that verse is plural. Think of it like this: He is going to prepare a place for each individual saint; and He is coming back to receive each individual saint of God, but when the individual saint gets to Heaven, they will be joined with other believers in the presence of Jesus. In other words, we believers in present day will not be going to Heaven alone! The saints of God from the Old Testament will be there too. The saints of God from the days of Jesus and from New Testament will be there too. The saints of God from the early church up until now will be there! Our redeemed loved ones will be there. Friends, family, and foes who have place their trust in the Lord Jesus Christ will all join us in that land someday. Not a single redeemed saint of God will be missing. Not a seat at the table in glory will be empty!

THE PERSONAL EFFECT OF HEAVEN

It is one thing to think about heaven from time to time; it is quite another thing to actually be affected by it in our life on earth. Obviously, Jesus wanted the thought of future glory to make a difference to us because He makes it the capstone of His prayer. He prayed, "O righteous Father! The world has not known You, but I have known You; and these have known that You sent Me. And I have declared to them Your name, and will declare it, that the love with which You love Me may be in them, and I in them." (John 17:25-26 NKJV). In other words, lost sinners may not know God or care about Heaven. But His followers do know God and should care about heaven. So, what can we do to build up our interest in our future home and motivate us to tell others about the Gospel of Jesus Christ? Let me ask you a few questions:

First, how real is Heaven to you? Most people don't think much about heaven until somebody they know dies and they attend a funeral. Suddenly, the thought of Heaven moves to center stage for a brief period of time. But Jesus talked about Heaven all the time. It was real to Him and He wants Heaven to be real to us. Here are some examples of how to make Haven real to you. First, learn about your future home. Take time to read your Bible daily. Look up Biblical descriptions of Heaven. Pray and ask God, through the Holy Spirit, to teach you more about Heaven. As you learn more begin to place yourself there and meditate at length on the descriptions of Heaven. Second, look at creation and listen to the beauty that God has created. For example, go outside on a clear night and look up. As you look up, think about where you are and what you are seeing. You live on a speck of dust in a galaxy known as the Milky Way. It is one of millions of galaxies, and this vast and complex universe is only temporary. One day, "the heavens will pass away with a great noise, and the elements will melt with fervent heat; both the earth and the works that are in it will be burned up" (2 Pet. 3:10 NKJV) all this will come to pass on the day of the Lord.

Then another question to ask yourself about Heaven is: How does Heaven motivate me? Do you care that some people are not going to be there with Jesus in His glory? Does the certainty of Heaven grip you so tightly that you are motivated to invite as many people as you can? Can you honestly be content to go to heaven alone? Jesus tells us to store up "for yourselves treasures in heaven" (Matt. 6:20 NKJV); that is, to put our temporal resources to work for future purposes. Earthly treasure can be used for God's glory by investing it in Heaven where it will las eternally. The way we spend our time and money indicates the condition of our hearts and the level of our preparedness for Heaven. Jesus asked, "For what profit is it to a man if he gains the whole world and is himself destroyed or lost" (Luke 9:25 NKJV). Ask yourself, "Do I have a saved soul but a wasted life?" You can prepare for Heaven right now by behaving as a fisher of men; using your time, talent, and treasure to help people come to know Christ, grow in Christ, and live for Christ. Paul writes, "Therefore, my beloved brethren, be steadfast, immovable, always abounding in the work of the Lord, knowing that your labor is not in vain in the Lord." (1 Cor. 15:58 NKJV). How do we do that? Teach them, along with the Gospel, about the return of Jesus Christ and Heaven.

Six Behaviors we Should have for the Coming of Jesus

First, we are to preach His coming. Paul tells us that we are to be "looking for the blessed hope and glorious appearing of our great God and Savior Jesus Christ." (Titus 2:13 NKJV). We are to be looking for that glorious appearing of Jesus. He goes on to say, "Speak these things, exhort, and rebuke with all authority. Let no one despise you." (Titus 2:15 NKJV). So, in other words, we are not to ignore this doctrine. A preacher or teacher who never speaks about this is only preaching a half truth. If they never mention the doctrine of the Second Coming of Jesus Christ is not obeying the Scriptures. Now, I don't mean that we should preach on this subject every Sunday, but we shouldn't stop speaking about it all together. Fishers of men should preach and teach all of the great doctrine of our faith, and never exclude this precious doctrine. The Book of Titus was written to a young preacher. The older preacher told him to speak often about the Second Coming. Surely, we, fishers of men, should study this subject and use it effectively in the Kingdom work. But a word of warning: "Don't set dates!" (Matt. 24:36 NKJV).

Second, we are to look for His coming. "So, Christ was offered once to bear the sins of many. To those who eagerly wait for Him He will appear a second time, apart from sin, for salvation." (Heb. 9:28 NKJV). Notice that phrase, "to those who eagerly wait for Him". That phrase implies that we are to be looking for Jesus with anticipation that He could come back at any second all the while doing God's Kingdom work. Do you remember how God thinned out Gideon's army in Judges 7 (NKJV)? God told Gideon to bring his ten thousand men down to the water to drink. Those who bent over and lapped up the water like a dog were to be left behind. Those who got down on their knees were also to be left behind. But the three hundred, who lapped up the water with their hands, while still looking toward the enemy, were chose. Even so, we are to be busy for Christ, while keeping our eyes open for His return.

Third, we are to pray for His coming. Jesus taught that when we pray, we should ask God for: "Your kingdom come. Your will be done on earth as it is in heaven." (Matt. 6:10 NKJV). What did Jesus mean by this? We should be praying "Come back Lord Jesus. Come back and establish Your kingdom. We cannot straighten things out here on earth. We need You to do it!" This is probably why you see the last prayer in the Bible refer to the coming of our Lord and Savior Jesus Christ. In Revelation 22:20 (NKJV), John was on the Isle of Patmos and Jesus says to John "Surely I Am coming quickly" (Rev. 22:20 NKJV). That is when John cries out "Amen. Even so, come, Lord Jesus!" (Rev. 22:20 NKJV). On any given Saturday in the fall, great crowds will gather in a football stadium. Soon the home team is almost on the goal line. The cheerleaders cry through the megaphone, "Go, go, go." Then the big bass drums begin to beat and the band chants, "Go, go, go." Then the student body and all the fans cry out, "Go, go, go." They are all anxious for a touchdown. But wouldn't it be wonderful if we, fishers of men, got excited about our worship and the return of Jesus? Then we could pray along with John: "Come down Jesus, come, come! Come down Jesus, come, come! Come down Jesus, come, come! Come and take us up to be with you! Come and reign as King of kings and Lord of lords!"

Fourth, we are to love His appearing. "Finally, there is laid up for me the crown of righteousness, which the Lord, the righteous Judge, will give to me on that Day, and not me only but also to all who have loved His appearing." (2 Tim. 4:8 NKJV). What Paul is saying is that he is getting a crown of righteousness, and you can have one, too, if you love His appearing. Some people don't love His appearing. They don't want Jesus to come back and break up their little world. Because He might keep them from shining in the social world like they hope to do someday. He might prevent them from getting some office of power they have set their hearts on. He might keep them from doing some things they were planning on doing. There is an old saying, "Well, bless their little pea picking hearts!" Don't you know if Jesus came and took you to heaven, it would be a million times better than all these things could ever be? Oh, how we need to behave as fishers of men and give up our sinful and worldly practices and get back to the kingdom work of our King! Oh, how I wish that we woold get back to have a dedicated heart serving God and sharing the Gospel. We should have a love that yearns for His coming. As a matter of fact, there are two words in the New Testament for love. One word is *"phileo"* which means love to eat, read, or sleep (*Strong's Concordance* 1984). Then the other word is *"agape"* this means a deep love, a yearning love, a heart-throb love (Strong's Concordance 1984). This is the word that Paul had in mind when he is talking about the appearing of His second coming.

Fifth, we ought to be comforted by His coming. "Therefore comfort one another with these words." (1 Thess. 4:18 NKJV). As Paul is writing to the Thessalonians, he tells them about the Second Coming of Jesus. He is doing this to comfort several of the Thessalonians who had lost their loved ones, and they wondered what had become of them. So, Paul told them plainly that Jesus was coming. And the dead would be raised first, then living Christians would be caught up in the air, and all would be together with the Lord. That is why he tells them and us that we are to comfort each other with these words. Would you like to be able to comfort someone who had just lost a loved one? Would you like to tell a lost person that they can have comfort in knowing that they will be going to heaven? Then tell them that one day the graves will be opened up, the bodies of your loved ones will be lifted up to meet the Lord in the air and they will be soon united with those whom they have loved. You want to be able to comfort someone who is seriously ill? Then tell them that when Jesus comes, He will take them to a land where there is no pain, no suffering, no deaths, no funerals, and no cemeteries! Oh, how these words should bring comfort to our hearts. One day Jesus is coming to free us from all of this. Until He does, behave as fishers of men by comforting one another with these words.

Then finally, we are to be purified by His coming. John writes, "Beloved, now we are children of God; and it has not yet been revealed what we shall be, but we know that when He is revealed, we shall be as He is. And everyone who has this hope in Him purifies himself, just as He is pure." (1 John 3:2-3 NKJV). What is John saying? He is saying to us as fishers of men, that since we know He is coming then we need to get ready for it by purifying ourselves by getting rid our sins. The reason so many Christians are living unworthy lives is because they do not remember that He is coming again. They go to cocktail parties and drink like those who do not know Jesus as their personal Lord and Savior. They read obscene magazines more than they read their Bibles. They watch lewd movies and surf pornographic websites more than they pray. They go to worldly clubs more than they go to their church. They make sure that their club fees are paid up and leave their church tithing unpaid. They spend time and energy on worldly organizations instead of using that time to serve Christ and sharing the Gospel. They do all these things because they have forgotten that one day Jesus is coming again and disapproves of the way that they are living.

Do you even shudder as you think of Jesus standing before you while you do the things you do on a daily basis? Listen; if God told us that He was going to come tomorrow at noon we would be busy doing His kingdom work and purifying our lives, right? We would throw all those things that doesn't matter and take a tighter grip upon the things of God. However, we don't know the day nor the hour that Jesus is coming back, therefore, we need to behave as fishers of men as though He is coming back at any second. Are you ready? Are you behaving? Maybe as a child of God you need to pray; "Dear God, there is something in my life that I am ashamed of. There is something that keeps me from behaving as a fisher of men. I have sinned, and worldlines and indifference towards others are guiding my behavior. But right now, Lord Jesus, I want to rededicate my life to You. From now on, count on me. I want to be ready when Jesus comes."

Again, if you are reading this book and you do not know Jesus Christ as your personal Lord and Savior, then you are not ready for His coming. Jesus says, "Therefore you also be ready, for the Son of Man is coming at an hour you do not expect" (Luke 12:40 NKJV). After the rapture of the church takes place, you will be left behind living in the Tribulation. And it quite probable that you won't have any chance to be saved. It is most definite that you will not have a second chance to be saved after the Second Coming. So, I plead with you come to Christ now by asking Jesus into your heart and ask Him to save you.

A little boy and his father got into an elevator in the Empire State Building and began their upward journey. As they kept going past each floor the boy got nervous. Finally, he grabbed his father's hand and blurted out, "Daddy, does God know we're coming?" The truth is God does know we are coming; He knows exactly when we'll arrive. The question is, are you ready of eternity when Jesus comes again?

CHAPTER SEVENTEEN

The Kingdom of God

Then He said, "To what shall we liken the Kingdom of God? Or with what parable shall we picture it?" (Mark 4:30 NKJV)

So, as Peter and the other disciples stood there on the shore of Galilee contemplating what they were going to do; surely all these teachings from Jesus and more came rushing together in their minds. If they gave it a little more thought, they probably could have connected the dots. Another area that should have motivated Peter and these six other disciples to go and behave as fishers of men was all those parables about the Kingdom of God. But what is the Kingdom of God? God's Kingdom has absolutely no boundaries. It's not a television season which, when it comes to an end, must resort to showing tired reruns as a way of maintaining our interest. It is not like a Saturday afternoon football game that keeps us on the edge of our seats through four exciting quarter only to suddenly come to an end, leaving us descending the bleachers with our empty popcorn boxes and hot dog wrappers, disappointed that there isn't any more.

No! The Kingdom of God is big and broad and beyond our wildest imaginations. Its fullness can never be attained. Its resources are never depleted. Its season is never over. You never get the feeling you have seen all this before. Unlike Solomon's research of everything that was under the sun, according to the Book of Ecclesiastes, the Kingdom of Heaven will not be vanity. Even while admitting that the Kingdom of God is indeed vast and unsearchable, God in His grace and wisdom has somehow made the Kingdom of God/Heaven simple for us. To be honest, the Kingdom of God can be adequately understood just by realizing that He is our King, and we are His people, that He is our Master and we are His servants, and that He sets the rules and we simply obey. Isn't that how God started out with nation of Israel (Gen. 17:6-8; Ex. 6:7 NKJV)? However, while this is simple in theory, it just isn't easy in practice; just ask the Old Testament people of the nation of Israel.

Knowing what truly ignites the heart of God is something that fishers of men desperately need to understand, yet we have a hard time defining it. We don't always know it when we see it. We don't always live by it when we do. And we don't recognize it when we are missing it. Therefore, we are brought to our knees, where we must always be, if we every truly want to understand the kingdom and its implications in our lives as fishers of men. The Kingdom of God has been God's plan and purpose for all eternity, and He has painted its colors from one corner of the Scriptures to the other; sometimes in muted shades; sometime in bold visible designs. Therefore, it is imperative that we open and read our Bibles and let God speak to us through the pages of His story, through the lives of His people, and through the love of His Son.

The Kingdom of God has always been central to our relationship with God, for it has always been His way of relating to us. His purpose has always been to raise up a people who would embrace His mission, embody His name, and obey His Word. Fishers of men are to behave as that people, for we are connected across time with God's people of every age, creed, and color. We are to be united with Him and with fellow fishers of men in Him living out His eternal message. So, again what is the Kingdom of God? The word "kingdom" comes from a Greek word which means "royal power, kingship, dominion or to rule or to reign". Let's look at several aspects of the Kingdom of Heaven.

The Prophecy of the Kingdom

It is clear when you read the Bible that God often promises that there will be a future kingdom of righteousness upon this earth. Over in Matthew 6:10 (NKJV), when Jesus is teaching us to pray, He tells us to pray "Thy kingdom come." (Matt. 6:10 NKJV) When we pray this, we are asking for our Heavenly Father to bring His kingdom to pass on the Earth. Essentially what we are asking God is to fulfill all His promises and prophecies concerning His earthly kingdom. There are several verses in the Bible that speak on this. "For unto us a Child is born, unto us a Son is given; and the government will be upon His shoulder. And His name will be called Wonderful, Counselor, Mighty God, Everlasting Father, Prince of Peace. Of the increase of His government and peace there will be no end, upon the throne of David and over His kingdom, to order it and establish it with judgment and justice from that time forward, even forever. The zeal of the Lord of host will perform this." (Isa. 9:6-7 NKJV). "And in the day of these kings the God of heaven will set up a kingdom which shall never be destroyed; and the kingdom shall not be left to other people; it shall break in pieces and consume all these kingdoms, and it shall stand forever." (Dan. 2:44 NKJV). "He shall be great and will be called the Son of the Highest; and the Lord God will give Him the throne of His father David. And He will reign over the house of Jacob forever, and of His kingdom there will be no end." (Luke 1:32-33 NKJV). "When the Son of Man comes in His glory, and all the holy angels with Him, then He will sit on the throne of His glory." (Matt. 25:31 NKJV). It is a fact that Jesus was born on this earth; that He lived here and died here, therefore, there will come a day when He will indeed reign and rule here in power, glory, and righteousness!

This future kingdom will be vastly different from any kingdom that has ever existed upon this Earth. All earthly kingdoms are tainted by the effects of sin. There is evil at their core. In fact, this world resides under the dominion of Satan right now (2 Cor. 4:4 NKJV). Right now, all creation groans to be free from its bondage (Rom. 8:22 NKJV). Now, all the world lies under the grip of sin. But there is a day coming when Jesus Himself will rule this world. This is the clear statement of the Bible: "Then the seventh angel sounded: and there were loud voices in heaven, saying, "the kingdoms of this world have become the kingdoms of our Lord and of His Christ, and He shall reign forever and ever!"" (Rev. 11:15 NKJV).

As of right now, Satan is the god of this world, blinding men to the truth of the Gospel. In that day, he will be cast into a bottomless pit, bound in chains and will be unable to hinder or tempt anyone (Rev. 20:1-3 NKJV). Today, Israel lives in blindness regarding their Messiah; one day they will bow down to Jesus and worship Him as God. Today, creation groans to be delivered from bondage; one day all the earth will be restored to what it was before sin tainted the world with its staining touch. Today, the church, the bride of Christ, exists in weakness and humiliation, tares and wheat grow up together; she is being defeated by enemies from without and from within; one day the church will be glorified, forever delivered from sin, and perfected in His image. What a day that will be! Jesus, and Jesus alone, can do these things and one day He will! He will bind the devil, restore all creation, glorify His bride, and claim dominion over all the Earth. That is the essence of His coming kingdom!

The Past of the Kingdom

In Matthew 3:2 (NKJV) we have the first occurrence of the phrase "kingdom of heaven", which is used 32 times only in Matthew's gospel. But let us define and describe the kingdom of Heaven/God. The kingdom is the sphere in which God's rule is acknowledged. The word heaven is used to refer to God. Daniel points this out for us in Daniel 4:25 (NKJV) where he says, "...the Most High rules in the kingdom of men and gives it to whomever He chooses." Then in the next verse Daniel says that "Heaven rules." (Dan. 4:26 NKJV). Wherever people submit to the rule of God, there the kingdom of heaven exists. Therefore, when we apply all these references to the kingdom of God in the Bible, we can begin to trace its historical development in five distinct phases.

PROPHESIED

We have already talked a lot about this phase but let me add that Daniel predicted that God would set up a kingdom that would never be destroyed nor yield its sovereignty to another people (Dan. 2:44 NKJV). Daniel foresaw the coming of Christ to exert His universal and everlasting dominion. However, I must point out that by the time Jesus arrives on the scene the eschatological hope of the kingdom took on a great variety of forms in the Jewish belief. The Jews, at the time of Jesus' ministry, were looking for the Messiah to come and restore David's kingdom and to renew the world. They could not see nor could they understand what Daniel saw about Jesus.

BEGINNING

John the Baptist was the first to preach the arrival of the kingdom of God (Matt. 3.2 NKJV), for the kingdom of God was present in the Person of the King. John preached a message of judgment and repentance, while Jesus preached that the kingdom included elements of judgment and repentance, all while pointing to the "gospel of the kingdom" (Matt. 4:23 NKJV) for that was the purpose He had been sent (Luke 4:43 NKJV). Now, when you begin to study how Jesus taught about the kingdom you notice that Jesus does not define the kingdom, He only describes it through parables. In Mark 4:30-32 (NKJV) we have Jesus' description of the kingdom using a mustard seed which is a powerful illustration. Jesus said that the kingdom was "like a mustard seed which when it is sown on the ground, is smaller than all the seeds on earth." (Mark 4:31 NKJV). While the mustard seed is not the smallest seed known to man, it was the smallest seed planted in the gardens of Jesus' day. The mustard seed itself is very tiny. It takes about 750 of them to make up a single gram. There are 28 grams in an ounce; thus, there are some 21,000 mustard seeds in an ounce. It may be a tiny seed, but it produces a large plant.

Remember that while Jesus is teaching about the kingdom of Heaven through the mustard seed, there were people who believed that nothing would become of the Lord Jesus and His ministry. The people could see the tiny seed, but they could not see the great tree. Consider some of the facts about the beginning of the kingdom of God: Jesus was born in the tiny town of Bethlehem in horrible poverty. Which by the way is another fulfillment of prophecy of the coming of the kingdom! Micah writes, "But you, Bethlehem Ephrathah, though you are little among the thousands of Judah, yet out of you shall come forth to Me the One to be Ruler in Israel, whose goings forth are from old, from everlasting." (Mic. 5:2 NKJV). Jesus was reared in Galilee, and no one believed that a man of God could come from there (John 7:52 NKJV). He was raised in Nazareth where the citizens were considered wicked and worldly by the Jews. He had no family connections, no money, no support from the religious leaders of that day. They considered Jesus to be nobody from nowhere, who would amount to nothing! Even His ancestry was question in John 7:41-42 (NKJV) by His enemies. Then there is His followers, who for the most part were the dregs of society. His own people rejected Him. He was despised and rejected by men. The Romans eventually nailed Him to a cross and buried Him a tomb. His followers preached His resurrection, but most people ignored their message and considered them fools for following a dead man. Even the Lord's message was hard to swallow. For some it still is!

Jesus in His ministry was teaching His disciples to be fishers of men. And some of what He taught them was that in order to get you must give away what you have. He told them to love their enemies. He counseled them to turn the other cheek. There is no question that the Kingdom of God was just like that tiny, insignificant mustard seed in the beginning. For no one could see what that tiny seed Jesus was sowing would become! There are still many in our day that mock Jesus and make fun of His claim to be God in the flesh and the only savior of men. There are many who believe that Jesus never rose again from the dead. There are many who deny that He ever existed. That is why it is important that the fishers of men continue to plant that Gospel seed!

BUILDING UP

"But when it is sown, it grows up and becomes greater than all herbs, and shoots out large branches" (Mark 4:32a NKJV). After Jesus was rejected by the nation of Israel, the King returned to heaven, leaving the kingdom in the hands of the fishers of men. While the King is absent, He has sent His Holy Spirit to live in the hearts of all those who acknowledge His Kingship. And to think, we, the fishers of men, have been given a great responsibility to continue the work of the Kingdom of Heaven. Therefore, we must behave as a fisher of men and do the work with urgency! To bring the King honor and glory!

When the tine mustard seed is planted in good soil, it germinates and produces a large shrub-like plant that eventually grows to resemble a tree. Some mustard plants have been known to grow as high as fifteen feet tall. Something so small, with such a humble beginning, can become something that is utterly amazing to behold. In the beginning there was just Jesus and a few ragtag followers. His followers consisted of some uneducated fishermen, a few revolutionaries, some women, and a traitor. By the time the Day of Pentecost came around, there were still just one hundred twenty devoted fishers of men (Acts 1:15 NKJV). On that day something amazing took place! Over three thousand people came to faith in Christ Jesus (Acts 2:42 NKJV). A short time later another five thousand were saved at one time (Acts 4:4 NKJV). The church began to grow at an astounding rate. It was not many days until the church in Jerusalem is said to have numbered fifty thousand believers. That was just the beginning of the kingdom and it was building up and up! As the Gospel seed was carried around the world, vast multitudes began to come to Jesus. Cities and nations fell on their knees in the face of the message of the Gospel of grace. All this growth was because the early believers were behaving as fishers of men, going out and bringing in; discipling and sending out more fishers of men. And this amazing building up, the growth of the kingdom has continued throughout history up to today! Who but God knows the true count of the souls that have been saved and the lives that have been changed by the Gospel! We need to behave as fishers of men because we need to continue the kingdom work. Just think that there will come a day when a vast multitude that cannot be counted will stand before the Lord in Heaven and praise Him for saving them by His grace (Rev. 7:9 NKJV).

God has a way of bringing great things out of humble beginnings. Look at David. He was a mustard seed. He was the youngest son in a family of eight boys. He was ignored and given the job no one else in the family wanted, taking care of the sheep. Yet, God took this mustard seed and made a giant-killing king out of his life.

Consider Gideon! He was a mustard seed too. He was from the smallest family in the smallest tribe in the nation of Israel. God took Gideon and used him as a great military leader. Now, look at your life. If you are a child of God today, meaning you have placed your faith in the Lord Jesus Christ as your personal Lord and Savior; then you certainly had a mustard seed beginning! According to the Bible, you were a sinner (Rom. 3:10-23 NKJV). You were "dead in trespasses and sin" (Eph. 2:1 NKJV). You were under a death sentence and you were headed to Hell (Rom. 6:23; Eph. 2:3; John 3:18, 36 NKJV). But God, in His grace, looked beyond what you were able to see, and saw what you could become through His grace: a fisher of men. He saved you, planted you in Christ Jesus, and now you are to continue building up (growing) in Christ. You are to behave as follower of Christ and behave as a fisher of men bearing fruit for the kingdom and for the glory of God.

APPEARANCE

The appearance phase of the kingdom is exactly what it implies; "Thy kingdom come". This refers to the thousand-year reign of Christ on earth which is pictured for us by the Transfiguration of Christ when He was seen in the glory of His coming reign. Peter standing there that day by the Sea of Galilee with the six other disciples should have remembered what had transpired on the Mount of Transfiguration. Peter did remember that he was a witness and it was privilege of seeing the glory of the kingdom. Peter said in 2 Peter 1:16-18 (NKJV), "For we did not follow cunningly devised fables when we made known to you the power and coming of our Lord Jesus Christ, bur were eyewitnesses of His majesty. For He received from God the Father honor and glory when such a voice came to Him from the Excellent Glory: "This is My beloved Son, in whom I am well pleased." And we heard this voice which came from heaven when we were with Him on the holy mountain." Peter got a glimpse of the appearing of the kingdom coming just as it was promised to them by Jesus in Matthew 16:28 (NKJV) which says, "Assuredly, I say to you, there are some standing here who shall not taste death till they see the Son of Man coming in His Kingdom." This was an assurance to Peter and the disciples, who at that time could not understand the cross. However, Peter, James, and John were sworn to secrecy until (catch this) the resurrection of Jesus Christ. "Tell the vision to no one until the Son of Man is risen form the dead" (Matt. 17:9 NKJV). Peter knew this and standing on that seashore he should have been about telling others about the coming kingdom.

In Peter's second letter we find that he is now telling people about the coming of Christ, because now he is having to refute the false teachings for the false teachers who are denying the promise of Christ's coming (2 Pet. 3:3 NKJV). Peter summed up the experience he had on that holy mount that day (2 Pet. 1:16-18 NKJV). For he saw Jesus Christ robed in majestic glory and witnessed the demonstration of the power and coming of the Lord Jesus Christ. Plus, Peter heard the Heavenly Father's voice. Peter was a witness to of the kingdom that day and it impacted his life, however, we must remember that sometimes our experiences fade but the Word of God remains. Peter was inspired to write down what he saw and heard so that we might behave as fishers of men by telling what we have seen and heard through the Word of God.

What is unique is the fact that the experience of Peter, James, and John is recorded in Matthew 17:1-9, Mark 9:2-8, and Luke 9:28-36 (NKJV); yet none of those writers participated in it! But let's briefly look at Luke's account of this event.

The climb to the top of Mount Hermon would have taken the better part of the day Luke tells us that Jesus began to pray when they arrived at the top of the mountain. Apparently, this prayer meeting lasted for a while because the disciples feel asleep (Luke 9:32 NKJV). So, the day has probably vanished, and night has fallen. The peaceful mountain is covered with a sky filled with a canopy of stars. Suddenly, Jesus changes! His face changes and garments changes; "As He prayed, the appearance of His face was altered, and His robe became white and glistening" (Luke 9:29 NKJV). Mark uses the word "transfigured" (Mark 9:2 NKJV) which means metamorphosis (*Dictionary* 1828). It is the same word that is used to describe the changes a caterpillar goes through when it is transfigured into a butterfly. In other words, Jesus change forms on the mountain. The glory that was concealed within Him was revealed on that mountain and Peter witnessed it.

However, this is not the first time that Jesus has experienced a transfiguration. When He was born in Bethlehem, Jesus concealed the glory of His deity behind the vail of His human body. On this occasion, the glory on the inside burst forth to the outside. The dark mountain was instantly bathed with a light that is brighter than the sun. Anyone looking up at Mount Hermon that night would have seen the mountain lit with the glory of God. And to think that Peter and the other two were given a glimpse of the glory that one day all of God's children will see when we get to Heaven. We will get to see Jesus in all His glory (1 John 3:2 NKJV).

Then, Moses and Elijah appeared there on that mountain with Jesus (Luke 9:30 NKJV). Mark says they were "talking with Him" (Mark 9:4 NKJV). Luke tells what they were discussing, His "decease" (Luke 9:31 NKJV). In other words, they were discussing His death upon the cross. But why Moses and Elijah? Again, let me point out that it is important for the fisher of men to understand prophecy! These two men represent the two ways the children of God will meet death. Moses died and was buried (Deut. 34:5-6 NKJV). Elijah was taken up alive into Heaven (2 Kings 2:11 NKJV). Like Moses, many have, and many will die. Like Elijah, some will be taken up alive into Heaven to meet God (1 Cor. 15:51-52; 1 Thess. 4:16-18 NKJV). Like Moses and Elijah, regardless of how you leave this world, if you know the Lord Jesus Christ as your personal Lord and Savior, you will be with Him in glory someday!

The final thing to know about the past of the kingdom is that the Kingdom of Heaven will be everlasting. Peter describes the kingdom as "the everlasting kingdom of our Lord and Savior Jesus Christ." (2 Pet. 1:11 NKJV). Meaning that Jesus is going to rule and reign forever and ever! Hallelujah! But where do you see the kingdom of God today? What has happened to Jesus's message of repentance in our society?

The Personal of the Kingdom

Just as surely as we are to pray for the appearance of a future kingdom, that will be everlasting, we are to pray for His kingdom to be realized in our own lives as fishers of men. Remember, the word "kingdom" means royal power, kingship, dominion or to rule or to reign. When we pray "Thy kingdom come" we are praying for God to rule and to reign in our personal lives. This petition expresses a desire for God to be our Lord and Sovereign King! It is a prayer that God will be enthroned within our hearts. As fishers of men, we should seek to dethrone ourselves and that God alone is the center of our hearts! The only way this can come to pass is if you are saved by faith. You cannot be under His rule until you know the savior. But you cannot have Him as Savior unless you also have Him as Lord of your life. He is the Lord Jesus Christ, and His Lordship cannot be divorced from His role as Savior. Jesus is not a buffet! When you ask Jesus into your heart you get the whole package!

That being said, think on this: God's kingdom in your life and mine is not a democracy! Jesus does not come asking for your obedience, He comes into our lives as King! He wants and commands absolute control over your life. By the way, the church is not a democracy either! It is an absolute Theocracy. The church is not under the control of a pastor or deacons, it is under control and authority of the Lord Jesus Christ! Now a lot of people don't like that concept, because they want a Jesus they can mold into their image. If you are going to behave as a fisher of men, then you must give Him control of your life and church. Jesus said, "If you love Me, keep My commandments." (John 14:15 NKJV).

While the literal reign of Jesus is a future event, it is true that those who are saved by His grace are citizens of that kingdom now. "For our citizenship is in heaven, from which we also eagerly wait for the Savior, the Lord Jesus Christ" (Phil. 3:20 NKJV). When you become a citizen of a kingdom, you are expected to keep the laws of the King. We are to pray that His kingdom will be lived out through our lives for His glory. And that everything having to do with our lives as fishers of men will be brought under His dominion. Anything less is rebellion! When there is no desire to see Jesus enthroned as Lord and King of one's life, it may be evidence that a person is not truly saved. If you can live like you want to, without regard for His will, then you probably aren't even saved (1 John 3:7-8; 1 John 2:29 NKJV). If you aren't fishing for men, then you're not behaving as a fisher of men.

The Application of the Kingdom

When we pray "Thy kingdom come", we are expressing a desire to see His work, His Word, and His will and Kingdom advanced in the world today. We might as well accept this fact: we will not make this world any better through human efforts. In other words, we will not be able to usher in His kingdom ourselves. He will bring it when He comes, and it will be established by His power alone. However, when we behave as fishers of men, we can have a part in seeing that our Lord's kingdom is spread abroad in the world around us. There are several ways in which we can do this.

First, fishers of men are to pray for the kingdom of God to come and His will do be done here upon earth. Second, fishers of men are to behave by submission to Jesus. We are to yield our lives to Him so that He can live through us. As we do, He demonstrates His love, grace, and saving power to a lost and dying world. "I have been crucified with Christ; it is no longer I who live, but Christ lives in me; and the life which I now live in the flesh I live by faith in the Son of God who loved me and gave Himself for me" (Gal. 3:20 NKJV). "For we are His workmanship, created in Christ Jesus for good works, which

God prepared beforehand that we should walk in them." (Eph. 2:10 NKJV). "But we have this treasure in earthen vessels, the excellence of the power may be of God and not of us." (2 Cor. 4:7 NKJV). The final way is through outreach. When fishers of men behave properly then we will become burdened over a lost and dying world, we will go into the world and spread the Gospel message. Our desire will be to see others saved and we will do everything in our power to bring that to pass. This world might be in darkness today, but there is light in every fisher of men and that light must be shared with this world. We have been commanded to do this (Mark 16:15; Matt. 28:18-20 NKJV). And we have all the resources we need (Acts 1:8; Rom. 1:16 NKJV) behave as fishers of men. May the Lord help us to get involved in His Kingdom work. We ought to ask ourselves this question: What am I doing as an individual to spread God's kingdom in the world today? What can I do to be more effective for the Kingdom of God?

CHAPTER EIGHTEEN

Come and Dine

Jesus said to them, "Come and eat breakfast." Yet none of the disciples dared ask Him, "Who are You?" knowing that it was the Lord. (John 21:12 NKJV).

AFTER PETER AND THE OTHER SIX MADE THE DECISION TO GO FISHING, they got in their boat and paddled out to sea. They began to let down their nets and cast after cast they continued to catch nothing. All night long they fished and fished never catching anything (John 21:3 NKJV). Then by morning light there was Jesus standing on the shore, and the disciples at that time did not know that it was the Lord. Jesus is concerned for them and asks "Children, have you any food?" (John 21:5 NKJV). They did not. Jesus being the wonderful teacher He was instructed the fishers of men to "cast the net on the right side of the boat, and you will find some." (John 21:6 NKJV). Of course, when they obeyed the Lord, they were "not able to draw it in because of the multitude of the fish." (John 21:6 NKJV). That is when John recognized this situation before and the miracle that took place that it was Jesus who was standing on the shore. When Peter heard this, he could not wait to get the boat to shore and just plunges right into the sea and swim to shore (John 21:7 NKJV). When they all get to shore, they see Jesus sitting there with a fire and He invites them to bring some fish to cook on the fire. But still what is the most memorable about this experience is the fact that Jesus invites these fishers of men to come and dine. He said, "Come and eat breakfast." (John 21:12 NKJV). With all that Jesus had taught them about being fishers of men this one lesson is the most important.

Let me break this event down. Jesus to the fishers of men to go cast your net (The Gospel message) on the right side (God's way). They did and they caught one hundred fifty-three fish (lost souls, which can also represent the different people groups of the world). They begin to bring them in, as Jesus invites the fishers of men to bring the fish to Him (discipleship). Then He invites the fishers of men to come and dine (have fellowship with the different kinds of fish). In this passage of Scripture, you can see the Great Commission on display for us. Not to mention the fact that Peter was witnessing firsthand a parable that Jesus taught him about the Great Commission in the Parable of the Great Supper recorded for us in Matthew 22:1-14 and Luke 14:15-24 (NKJV). The lesson for fishers of men is that not only are we commanded to go but we are compelled to come. When we bring in the fish of lost men, we are to disciple them and fellowship with them at the Master's table. Someone said, "That how we treat other people", people of other race, "is just practice for when we all get to heaven." Let me just add to that; when you are out of sorts with your fellow man, then most likely you are out of sorts with God. When you are disregarding God, you are going to disregard people. Isn't that what the two greatest commandments teach us (Matt. 22: 37-40 NKJV)?

In Luke 14 (NKJV) Jesus is teaching His disciples about hypocrisy. The chapter opens with Jesus being invited to the home of one of the chief Pharisees (Luke 14:1 NKJV). Which is common during those days for a teacher to be invited home for a meal after services at the synagogue, much like people would invite the preacher home for a Sunday lunch. This gave the host and hostess the opportunity to exercise the spiritual gift of hospitality. However, on this day it would not be a time for hospitality; it was going to be a time of hypocrisy.

The Pharisee had also invited a man with "dropsy" (Luke 14:2 NKJV) and had made sure that this man was placed where Jesus could not miss him. "Dropsy" is a condition in which the tissues of the body retain water. It was caused by problems with the heart, the kidneys, or the liver. In that day, it was an untreatable, incurable condition. The Pharisee brought the man there that day to catch Jesus in a trap. If He merely ignored the sick man, they could claim that He lacked compassion. If Jesus healed the sick man, they would accuse Him of breaking the Sabbath. Jesus, knowing what was in their hearts, turned the tables on them (Luke 14:3 NKJV). He asked them if it was lawful to do good on the Sabbath, then Jesus healed the sick man and sent him away for the man's safety. The Pharisee did not answer (Luke 14:4 NKJV). That is when Jesus exposed their hypocrisy (Luke 14:5 NKJV). He reminded them that they would go out of their way on the Sabbath to save a valued animal, but they lack the decency to help a fellow human who was created in the very image of God. Jesus left them speechless (Luke 14:6 NKJV).

So, Jesus being the compassionate teacher He is, shared a couple of parables with His host. These parables were designed to teach these hard-hearted men the value of true humility. Instead of trying to promote self by seeking the seats of honor in a feast, they were to just take a seat and leave their advancement to the host of the feast (Luke 14:7-14 NKJV). Then, He challenged them to reach out to people who could not return the favor, instead of only reaching out to those who they could benefit from later (Luke 14:12-14 NKJV).

This brings us to the parable of the Great Supper. What initiated this parable is that one of the guests hears all this talk about breaking bread and tries to be super-spiritual. You know people try to do that all the time when they are being confronted by the truth. They try to act all spiritual, but all they do is reveal how unspiritual they truly are. The man said, "Blessed is he who shall eat bread in the kingdom of God!" (Luke 14:15 NKJV). Basically, what this man said was, "Praise God! We are going to a real feast some day!" The Jews believed that the Kingdom of God was like a feast. They believed they would sit down with Abraham, Isaac, and Jacob and break bread. This fellow talked like he believed that he would be there. This event should have been something that Peter remembered when Jesus invited them to "come and eat breakfast" (John 21:12 NKJV) in then "Jesus came and took the bread and gave it to them, and likewise the fish." (John 21:13 NKJV), they were feasting at the master's table and the parable of the Great Supper should have come to mind.

So, after the man had said what he said about eating in the kingdom of God, Jesus used this opportunity to confront the hypocrisy of the Jews; to challenge the false confidence of those who believed they were right with God; and to teach them how the invitation to God's feast "Come and dine" really worked. As we look at this parable may it confront us that we need to behave as fishers of men sharing the Gospel to the lost.

The Invitation Extended

Jesus tells us that this would be a "great supper" (Luke 14:16 NKJV), meaning that it was going to be a magnificent, grand event. It would be a time of lavish entertainment for those attending. When everything was ready the host sent his servants to go and tell those invited "Come, for all this are now ready." (Luke 14:17 NKJV). The people who were invited to this feast were probably the cream of the crop, the rich, the most influential, the movers, the shakers, the who's who of who's who. Everyone that was anyone would have been invited to come. Jesus is using this feast to illustrate the glory of God's kingdom. For those who will attend the Lord's feast in Heaven, it will be an event so grand and so glorious that we cannot even begin to comprehend it. And there on that morning Peter and the other disciples with their fish were invited by Jesus to sit by the fire and eat breakfast. How humble the Master's table was that day; and yet it was so peaceful by that seashore. What a day that is going to be when we feast with Jesus!

However, look at the grandeur of this world, and remember that this world is tainted and spoiled by sin. Then, imagine if you will a world that is perfect just like that picture of Jesus, Peter, the other six disciples on that beach that day. It will be a world that is free from sin, free from the influence of the devil, free from pain, suffering, sorrow, and tears (Rev. 21:4 NKJV). Imagine a world that is lit by the very glory of God.

Imagine a world that is filled with holiness and righteousness. Imagine a feast attended by the great saints of the ages, Abraham, Isaac, Jacob, Noah, Matthew, Mark, James, John, Paul, and Peter. Everyone who has placed the faith in the Lord Jesus Christ as their personal Lord and Savior from every tribe, creed, culture, and race will be there. If you can imagine a scene like that, then you have a small idea where we are headed and what we will see and experience when we arrive there. It will be the social event of eternity, and you will not want to miss it, you will not want others to miss out. When we behave as fishers of men, we are the servants of the Host of this parable and we are to go out and invite them to "come, for all things are now ready!"

The Invitation Extinguished

When a feast of this magnitude was planned in the ancient world, it was not a spur of the moment event. All of those invited would have been informed of the date and the event well in advance. Each one of them would have already promised that they would attend the event because the host would need to know how much food to prepare by having an accurate count of those who were coming. When the day of the feast had arrived, the host would send out his servants to call those who had been invited to come to the feast. They knew the date and they were to be prepared and ready.

There is an application in this parable that we can apply to our lives before we dig any deeper. God the Father began planning the feast of Salvation from the beginning of time and started inviting the most important people, the children of Israel, to come and dine. The children of Israel were to set the example for all other nations and bring them when they came to the feast. Then when God sent His Servant Jesus to Israel to tell them about the feast of Salvation, they rejected the invitation by crucifying Jesus on the cross at Calvary. Which by the way made "all things now ready!" Then God the Son promised that He would send another Servant God the Holy Spirit into the world and He would invite sinners to come to Jesus. Yet, like Israel of old, men turned a deaf ear to the pleading of the Spirit of God. Most men do not realize that without His call His drawing, man cannot be saved. Jesus said, "No one can come to Me unless the Father who sent Me draws him; and I will raise him up at the last day" (John 6:44 NKJV). He goes on to say, "Therefore, I have said to you that no one can come to Me unless it has been granted to him by My Father." (John 6:65 NKJV). Understand, the Gospel of Jesus Christ and the salvation it brings is available to everyone; and the Holy Spirit reaches out to every human being. However, not every human is going to receive this urging from the Holy Spirit. They just make excuses.

Notice some of the excuses in this parable and how they represent the areas of people's life and the reasons they use for not coming and dining with Jesus.

THE EXCUSE OF MATERIAL POSSESSIONS

"The first said to him, 'I have bought a piece of ground, and I must go and see it. I ask you to have me excused.'" (Luke 14:18 NKJV). This man had purchased a piece of property, without seeing it first. Who does that? But then, in the evening when it came time for supper, now he must go and see it. How can you look at a mystery piece of property one you never seen at dusk? Well, this man and his excuse is a picture of the sinner who is so materially minded that he refuses the call of the Gospel sot that he can continue to life for this world and all that it gives. The Bible has this to say about this type of individual in Mark 8:36-37 (NKJV), "For what will it profit a man if he gains the whole world, and loses his own soul? Of what will a man give in exchange for his soul?" Jesus said the same thing about the foolish man in Luke 12:20 (NKJV), "But God said to him, 'Fool! This night your soul will be required of you then whose will those things be which you have provided'" (Luke 12:20 NKJV). The most important thing in life is not, "How much am I worth?" It is, "Am I saved?" How do you answer that question today?

THE EXCUSE OF PROFESSIONAL ADVANCEMENT

"And another said, 'I have bought five yoke of oxen, and I am going to test them. I ask you to have me excused'" (Luke 14:19 NKJV). This man had bought ten oxen, without trying them out; and yet, he wants to be excused so he can go at supper time and plow a field. What a lame excuse, but most importantly who buys cattle without looking at them. Looks like this man is trying to get ahead in the world and he is not alone. There are many people who allow their occupations, their businesses, their pursuit of material gain keep them from coming to Jesus. There is nothing wrong with hard work and making money to earn a living, but when those things come ahead of God, they are sinful! God doesn't give people jobs that move them away from Him. He provides the blessing of work and income for you offer thanks to Him. There have been so many people who have place their career ahead of God and as a result they will die and go to Hell.

THE EXCUSE OF PERSONAL RELATIONSHIP

"Still another said, 'I have married a wife, and therefore I cannot come'" (Luke 14:20 NKJV). Now, we can understand being newly married and wanting to spend time with his new bride. Still, weddings in the Middle East are extravagant events planned months in advance. He knew about the wedding when he accepted the invitation to the feast. This man placed his personal relationship ahead of everything else in life. There are many who do the same thing today. They won't come to Christ because there are afraid of their family or friends might make fun of them. Some let their family events or outings keep them from coming to Jesus. People still make their excuses and these excuses that these people made back then mean as much as they do today, diddly squat! Not a single person who rejected this invitation had a valid reason for doing so, and not a single person who rejects Jesus Christ has a valid reason for turning a deaf ear to the invitation of the Gospel. There will be people at the Great White Throne of Judgment offering these same excuses to Jesus for reason why they need to be let into Heaven and Jesus is going to say, "I never knew you; depart from Me, you who practice lawlessness!" (Matt. 7:21-23 NKJV).

The Invitation Expanded

When the servant returns with the responses of those who were invited, the master of the house becomes angry (Luke 14:21 NKJV). He is angry because he invited those people specifically and wanted them there at his feast. They all promised to come when he called; but now the time has come, and they reject his invitation. Therefore, their rection anger the master of the house. Understand this is a picture of God's invitation of salvation to Israel first. As it is said in Romans 1:16 (NKJV), "For I am not ashamed of the gospel of Christ, for it is the power of God to salvation for everyone who believes, for the Jew first and also for the Greek." In this parable, the man who is having the feast sends his servant (Jesus: The Messiah) out to invite the chosen attendees (Israel: God's chosen people) when they reject the servant, the master sent the servant "out quickly into the streets and lanes of the city, and bring in here the poor and the maimed and the lame and the blind" (Luke 14:21 NKJV). So, as the servant invites as anyone (the Gentiles) he can find he fills the feast with people. You see, God did not have a plan B. God knew that when He sent Jesus into the world that His offer of salvation would be rejected by the nation of Israel. He knew that the poor, the diseased, the outcast, and the downtrodden would come to Jesus. He also knew that the rich, the powerful and the religious would not. God invited His people (Israel) to come, just as He told them He would. When they refused, He expanded His invitation to include "whosoever will." Let's look at this expansion of God's invitation and what the Bible says about the plan of God to save the lost and how we are to further behave as a fisher of men.

THE EXPANSION IS CRITICAL

In Luke 14:21 (NKJV), we see that the master of the feast sends his servant out and tells him to "quickly" find enough people to fill the feast. There is a sense of urgency and haste to this command. We as fishers of men need to share the Gospel of Jesus Christ with urgency. It is urgent for this servant to find a multitude of people because the feast is ready and the food will spoil in a short time. The master of the feast knows that time is short. The Lord Jesus knows that time is short for lost people as well. People all around us live like they are going to live forever, but that is not the case. Our lives are short, regardless of how long we last. The human life is but a vapor. James writes, "Whereas you do not know what will happen tomorrow. For what is your life? It is even a vapor that appears for a little time and then vanishes away." (Jam. 4:14 NKJV). When God made you, God breathed into your nostrils the breath of life; you became as living soul. You could no more cease to exist than God Himself could cease to exist. Your soul will be in existence somewhere when the sun, moon, and stars have grown cold. You have everlasting existence. What you need is everlasting life. You are going to spend eternity somewhere, therefore, you must decide if you want to spend your eternity in the smoking section or the non-smoking section!

After this life, there is a long eternity that will be spent in Heaven with the Lord Jesus or in Hell with the Devil and other lost people. The only way to avoid Hell and enter Heaven is through a relationship with the Lord Jesus Christ. Jesus is the dividing line between Heaven and Hell. "Nor is there salvation in any other, for there is no other name under heaven given among men by which we must be saved." (Acts 4:12 NKJV). "Jesus said to him, "I am the way, the truth, and the life. No one comes to the Father except through Me."" (John 14:6 NKJV). That is why we must behave as fisher of men with urgently telling others about Jesus. Someone said that fishers of men are just "beggars telling other beggars where to find bread." The fact is, the Great Commission is urgent, because time is running out for men, women, boys, and girls to repent of their sin and call on the Lord. It is my prayer that as you have read through this book that God will impress upon your heart the lateness of the hour. People are perishing and it seems that we are doing little to reach them!

THE EXPANSION IS COMPREHENSIVE

When the master of the feast sends his servant out to call the people to the feast, he sends him out to call all those that polite society would never have no fellowship with. So, let's consider who this man calls, then let's stop and think about the kind of people God reaches out to with the Gospel. The first people the master sends the servant out to is the poor (Luke 14:21 NKJV). The poor are those people who could never pay him back. For example, those that did not have money to pay bills or could even afford to put food on their tables or a shelter over their heads. This group would also include children or youth of the next generation. (We will expand on this part of this group in the next chapter). But notice, what a beautiful portrait of God's grace. He reaches down to men who will never be able to repay Him for His salvation. Yet, God askes for no repayment, He just asks men to come to Him. "Ho! Everyone who thirsts, come to the waters; and you who have no money, come, buy and eat. Yes, come, buy wine and milk without money and without price." (Isa. 55:1 NKJV). "And the Spirit and the bride say, "Come!" and let him who hears say, "Come!" and let him who thirsts come. Whoever desires, let him take the waters of life freely." (Rev. 22:17 NKJV). As fishers of men, we need to be offering this free gift of salvation to the poor.

The next group the servant was sent to is the maimed (Luke 14:21 NKJV). This refers to people who have deformed, twisted, and broken bodies. These are the kind of people society feels uncomfortable being around. These are the people who are considered to be the defects and the rejects of society. Yet, this gracious man reached out to them. God loves the spiritually maimed. Every person in this world possesses a twisted old nature, because sin entered the world and this old nature is drawn towards sin. The Bible calls that drawing towards sin "iniquity".

Society and the church often draw back from these people, but Jesus loves them and died to save their souls. He calls the most twisted to leave their old life behind and come to Him. In fact, there is no sin so vile in this world today that will ever cause God to stop loving the sinner (Jer. 31:3 NKJV). The Bible is clear "For whoever calls on the name of the Lord shall be saved." (Rom. 10:13 NKJV).

The next group the servant was sent to is the lame (Luke 14:21 NKJV). These are the crippled, the people who are unable to get around on their own. In fact, to come to the feast, these would have had to have help. Again, this is a picture of the lost person, crippled by sin and unable to get to God for sinners need the help of the fishers of men to come to God. "But your iniquities have separated you from your God; and your sins have hidden His face from you, so that He will not hear." (Isa. 59:2 NKJV). Remember the crippled man in Mark 2? His friends brought him to Jesus by letting him down through the roof of a house. His friends' actions preached a message that still reverberate through the ages. This is the very reason that Jesus seeks sinners. "For the Son of Man has come to seek and to save that which was lost." (Luke 19:10 NKJV). He knows that in themselves, lost people cannot get to God. They need help and Jesus is that help through fishers of men. It doesn't matter what degree of "crippled' a person may be, they cannot get to Jesus on their own. Lost sinners are dead (Eph. 2:1 NKJV). They need someone to come to them. The Lord comes to them through His followers who behave as fishers of men. As we behave, we are carrying the Gospel to those perishing in their sins. That is our mission and they are our mission field.

The next group that the servant is sent to is the blind (Luke 14:21 NKJV). These are the people who are trapped in their own little world of darkness. They do not possess the resources to get to the Lord by themselves. They need a guide. They need someone to show them the light. There are millions who are wandering around in spiritual darkness and headed to Hell (2 Cor. 4:4 NKJV). These people need someone to show them the light. That is what the Holy Spirit does! He come in and He illuminates the darkness. He makes it possible for the blind sinner to see his need for a Savior. Quite often, Jesus uses those who have already been delivered from blindness to hold the light for those who still cannot see. That is why we must behave as fishers of men!

The last group that the master sends the servant to is the highway and hedge dwellers. "Then the master said to the servant 'Go out into the highways and hedges and compel them to come in, that my house may be filled." (Luke 14:23 NKJV). After the servant had found all the wrecks of humanity he could find and had brought them in, the master's house still had room. Now he sends the servant into the streets and the hedgerows. Here he is going the find the worst of the worst; those whom no one else wanted anything to do with. These people were the scum of all humanity. Mixed among these assorted homeless and wanderers would be found those who were journeying out on business. In other words, the servant would meet anyone and everyone in the streets and hedges. This is how we are to behave as a fisher of men. We should see that everyone everywhere needs to hear about Jesus Christ and the way to God.

God has a plan to save the lost and fishers of men are part of that plan. We are to take the Gospel to the world and tell them about a loving, saving Lord. Salvation comes to those who hear the Gospel. "For since, in the wisdom of God, the world through wisdom did not know God, it pleased God through the foolishness of the message preached to save those who believe." (1 Cor. 1:21 NKJV). For them to hear, someone must take the message to them (Rom. 10:13-17 NKJV) and fishers of men are those someone's! The Spirit of God works through us to enable us to carry the message of life to the lost. It is challenging mission, but it is a mission that should be carried out with a sense of urgency. The time is now; the one we should tell is everyone we meet. That is our mission; that is our mandate; we must behave as fishers of men.

CHAPTER NINETEEN

The Invitation to Generation Now

But Jesus said, "Let the little children come to Me, and do not forbid them; for of such is the kingdom of Heaven." (Matthew 19:14 NKJV)

As stated in the previous chapter, I want to expound on the poor that the servant from Jesus' parable of the Great Supper was sent by the master of the feast to invite (Luke 19:21 NKJV). The poor were those who cannot pay the master back and this would also include children and/or youth. Children up to a certain age would have stayed at home and could not repay the master of the feast by inviting him to a feast. When children got up to an age where they could go to work, and even in their youth, they were paid but it was given to the parents. Children and youth did not handle the money in those days. Therefore, they could not repay the master of the feast by inviting to a feast. And yet the master of the feast sent his servant out to invite the poor, including the children and the youth, to come to the feast.

In Matthew 19:13-15 (NKJV), we see one of the most precious and most ignored invitation in the Word of God. I am referring to the invitation of generation now. Jesus had just finished teaching about the very serious matter of marriage and divorce. As soon as that discussion is finished, Jesus turns His attention to some little children that are being brought to Him by their parents. It was a Jewish tradition to bring small child to a great rabbi so he could bless them and pray for them. It was also common for parents to take their children to the synagogue, where each of the elders would take the child in his hands and pray for the life of the child. This is much the same thing we still do today when we dedicate a child and parent to the Lord at a baby dedication.

However, as these parents of these children get near, they are severely rebuked by Jesus' disciples. Apparently, they felt the Master's time was too valuable to spend on small children. Jesus, in turn, rebuked them for their behavior regarding these children. He told the disciples in no uncertain terms that little children was what the Kingdom of Heaven was all about. But let's be honest, children can be noisy in church; they require a lot of special attention and special programs; and they cannot contribute to the financial burden of the church. But children are not a cursed to be endured; they are a blessing to be enjoyed! Psalm 127:3 (NKJV) says, "Behold, children are a heritage from the Lord, the fruit of the womb is a reward." We can count ourselves blessed when we have children. And a church is blessed when there are children coming!

In Matthew 19:13-15 (NKJV) it has something to say about child and about the Savior's invitation for them to come to Him. But it also has something to say to fisher of men and how we must be sharing the Gospel of Jesus Christ with urgency to the generation now!

A Word about Responsibility

The first thing that we as fishers of men are responsible for is evangelizing the generation now. "Then the little children were brought to Him that He might put His hands on them and pray, but the disciples rebuked them. But Jesus said, "Let the little children come to Me and do not forbid them; for of such is the kingdom of heaven." And He laid His hands on them and departed from there." (Matt. 19:13-15 NKJV). In this passage, it nowhere implies that Jesus was saving these children. He was merely praying for them and pronouncing a blessing on their young lives. This scene teaches us that these parents cared enough about the spiritual condition of their children to bring them to Jesus so that they might be blessed through His praying and His touch.

From the earliest passages of the Bible God's people have been challenged to share the things of God with their children. "Now this is the commandment, and these are the statues and judgments which the Lord your God has commanded to teach you, that you may observe them in the land which you are crossing over to possess, that you may fear the Lord your God, to keep all His statutes and His commandments which I command you, you and your son, and your grandson, all the days of your life, and that your days may be prolonged." (Deut. 6:1-2 (NKJV). The New Testament renews that challenge to parents in Ephesians 6:4 (NKJV) which says, "And you, fathers, do not provoke your children to wrath, but bring them up in the training and admonition of the Lord." Parents should do everything in their power to ensure that their children are exposed to the Gospel. Because parents should behave as fishers of men in the home and in front of their children in order to fulfill the Great commission in the home. That means bringing them to church on a consistent basis, giving them opportunity, to be in Sunday School, Bible Study, Choir, and Vacation Bible School. It means praying with your children and for them, reading the Bible with them, talking about your faith, and discussing what they might need to grow their faith. Yes, it is true that the Sunday school teacher share the Gospel with the children. And yes, it is true that the Gospel should be preached from the pulpit. And yet, the primary responsibility for evangelizing the children are the parents.

Another area that we as fishers of men are responsible for is educating generations now. By bringing their children to Jesus, parents were telling their children that they saw something special in Him. Like those ancient parents, fishers of men in our day have the responsibility of modeling our faith in Jesus so the babes in Christ, and the younger generation can see that He is worth knowing. If my faith does not change my life and I don't behave as a follower of Christ, and I don't behave as a fisher of men; then my walk with Christ translates into hypocrisy in the eyes of my daughter who is learning how to behave as a fisher of men. Young people are quick to spot a phony! We are responsible for educating our children about the things of God! It is our duty to bring them face to face with a saving Lord. If we make Jesus the main thing in our lives, they will be far more likely to come to Him at an early age and remain faithful to Him as they mature.

One last area that we as fishers of men are responsible for is encouraging generation now. When these parents came to Jesus with their children, they were encouraging them to approach Jesus as well. Christian parents are told to "bring them up in the training and admonition of the Lord" (Eph. 6:4 NKJV). The word "admonition" has the idea of encouragement. Fishers of men ought to encourage our children to seek the things of God. Teach them to pray at an early age. Make the Bible a big part of their daily lives. Pray with them and in front of them. Get them involved in the worship service, meaning let them see us worshipping God. We need to expose them to everything that godly that is available in our world; especially since we are living in perilous times. Teach them to know what it means to abide in Christ (John 15:2 NKJV). One of the best things a fisher of men can do for children and/or youth is help them to grow in love with Jesus Christ (John 14:15 NKJV). When mature adults love Jesus with a sincere devotion, it encourages children to love Him too!

A Word about Redemption

Now while this event involving Jesus, the disciples, the parents, and the children (Matt. 19:13-15 NKJV) certainly highlights adult responsibilities toward a child's spiritual foundation, it also speaks about the matter of salvation. Notice first what it implies. The fact that the poor was invited to the feast in Jesus' parable of the Great Supper, and since children and youth are part of that group would mean that children and youth need a Savior. Now, there are some folks that don't want hear this, but children are sinners too! "Behold, I was brought forth in iniquity, and in sin my mother conceived me." (Ps. 51:5 NKJV). "The wicked are estranged from the womb; they go astray as soon as they are born, speaking lies." (Ps. 58:3 NKJV). "Foolishness is bound up in the heart of a child; the rod of correction will drive it far from him." (Prov. 22:15 NKJV). "Surely you did not hear, surely you did not know; surely from long ago your ear was not opened. For I knew that you would deal very treacherously, and were called a transgressor from the womb." (Isa. 48:8 NKJV). "And you He made alive, who were dead in trespasses and sins, in which you once walked according to the course of this world, according to the prince of the power of the air, the spirit who now works in the sons of disobedience, among whom also we all once conducted ourselves in the lust of our flesh, fulfilling the desires of the flesh and of the mind, and were by nature children of wrath, just as the others." (Eph. 2:1-3 NKJV). While children may possess certain innocence, they still stand in need of salvation. That is why parents and other concerned adults must behave as fishers of men to bring children face to face with the claims of the Gospel of Jesus Christ. It is not our duty to save them, but it is our duty to expose them to the Word of God. When children hear the Gospel preached, taught, and lived out, they are far more likely to come to Jesus at an early age (Rom. 10:17 NKJV). Paul told Timothy about exposing children to the Word of God. Paul said, "and that from childhood you have known the Holy Scriptures, which are able to make you wise for salvation through faith which is in Christ Jesus." (2 Tim. 3:15 NKJV).

The second thing about redemption is what it involves. Whenever a discussion about childhood salvation comes up, someone always mentions "the age of accountability". Now it may surprise you but the Bible never mentions a specific "age of accountability". A child becomes accountable for his or her sins when they come to the place where they can understand the difference between right and wrong. When they are capable of choosing between right and wrong (Isa. 7:16 NKJV). Listen when you are teaching you child how to make right or wrong decisions and the consequences thereof in and around the home, school, or in a store then now is the time to start telling them about the Gospel of Jesus Christ. The term "age of decision" might be a better term to use than the phrase "age of accountability", because when a person reaches a level of mentality of understanding regarding the nature of sin and its consequences and are able to make a decision for or against Jesus Christ, they have reached the "age of decision."

So, when is that age? Well to be honest it is different for every child. My brother was saved at the age of six. I was saved at the age of five during a revival at Auburntown Baptist Church in Auburntown, Tn. Bro. Eddie Rushing was the evangelist and something in the sermon made me realize that I was lost and that I need to be saved. So, I walked the isle and took the pastor by the hand, which happen to be my dad, and told him I wanted to be saved. We knelt down at the front pew and I prayed and asked Jesus to come into my heart. When we got home, I heard mom and dad discussing what I had done at church. Mom said, "Do you think he understands what he has done?" Dad said, "We will know for it will come out." A year later and another revival, I went forward because I wanted to be baptized. Dad looked at me, while everyone else was singing, and said, "Now, you know in order to be baptized you have to be saved?" I looked up at him and said, "Dad! Don't you remember I got saved last year?" That is when dad realize that I genuinely got save at the age of five. Listen it does not matter the age, because when you reach a place in your life where you understand that you are a sinner; where you understand that you are going to Hell because of your sin; and you understand that Jesus Christ died and rose again from the dead to save you, you need to be saved. You need to come to Jesus and put you trust and faith in Him alone.

If you are a parent, just because your children are young, do not assume that they do not need to be saved. Children grow up quickly, and pick up things faster than you think, and they need to know about Jesus Christ. Tell them about Jesus from the day they are born and watch God save them at an early age! Let me touch on something else, when children come to you and talk to you about salvation, do not; I repeat "Do Not!" put them off. Take the time to ask them some pointed questions like: "What does it mean to be saved? Why do you feel that you need to be saved? Can you explain to me how a person gets saved? Can you explain to me what sin is?" There are many other questions you can ask, but you get the idea. If they do not understand, keep praying for them, keep taking them to church and let them see you that God is real in your life, keep talking to them about Jesus. They will come back when they are ready, you will know because the truth will come out.

When they are ready to receive Jesus, be careful that you point them to Him and allow them to come to Him by faith. In other words, do not put words in their mouth. You might can help them to understand the kind of things they should pray about when they are getting to ask Jesus into their heart. For example: help them to pray about confession of sin, expression of faith in the finished work of Jesus Christ, asking Jesus into their hearts; but never, never, never tell them exactly what they should say. If they understand what they are doing and they are really under the Holy Spirit conviction, they will know what they need to do.

What about children who die before they reach the "age of decision"? What happens to them? The Bible holds the answer for us on this question. When David lost an infant son in 2 Samuel 12 (NKJV), he was convinced that his son had gone to be with the Lord (2 Sam. 12:23 NKJV). Children and others who cannot choose for themselves are not saved, but they are "safe" in Jesus Christ. The saving power of the atoning work of Jesus is applied to them. When they die in that "safe" condition, they are regenerated and taken to Heaven! Parents who have lost children to death, miscarriage, or still birth should never fear because their little ones are in Heave with the Lord Jesus today. My wife and I had two miscarriages and we don't know if they were a boy or a girl. However, we take comfort in knowing that one day we will know and get to meet them in Heaven!

The last thing about redemption is what it illustrates. This whole matter of children coming to Jesus was used by our Lord to illustrate the way all believers must come to Him. Jesus said, "Assuredly, I say to you, unless you are converted and become as little children, you will by no means enter the kingdom of heaven. Therefore, whoever humbles himself as this little child is the greatest in the kingdom of heaven. Whoever receives one little child like this in My name receives Me." (Matt. 18:3-5 NKJV). Listen, all who come to Jesus must come to Him with a childlike faith. He is referring to a few of the special characteristics that separate children from adults. Children are trusting, humble, and dependent. Those are the requirements for a person to come to Jesus.

For a person to be saved, regardless of their age, they must be willing to humble themselves before God. They must be willing to lay down their pride over their lives they have lived and the achievements they have accomplished and surrender all to Jesus. They must be willing to confess all their sins before God, willing to admit that their works and religious activity can never save them. This lesson about child like faith, that Jesus taught, can be seen in the next chapter of the Book of Matthew. When the rich young ruler came to Jesus (Matt. 19:16-22 NKJV), he would not turn loose of his pride, his money, or his self-righteousness. He left with all his possessions, but he left without Jesus! A person must look to Jesus by faith, trusting Him and His finished work upon the cross at Calvary for their soul's salvation. This requires childlike qualities of trust, humility, and dependence. This is the only way anyone ever receives salvation.

A Word about the Redeemer

As you meditate on this event involving the children in Matthew 19:13-15 (NKJV), you get to watch Jesus as He ministers to the children, and you get to see Jesus' personality. First, we can see His heart (Matt. 19:13 NKJV). The disciples thought Jesus was too busy for a bunch of children. Notice the phrase "brought to Him", this phrase has the idea that there was a long line of parents and children. Parents from all over the area had brought their children to Jesus so that He could pray for them and pronounce a blessing over them. When the disciples rebuked the parents, Jesus then rebukes them (Matt. 19:14 NKJV). In Mark's account of this event, he says that Jesus was "greatly displeased." (Mark 10:14 NKJV) This means that Jesus was very upset, possibly even angry with the disciples for trying to prevent children from coming to Him. Just think, Children hold a special place in the heart of God! In fact, Matthew 18:6 (NKJV) reminds us, "Whoever causes one of these little ones who believe in Me to sin, it would be better for him if a millstone were hung around his neck, and he were drowned in the depth of the sea." Jesus always defends the defenseless! This scene reveals a lot about

Jesus. Children cannot serve Him like those who are older. They cannot contribute as much money as those who are older. It appears to me that Jesus holds a special place in His heart for children. Still, He loves them and reaches out to them in grace. This reminds us that God is not interested in what we can do, what we can give, or how old we are. Go out into the highways and byways and compel them to come in! Just simple invite people to come to Him on the basis of pure grace! Jesus loves the sinner and He invites them all to come to Him (Rev. 22:17; Matt. 11:28; John 3:16 NKJV).

Second, we can see His hands (Matt. 19:15 NKJV). In this verse, we are told that Jesus "laid His hands on them". This indicates that He took the time to bless each individual child that came before Him. No matter how young they were or how insignificant they appeared, Jesus cared about them and took time for them. Never think for an instant that Jesus does not care about you. He loves you and He will not turn you away if you come to Him. No matter where the path of life has taken you; no matter what you may have done; no matter how insignificant you may feel; Jesus Christ will save you and change your life if you will come to Him. He cares about your condition and He will take the time to touch your life if you will only come to Him by faith.

CHAPTER TWENTY

A Tender Moment

Then His disciples answered Him, "How can one satisfy these people
with bread here in the wilderness?" (Mark 8:4 NKJV)

As Peter and the six other disciples were standing there on
the shore of Galilee that morning after seeing Jesus, they were
contemplating the question as to what they should do next. As we have
discussed this far there are several teachings of Jesus that they should
have remembered especially about going and sharing the Gospel. But
here in Mark 8 is another question that could have come to mind that
they asked which should have reminded them to go out and share the
good news about the Bread of Life.

The sad question they asked on that day was "How can one satisfy
these people with bread here in the wilderness?" (Mark 8:4 NKJV).
Understand, Jesus had just told them that He had "compassion on
the multitude, because they have now continued with Me three days
and have nothing to eat. And if I send them away hungry to their
own house, they will faint on the way; for some of them came from
afar." (Mark 8:2-3 NKJV). Now, these disciples must have forgotten
what they have seen Him do, especially after seeing another multitude
of this size. As we know it was 5,000 men (not to mention women
and children also in addition to that number) as recorded in all four

Gospels (Matt. 14:13-21; Mark 6:30-44; Luke 9:10-17; John 6:1-14 NKJV). So, upon hearing Jesus wanting to feed this multitude of about 4,000 (Mark 8:9; Matt. 15:38 NKJV) these disciples if they had remembered should have been saying: Jesus all we have is "seven loaves of bread and a few little fish" (Matt. 15:34 NKJV). It's all we have but we know that you can use this to feed the multitude." However, they instead asked Jesus, "How can one satisfy these people with bread here in the wilderness?" Now, it could have been the fact that they were in Gentile territory and perhaps thought the Jesus might not perform that kind of miracle here.

Let me point out there are two different events of the feeding of the multitude: the feeding of the five thousand (recorded in all four Gospels) and the feeding of the four thousand (which only Matthew and Mark record). There are some clear similarities between the two. Obviously, both involved huge crowds and took place in a location where there was no food. In both miracles, Jesus involved the disciples in which both times they doubted the Lord's ability to meet the need of the multitudes. In both miracles, Jesus asked "How many loaves do you have?" (Matt. 15:34; Mark 6:38 NKJV). In both, He would take what they had, give thanks to God for it and broke, and gave to the disciples to distribute among the multitude. In each miracle crowds were entirely satisfied and there were large amounts of food left over.

However, there are some differences between the two miracles. The first miracle took place in Galilee, near Bethsaida, and involved predominantly Jews. The second miracle took place near Decapolis and involved mostly Gentiles. In the first Jesus started with five loaves and two fish where as in the second He had seven loaves and a few fish. In the first the multitude had been with Jesus for one day, while in the second the crowd was with Him for three days. After every person had their fill of food in the first, there were twelve small wicker lunch baskets of fish and bread. In the second, after everyone had their fill there were seven large baskets, big enough to hold a man (Acts 9:25 NKJV), that was filled with the leftover fragments. After the first miracle Jesus preached a message on the subject "The Bread of Life", while He did not preach a message to the Gentiles, because the Old

Testament manna and the "Bread of God" would have been foreign to these Gentiles.

So, with the message of the "Bread of God" behind them they should have associated the message Jesus preached to the needs of the four thousand. Little lone, immediately after asking Jesus about how can One (Jesus) going to satisfy (Jesus satisfies every need) these people with bread (the Bread of Life) in the wilderness should have cause them to stop and as least say, "Oh, wait Jesus I believe we have seven loaves for you to use!" But let's not be too hard on them. How many times have we forgotten the mercies of God? We need to remind ourselves that Jesus Christ is still the same yesterday, today, and tomorrow. And He is the solution to every problem. "Casting all your care upon Him, for He care for you." (1 Peter 5:7 NKJV). So, let's remind ourselves by looking at the message that Jesus taught about the Bread of Life.

The Personality of the Bread

Over in John 6:35, Jesus said, "I am the bread of life." This simple truth should serve to remind us that we can never be saved by some religious system, method, or ritual. Salvation comes through faith in Jesus alone. "Nor is there salvation in any other; for there is no other name under heaven given among men by which we must be saved." (Acts 4:12 NKJV). Jesus goes on to say, "He who comes to Me shall never hunger, and he who believes in Me shall never thirst." (John 6:35 NKJV). What Jesus is telling us is that He has the power to save, secure, and satisfy every sinner who comes to Him by faith. This is what separates Jesus from all man-made religions and self-proclaimed messiahs of the worlds. While they may promise great things, they can only deliver. Proverbs 16:25 (NKJV) says, "There is a way that seems right to a man, but its end is the way of death." Jesus promises life, salvation, security, satisfaction, and absolute safety for a man's soul. When Jesus is received by a sinner, by asking Jesus into the sinner's heart; the sinner is given salvation that last for all eternity. Nothing can ever take that away from the child of God. The simple fact is this, every person who places their faith in Jesus for salvation is going to live forever! Again, before the Bread of Life can be enjoyed by the sinner, the Bread of Life (Jesus) must be received by the sinner. This is so simple, and yet so many seem to stumble right here. They can believe that Jesus was real, that He died on the cross, that He was buried, and even that He rose from the dead. However, to come to Jesus and accept His sacrifice and the salvation He offers, is where most people have trouble coming to Jesus.

The Presentation of the Bread

In both feedings of the multitude, Jesus presented Himself as the Bread of Life. This can be seen in the His compassion He had on them. By caring for them, providing for them, and satisfying the multitude Jesus was presenting Himself as the "Bread" they need. You see, the implication is that Jesus, like the loaves and fish, is sufficient for the physical and spiritual need of mankind. Jesus is the all-sufficient Savior. Just think in both miracles it says that they ate "as much as they would" (John 6:11 NKJV) or "So they ate and were filled" (Mark 8:8 NKJV). Every person had as much as they could eat of the fish and bread. Plus, there was still enough go around afterwards (John 6:13 NKJV). Here is the application, even though hundreds of millions have been saved by the grace of God, there is always grace for ONE more! Jesus is sufficient for the needs of the entire world!

What is so unique of the first miracle is the fact that the Jewish religious leaders come to Jesus after they ate of the bread and fish and request a miracle from Jesus (John 6:30-33 NKJV). Now, wait! What do you call this feeding of the five thousand? In any case, these Jewish religious leaders point out that the Old Testament miracle of the manna was given to the children of Israel by Moses and they are wanting to know how Jesus was going to top that miracle. Jesus responds by telling them that Moses had nothing to do with the manna from Heaven. That it was a provision by God. He then tells them that the true bread from Heaven is a person. In fact, it is Jesus Himself who is the Bread of Life (John 6:33 NKJV). What Jesus is saying is that the Manna was a type of Himself. So, let me give you a quick over view as to how the Manna speaks of Jesus.

First, it was small (Ex. 16:14 NKJV). This speaks of Christ's humility. He wasn't born in a king's palace, but in a manger. He never employed the riches at His disposal, but lived a poor life all the time He was in this world (Mark 8:20 NKJV). He came this way in order to identify Himself with the sinners he came to save. Next, it was round (Ex. 16:14 NKJV). This speaks of Christ's eternal nature. Jesus did not have His beginning in Bethlehem, but He has always been (John 1:1 NKJV). Jesus is the eternal Son of God! There has never been a time when He wasn't, there will never be a time when He will not be! He is the Great I AM! Third, the manna was white (Ex. 16:31 NKJV). This reminds us of the sinless, Holy nature the Lord Jesus Christ. He was born without sin, lived without sin and died without sin, and yet He became sin when He took our sin upon Him and carried them to the cross to pay our sin debt. Jesus is the sinless Son of God. Next, the manna came at night (Ex. 16:13-14 NKJV). Jesus came to a world lost in spiritual darkness to give the world light and life. Fifth, the manna was misunderstood by those who found it (Ex. 16:15 NKJV). The Israelites called it manna which means "what is it?" Jesus when He came into this world was misunderstood by the very people He came to save. "He came to His own, and His own did not receive Him." (John 1:11 NKJV). Today, Jesus is still misunderstood. Jesus is more than a teacher, a prophet, a poor unfortunate man who got Himself killed. He is the Son of God! He is the King of kings and the Lord of lords! Next, the manna is sufficient for every man's need (Ex. 16:17-18 NKJV). This reminds us that Jesus is the all-sufficient Savior. He meets the need of man's soul. Some go deep in their Christian walk with Christ, while other just get saved and choose to stay babes in Christ and not mature. However, wherever you find yourself in your Christian walk, as long as you are behaving as a fisher of men you will find that He is sufficient for every need. Another thing about the manna is that it was sweet to the taste (Ex. 16:31 NKJV). Those who partook of the manna found it sweet and satisfying. That is the way it is with Jesus when you accept Him as your personal Lord and Savior.

David says to "taste and see that the Lord is good." (Ps. 34:8 NKJV). And then lastly the manna was to be kept and passed on to others (Ex. 16:32 NKJV). The Israelites were to pass on to the next generation the experience of how God took care of them in the wilderness to the next generation. The next generation was to pass this on to the next generation and on and on the testimony of God's provisions would go. It is the same way with Jesus; He is to be shared with those who God puts in our path. We are to teach them all thing whatsoever God has showed us (Matt. 28:18-20 NKJV) with the next generation, and so on and so forth. There is more that could be said about the manna but needless to say the manna is the perfect type of Jesus for Jesus is the real Bread of life!

The Performance of the Bread

Man can try any method of salvation he chooses, because God has created man with the privilege of free will. We have the ability to choose how we will live our lives. However, regardless of how a man lives or what path he chooses, salvation will never be produced in the life of any person anywhere unless they come to Jesus Christ by faith (Eph. 2:8-9 NKJV). That may seem narrowminded and simple, but that is what the Bible teaches and that is how it will always be (Acts 16:31; Acts 4:12; John 3:16 NKJV).

Not only does the Bread of life have the ability to satisfy the needs of man, but it also has the power to guarantee security. Jesus said, "All that the Father gives Me will come to Me, and the one who comes to Me I will by no means cast out. For I have come down from Heaven, not to do My own will, but the will of Him who sent Me. This is the will of the Father who sent Me, that of all He has given Me I should lose nothing, but should raise it up at the last day. And this is the will of Him who sent Me, that everyone who sees the Son and believes in Him may have everlasting life; and I will raise him up at the last day" (John 6: 37-40 NKJV). This is the security of the believer; faith in the Lord Jesus Christ guarantees us perfect and absolute security in our salvation relationship. Jesus didn't save us to lose us along the way, He saved us to take us home with Him someday.

There are many who doubt the security of the believer. They feel that their security depends upon them and what they can do or have done. They have the opinion that they are responsible for maintaining their salvation and that if they let down their guard, or if they are guilty of some sin, they will lose what they have and will have to start all over again, if they don't die first. This couldn't be any farther from the truth! Salvation is a GIFT of God; He gives it to those who place their trust in Him and He is not going to take it back like an Indian giver. Man has nothing to do with the gift of salvation, man doesn't even possess the power to keep himself save. Think about it this way. Man cannot earn it, keep it, or lose it. Salvation is totally 100% a work of the Almighty God through His Son Jesus when He completed the work upon the cross. When He gives, He gives forever!

From the message that Jesus preached to His disciples that day after feeding the multitude, it is plain to see that Jesus is the only hope for the world. He is what the soul of man needs before it can experience eternal life. Therefore, as Peter and the six other disciples were standing there on the shore of the sea of Galilee contemplating what to do next, they should have been eager to go and tell others what they had seen and heard from the teachings of Jesus and that all that He had taught them concerning His death, burial, and resurrection had come to pass. But instead, they decided to go fishing. They spent all night and caught nothing (John 21:1-3 NKJV).

In the morning Jesus comes to the shore of the sea of Galilee just like He said He would, and calls out the disciples and asks "Children, had you any food?" (John 21:5 NKJV). When they reply "no", He proceeds to tell them to let their nets down on the right side of the boat (John 21:6 NKJV). When they do, the nets become heavy with a multitude of fish. That is when John "that disciple who Jesus loved said to Peter, "It is the Lord!" (John 21:7 NKJV). Peter jumps out of the boat swims to shore, while the other six come in the boat with the fish. When they come to where Jesus was, He had a fire burning and He tells them to bring some of the fish which they just caught (John

21:10 NKJV). Jesus then invites them to "Come and eat breakfast." (John 21:12 NKJV).

These disciples did not dare ask who it was, because they knew who it was (John 21:12 NKJV). Could it be that it may have dawned on them that they were not behaving as fishers of men? Could it have dawned on them that this is the same predicament that were in before when they did catch any fish after a night of fishing? Could have been the words of Jesus who said to "cast your nets on the right side of the boat" (John 21:6 NKJV) that brought back all that Jesus taught them and they knew that they weren't behaving as fishers of men? Were they afraid that Jesus was going to rebuke them for not behaving as fishers of men? Well, this is where we see the tenderness of Jesus on display.

This reminds me of a story I once heard. There was a certain man who had been faithful in worship with other believers for many years. Then without warning he stopped coming to church. The pastor was burdened for his spiritual welfare, so one day he went to see him at home. The man invited him in and offered him a chair by the fire. The pastor mentioned to the man how much he missed seeing him in worship services. The man replied that he was saved and saw no need to go to church. He felt that he could worship just fine at home. For several long moments they sat in silence and watched the burning embers. Then, the pastor take the tongs, removed a hot coal and laid it by itself on the hearthstone. As it began to cool, its red glow soon faded. The man, who had been expecting a verbal rebuke, quickly caught the message. He was at church for the next service.

These disciples were probably expecting a rebuke for not behaving as fishers of men. And I know that on many occasions when I have not behaved as a follower of Christ nor behaved as a fisher of men that I have expect a rebuke from Jesus. However, when those times came, like the disciples; Jesus just invites me to "Come and eat breakfast." In other words, I had to come before the Lord Jesus Christ, confess my sins and bad behavior, and seek the forgiveness and restoration of my Savior (1 John 1:9 NKJV). Each time I had breakfast with Jesus, I have found Him to be a faithful Friend even to those who have fallen by the wayside.

In John 21 (NKJV), we see Peter come face to face with the risen Lord Jesus. As Peter sat there with Jesus quietly eating breakfast, Peter was probably remembering back to that night when he denied Jesus three times. As we look at how Jesus handled Peter that morning, I want you to know that this is how Jesus deals with His children who are not behaving as fishers of men. Notice this tender moment between Peter and Jesus,

The Purpose of the Moment

Looking back on that night that Jesus was arrested we can see that Peter was in the wrong place altogether (Matt. 26:69-75 NKJV). Luke records Peter's boast that he would never forsake the Lord. Peter said, "Lord, I am ready to go with You, both to prison and to death." (Luke 22:33 NKJV). Yet, when the time came and Jesus was arrested, Peter, like all the others left Jesus behind and fled (Matt. 26:56 NKJV). However, he did decide to follow Jesus and see what happened, but he would only follow from "afar off" (Matt. 26:58 NKJV). When Peter found himself surrounded by the Lord's enemies, it became hard for him to behave as a follower and make good on his boast (Matt. 26:69-74 NKJV). Listen when you are not behaving as a fisher of men nor a follower of Christ, we tend to call that backsliding. Instead of staying as close to the Lord Jesus as we should, we begin to follow Him "afar off". It may begin as simply as not sharing the Gospel when the opportunity comes, missing out on evangelism events, not serving, not going to church as often as you should, or just not communing with Jesus altogether. Wherever your backsliding begins, it will eventually lead to the same place. It will lead you to a cold condition and the things you do will produce a night of no fish. Peter's problem, that night of Jesus' arrest, was that he found himself in the wrong place with the wrong people.

After Peter denied the Lord that night, the Bible tells us that he went out and "wept bitterly" (Matt. 26:75 NKJV). Peter was miserable from that night until that morning when he sat down to have breakfast with the risen Savior. He knew that he had wronged the Lord. He knew that he had violated something very precious and sacred. He was a miserable man, and because he was in this condition could have been the reason as to why he chose to go fishing instead of behaving a fisher of men. But that is how every child of God behaves who decides to walk away from the will of God. You will soon realize that sin brings pain, suffering, and misery. Proverbs 13:15 (NKJV) says, "Good understanding gains favor, but the way of the unfaithful is hard." Gone will be the peace of God and the sense of God's presence. God will be His power and His joy unspeakable and full of glory. Sin is a thief and a robber! It steals your youth, your beauty, your innocence and your effectiveness as fisher of men. Sin has the ability to make you into a very miserable person! In the story of the Prodigal Son (Luke 15:11-17 NKJV), he was not happy in that pig pen, because the money was gone and he had no friends. His primary thought was of how much better off he had been back in his father's house. Sin will make you miserable, and if it doesn't then you probably aren't saved (Heb. 12:8 NKJV).

After the resurrection, Peter must have assumed that his ministry was over. That is probably the reason why on the shore of Galilee he decided to go back to his old way of life. "I am going fishing." (John 21:3 NKJV) was his decision and his reasoning, "Well, I have a family to support." Whatever the motivation, Peter was still called to be a fisher of men (Matt. 4:19 NKJV). And that's the thing, people who are out of God's will are prone to make the wrong choices! It seems that they tend to make fleshly decision instead of spiritual ones, and when they do this, they have failed to hear the voice of the Holy Spirit. After all, the Holy Spirit is your moral compass and the failing to hear Him will cause you to go off course.

When Peter went back to the old life, he took with him six other disciples. "They said to him, "We are going with you also." (John 21:3 NKJV). If those six were in the right place they would have been behaving as fishers of men, for Jesus told them to go into Galilee and wait for Him (Matt. 28:10 NKJV). You see, when a child of God misbehaves, they usually aren't content to go all alone and they will try to drag others down with them. What a shame it is when we feel the need to drag others into the same foolish pit into which we have place ourselves. What is equally sad is the fact that there always seems to be those who are willing to follow the wayward child of God! Why? Because we like to surround ourselves with people who are on the same level as we are. If we are right with God as fishers of men, then we will want to be around other fishers of men who are right with God. If we are out of God's will, we feel rebuked by our bad behavior and seek out those who are like we are to remove that feeling.

Peter and the other six disciples fished all night and did not catch a single fish! Most of these men were professional fisher before being called to be fishers of men and this have been devastating for them They toiled and labored all night and produced nothing of value. This just the way it works for those who are not behaving as fishers of men. No matter what they try to accomplish in their own strength, it always comes to nothing! Jesus said, "for without me you can do nothing." (John 15:5 NKJV). Some might argue that they have been living a slack Christian life and that they are still thriving and prospering materially and physically. May I remind you that both of those things are temporary and will soon pass away? In the final analysis, all that last are those things you do when you behave as a fisher of men through Jesus Christ (1 Cor. 3:11-15 NKJV). What will happen when you face Jesus?

The Provision of this Moment

Notice that in the morning after Peter and the six disciples had fished all night that Jesus knew exactly where to be. "But when the morning had now come, Jesus stood on the shore." (John 21:4 NKJV). Jesus stepped onto the scene and in a few minutes turned everything around and made things like they ought to be. What made the difference? There was a change in Peter. The first difference was the fact that Peter had to confess his failure (John 21:5 NKJV). Confession is the first step to coming back to Jesus. We must acknowledge that we were not behaving as a fisher of men. The next difference was that Peter stared obeying Jesus again (John 21:6 NKJV). Peter stopped doing things

Peter's way and started doing them the Lord's way. This brought success where there had been only failure! The other noticeable difference was there was a renewed desire to be near Jesus (John 21:7 NKJV). Peter didn't want to wait for a more convenient time but went to meet Jesus immediately. If you are one of those who have not been behaving as a fisher of men, then you need to know that you still have a Friend in Jesus. He hasn't forgotten you and knows exactly where to show up in your life. Jesus still loves you as much right now as He ever has. He just wants you to come to the place Peter came to. He wants you to be willing to confess your sins, begin again to behave as a follower of Christ and behave as a fisher of men.

When Peter and the six disciples reach the shore, they find Jesus, a fire, and a prepared meal. They found Jesus, the Bread of Life, satisfying the things they needed after being out on the boat all night. They found a Savior who loved them and who had all the provisions in place for what they could not find out on that boat. Listen, you may have toiled and labored and have not been behaving as a fisher of men and you are miserable, there is no peace and no joy, and what you need is to come to Jesus. Come and eat breakfast with Him. When you do you will find that He still loves you and the He has all the things you lack while you were away from Him.

In John 21:15-17 (NKJV), we find Jesus dealing directly with Peter. "So, when they had eaten breakfast, Jesus said to Simon Peter, "Simon, son of Jonah, do you love Me more than these?" He said to Him, "Yes, Lord; You know that I love you." He said to him, "Feed My lambs." He said to him again a second time, "Simon, son of Jonah, do you love Me?" He said to Him, "Yes, Lord; You know that I love you." He said to him, "Tend My sheep." He said to him a third time, "Simon, son of Jonah, do you love Me?" And he said to Him, "Lord, You know all things; you know that I love You." Jesus said to him, "Feed My sheep."" (John 21:15-17 NKJV). In these verses, we find the Lord Jesus recommissioning Simon Peter for service by reminding him of the two greatest commandments (Matt. 22:37-40 NKJV). The first commandment is represented in the question that Jesus asked Peter, "Do you love Me?" (John 21:15-17 NKJV). The second command is represented in the next statement that Jesus says to Peter, "Feed My sheep." (John 21:15-17 NKJV). The lesson is obvious that no matter what we have done in our Christian walk with Jesus, we are to still keep His commandments. Because if you are out of fellowship with God, chances are you will be out of fellowship with people. If you are out of fellowship with people, then you are out of fellowship with God.

I am sure that Peter felt that his work and ministry was forever gone, but Jesus came to call him back to behave as a fisher of men. This was a time of unique fellowship and restoration between Jesus and Peter. Because in these verses, Jesus freed Peter from the bondage of his sin and failure; and set him back about the business of serving the Lord and sharing the Gospel. The same will be true for every backslidden fisher of men who returns to the Father's house. Not only will He forgive your sins, but He can restore you to a place of service and sharing the Gospel. He will help you to behave as a fisher of men because you done have to behave as a fisher of men alone! The Holy Spirit is there to help you every step of the way. So, go out in the power of the Holy Spirit and behave as a fisher of men.

The Promise of this Moment

Jesus told Peter about some promised that he would see in his life. Jesus said, "Most assuredly, I say to you when you were younger, you girded yourself and walked where you wished; but when you are old, you will stretch out your hands, and another will gird you and carry you where you do not wish." This He spoke, signifying by what death he would glorify God. And when He had spoken this, He said to him, "Follow Me."" (John 21:18-19 NKJV). The first promise Jesus gives Peter is that of sacrifice. Peter would eventually give his life for the Lord who had saved him and who had restored him. Peter's call was literally to follow Jesus as a fisher of men unto death. Tradition states that Peter was eventually put to death by crucifixion and that at his own request, he was crucified upside down because he did not feel worthy to die like his Lord.

The next promise that Jesus shares with Peter is that of service. Peter is told that his life, from this moment forward, to glorify God by behaving as a fisher of men. He is no longer to live for self, but in everything, he is to live for the glory of the Lord. That is how we are to behave as fishers of men. "Therefore, whether you eat or drink, or whatever you do, do all to the glory of God." (1 Cor. 10:31 NKJV). The last thing Jesus promises Peter is actually a command. He said, "Follow Me." (John 21:19 NKJV) Notice that the last call is the same as the first cal. When Jesus found Peter and called him the first it was a command "Follow Me, and I will make you fishers of men." (Matt. 4:19 NKJV). When He recommissions Peter, He issues the same call. This tells us that the Jesus hasn't changed His mind about Peter, or about Peter's duty as a follower of Christ. Regardless of how deep you may have fallen away from Jesus, please know that the Jesus has changed His mind about you! God gives the same command to you today that He gave to Peter then, "Follow Me, and I will make you fishers of men." (Mark 4:19 NKJV). All Jesus wants from you is a surrendered life; one that is lived for the glory of God; one that exalts Him and one that is lived for His will and service; one that goes out and behaves a fisher of men.

Peter and the six disciples were standing on the shore of Galilee contemplating what to do next. Peter said, "I am going fishing." (John 21:3 NKJV) And the other disciples said, "We are going with you also." (John 21:3 NKJV). Dear child of God every day you are faced with the same question "what to do next?" The question is: Are you going fishing or are you going to behave as a fisher of men? It is my prayer that you will choose to behave!

REFERENCES

Ackley, Alfred H. 1991. "He Lives." *The Baptist Hymnal*. The Convention Press.

Anonymous. n.d. "The Waterbearer and the Pot."

Bates, Katharine L. 1991. "America the Beautiful." *The Baptist Hymnal*. Convention Press.

C. Truman Davis, M.D. n.d. In *The Expositor's Bible Commentary, Vol. 8*.

Crosby, Fanny J. 1991. "Rescue the Perishin." *The Baptist Hymnal* . Nashville: Convention Press.

Dictionary, Merriam-Webster. 1828. "Merriam-Webster Dictionary." In *Merriam-Webster Dictionary*. Merriam-Webster Dictionary.

Lowery, Robert. 1991. "Low in the Grave He Lay." *The Baptist Hymnal*. The Convention Press.

Stanphill, Ira F. 1991. "Room at the Cross." *The Baptist Hymnal*. The Convention Press.

1984. *Strong's Concordance*. Nashville: Thomas Nelson Publishers.

The Chrildren Defense Fund. 2019. *Every Day in America*. Accessed 2020. https://www.childrensdefense.org/wp-content/uploads/2018/06/state-of-americas-children.pdf.

2021. *Who's Your One*. Accessed Feburary 2021. https://whosyourone.com.

Printed in the United States
by Baker & Taylor Publisher Services